CW00665907

THE REAL GLADIATOR

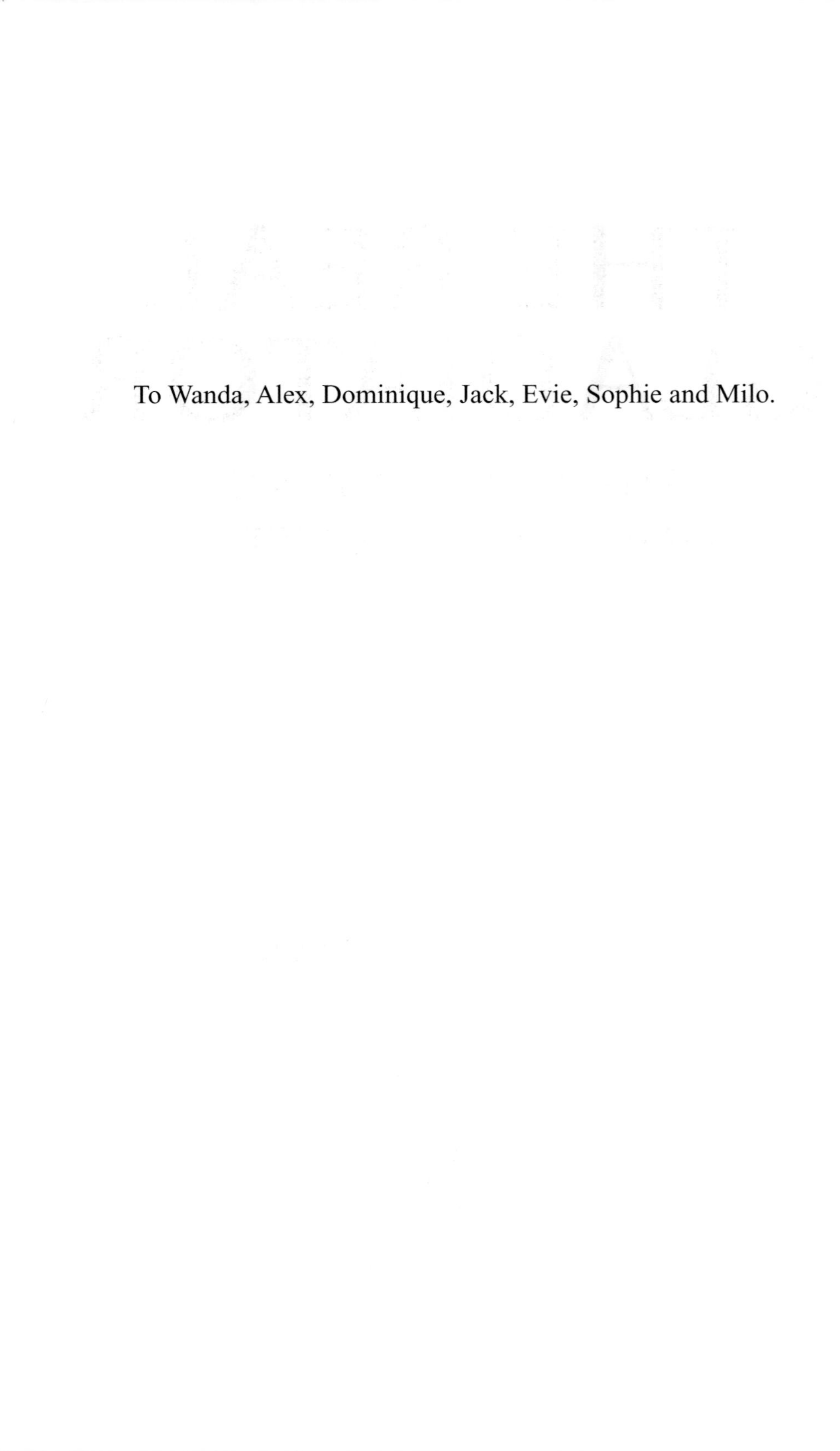

To Wanda, Alex, Dominique, Jack, Evie, Sophie and Milo.

THE REAL GLADIATOR

THE TRUE STORY OF MAXIMUS DECIMUS MERIDIUS

TONY SULLIVAN

AN IMPRINT OF PEN & SWORD BOOKS LTD.
YORKSHIRE – PHILADELPHIA

First published in Great Britain in 2022 by
PEN AND SWORD HISTORY
An imprint of
Pen & Sword Books Ltd
Yorkshire – Philadelphia

Copyright © Tony Sullivan, 2022

ISBN 978 1 39901 757 2

The right of Tony Sullivan to be identified as Author of this work has been asserted by him in accordance with the Copyright, Designs and Patents Act 1988.

A CIP catalogue record for this book is available from the British Library.

All rights reserved. No part of this book may be reproduced or transmitted in any form or by any means, electronic or mechanical including photocopying, recording or by any information storage and retrieval system, without permission from the Publisher in writing.

Typeset in Times New Roman 11/13.5 by
SJmagic DESIGN SERVICES, India.
Printed and bound in the UK by CPI Group (UK) Ltd.

Pen & Sword Books Limited incorporates the imprints of Atlas, Archaeology, Aviation, Discovery, Family History, Fiction, History, Maritime, Military, Military Classics, Politics, Select, Transport, True Crime, Air World, Frontline Publishing, Leo Cooper, Remember When, Seaforth Publishing, The Praetorian Press, Wharncliffe Local History, Wharncliffe Transport, Wharncliffe True Crime and White Owl.

For a complete list of Pen & Sword titles please contact
PEN & SWORD BOOKS LIMITED
47 Church Street, Barnsley, South Yorkshire, S70 2AS, England
E-mail: enquiries@pen-and-sword.co.uk
Website: www.pen-and-sword.co.uk

Or
PEN AND SWORD BOOKS
1950 Lawrence Rd, Havertown, PA 19083, USA
E-mail: Uspen-and-sword@casematepublishers.com
Website: www.penandswordbooks.com

Contents

Tables

Maps

Figures

Pictures

Acknowledgements

Many thanks to Matthew Parkes of 'Peturia Revisited' project in East Yorkshire for the use of pictures and the Legio VI Victrix, Eboracum re-enactment group based at York. Also for his advice and guidance on my first draft. Many thanks also to Ross Cronshaw from Magister Militum Facebook and re-enactment group for the use of photographs and his advice. Also to Glenn Higgins for reading a first draft and giving much needed advice. Any remaining mistakes are my own.

Introduction

The 2000 film *Gladiator*, directed by Ridley Scott and starring Russell Crowe, was a huge box office success grossing over $450 million worldwide. Based on *Those About to Die*, a 1958 book by Daniel Mannix, it won five academy awards: Best Picture, Costume Design, Visual Effects, Sound and Best Actor for Russell Crowe. It followed the career of a Roman General, Maximus Decimus Meridius, through the reign of two emperors. The first, a conscientious Marcus Aurelius, played by Richard Harris. The second, a brilliant performance by Joaquin Phoenix of the murderous psychopath Commodus. One memorable scene has Maximus, reduced to fighting as a gladiator, single-handedly killing several opponents in the arena, before turning to the crowd and shouting: 'Are you not entertained?' The answer for the majority of cinema goers and those watching at home was surely 'yes!' we were indeed entertained.

The question that often occurs to history lovers is, would we have been any less entertained if the plot had been more historically accurate? In the film Commodus dies in the arena, but is this more dramatic than the truth? In reality, after a poisoning attempt by his mistress failed, Commodus was strangled to death in his bath by his wrestling partner, Narcissus. One of the historical figures Maximus's career most closely resembles is that of Tiberius Claudius Pompeianus c. AD 125–193. He was indeed a general and favoured by Marcus Aurelius. In the film there is a love interest with Lucilla, daughter of Marcus Aurelius. In reality they were in fact married and Lucilla reportedly hated her new husband. Not just because he was much older than her, but more because of his lowly position. Having been previously married to Lucius Verus, co-emperor to her father, she had a very high opinion of herself. She was eventually executed by her brother Commodus two years into his reign. Her husband was not implicated in the plot and survived. Pompeianus never fought in the arena but interestingly, turned down the offer of emperor three times.

Another interesting figure is Marcus Valerius Maximianus. He too was a general in the northern legions during the Marcomannic Wars that raged across the Danube and Rhine during the second century. One of his exploits during this war was to kill a tribal chief of the Naristi in a single combat. He went on to command the army at the final battle, the one depicted in the film, just before the death of the emperor. Like Pompeianus he never became a gladiator but remained in favour of the new emperor, even being appointed consul. The gladiator was actually Commodus, who scandalised Romans of the day, by appearing in several contests against both men and beasts. Hopefully this book will demonstrate that not only is fact stranger than fiction, it can be just as entertaining, if not more so.

Before we begin it is worth summarising the plot of the film so we can compare and contrast significant points as we go through. The film starts in AD 180. Rome is said to be at the height of its powers, stretching from the deserts of Africa to northern Britain. Marcus Aurelius has spent twelve years subduing Germanic tribes and one last stronghold stands out. Victory will apparently promise peace throughout the empire. The opening scenes are of a battle in a forested area, supposedly near Vindobona in modern Austria. We will discuss how realistic some of the battle and gladiatorial scenes are later. The general Maximus wins the battle for the watching emperor, Marcus Aurelius, just before Commodus and his sister Lucilla arrive.

Marcus Aurelius privately tells his general that Commodus is unfit to rule and asks Maximus to succeed him as regent to restore the Roman Republic. When Commodus discovers this he murders his father, proclaims himself emperor and asks Maximus to support him. Maximus predictably declines and is arrested by the Praetorian Guard . He is taken to the forest to be executed but manages to kill his captors and escape. He races across Europe to his home in Spain only to find Commodus's men have got there first. His home has been destroyed and his wife and son murdered. He manages to bury them before collapsing unconscious, presumably from exhaustion and his injuries. Found by slavers he is transported to Mauretania Caesariensis in North Africa.

There he is sold to a gladiator trainer called Proximo, played by Oliver Reed. He soon becomes a crowd favourite and it is at this point we get the dramatic 'are you not entertained?' moment. The reluctant Maximus is persuaded to fight by Proximo, who explains that he too was once a gladiator and won his freedom in the arena, granted coincidently by the Emperor Aurelius. Commodus has organised 150 days of games at the Colosseum in Rome and Maximus sees his chance of freedom and revenge. The drama then moves to Rome and we have a dramatic view of the Colosseum. The games soon begin.

Maximus uses a masked helmet to disguise himself and debuts in a re-enactment of the Battle of Zama. Heavily outnumbered and playing the part of the Carthaginians, Maximus and his fellow gladiators are expected to be wiped out. He takes leadership of his small band as they are attacked by scythed chariots used as mobile platforms to fire arrows and spears at the gladiators. His experience and skill enables him to lead his men to victory, winning over the crowd as he does so. The watching Commodus comes down to the arena to congratulate him and orders he remove his helmet. Maximus eventually does so and we get the dramatic confrontation where Commodus realises the execution didn't take place and Maximus promises revenge for the death of his family. Commodus is compelled by the crowd to let him live, but quickly plots a way to get rid of him. He organises a fight against a legendary gladiator called Tigris of Gaul, hoping he will kill him. Maximus wins the fight and refuses the emperor's order to kill his opponent. The crowd cheer 'Maximus the merciful', which angers Commodus even more.

Meanwhile, a plot to topple Commodus grows. Lucilla, Commodus's sister, and a senator, Gracchus, meet Maximus in prison and plan to help him escape. Outside Rome soldiers loyal to Maximus are camped and the plan is to remove the emperor by force and hand power back to the senate. Unfortunately Commodus discovers the plan, has Gracchus arrested and attacks the gladiators' barracks. Maximus escapes but is captured en route to his awaiting troops. In a bid to win the crowd's support and kill Maximus once and for all, Commodus arranges a gladiatorial contest between himself and Maximus. Before the fight Commodus stabs Maximus to weaken him and ensure victory. Despite this, Maximus manages to defeat and kill the emperor before succumbing to his injuries.

It is worth briefly mentioning some of the more glaring historical inaccuracies before we delve into the history. Firstly Marcus Aurelius was not murdered by Commodus, although he did die in AD 180 at Vindobanda, modern Vienna. There were rumours of poisoning but the cause of death was most likely the Antonine plague that was sweeping through the empire at that time. This was likely smallpox, brought back from the East after the Roman Parthian War of AD 161–166. The death of Commodus did not bring about peace and a return to the republic. Rather the year of the five emperors in AD 193 continued the civil war, bloodshed and corruption that bedevilled much of Roman history.

Chapter one will give a brief background of that history up to the beginning of the reign of Marcus Aurelius. Chapter two will look at the battle scene and historical background behind the Marcomannic Wars.

This will lead into a look at weapons, warfare and contemporary battles of the period in the next chapter, followed by a detailed look at the life of Marcus Aurelius and whether the depiction of the kindly old man yearning for a return to peace and some sort of democracy is accurate. Chapter five is devoted to gladiators and the games and the reality behind the bloody spectacles. The penultimate chapter will investigate Commodus and discuss whether his historical portrayal as a psychopath is deserved. We will finish with the aftermath of his death. Hopefully the reader will be not only entertained, but gain an insight into this fascinating period of history.

Chapter 1

From Republic to Empire

Early history

One of the features of the film is a desire to return Rome to a republic. We will of course cover the accuracy of this, but first we need to understand what Rome was and what it became. What is this republic to which some yearned to return? What was this empire it had become? It is therefore important to cover briefly the early history of Rome and how it evolved from the early kings to a republic, and then later to imperial rule.

The traditional date for the founding of Rome is 753 BC, on seven hills above the Tiber sixteen miles from the coast of the Tyrrhenum sea. Over time two separate foundation myths became fused together. The early history and myths are important as they influence the mindset and cultural identity of Romans up to Commodus and beyond. The first is recorded by Virgil in the first century BC. After the fall of Troy, Aeneas, a Trojan prince, led survivors to settle on the west coast of the Italian peninsula. An initially separate legend has Romulus and Remus as the founders, but later they are made descendants of Aeneas. The story told by the Roman historian Livy is interesting as it mirrors much of the later bloody historical events and describes a Rome built on fratricide.

In the town of Alba Longa in the Alban Hills, just south of where Rome was founded, Numitor was overthrown by his brother Amulius. Fearing possible future rivals he forced his niece, Rhea Silvia, to become a priestess against her will, a role that required chastity. Unfortunately for Amulius this plan failed when she was raped by Mars, the god of war, and gives birth to two boys, Romulus and Remus. Livy, though doubtful of this tale, records that Amulius orders the twins to be thrown into the Tiber and drowned. Unable to go through with their grisly task the servants simply abandon the infants to their fate. It is at this point a nurturing she-wolf finds and suckles the babes. Livy attempts to rationalise the story at this point and notes the Latin word for wolf, Lupa, was also a colloquial term for prostitute.[1] The boys are then rescued and raised by a shepherd, Faustulus, and his wife, Acca Larentia.

When fully grown they return to Alba Longa, restore their grandfather and set out to establish their own city on seven hills next to the Tiber. They soon quarrel and Romulus chooses what later becomes the Palatine Hill with Remus choosing the Aventine. When Remus jumps over his brother's palisade Romulus kills him in a scene similar to the biblical Cain and Abel. Romulus declares Rome an asylum and attracts exiles, refugees, runaway slaves, convicts and the 'rabble and dispossessed of the rest of Italy'.[2] Lacking women Romulus plans a trick. He invites the neighbouring tribes, the Sabines and Latins, to a festival and, on a given signal, abducts the women.

A war ensues and the Romans defeat the Latins but are hard pressed by the Sabines. It is the intervention of the abducted Sabine women on the battlefield that stops the fighting. Rome becomes a joint Roman-Sabine town until the Sabine king, Titus, is murdered, leaving Romulus once more as sole ruler. He is the first of seven kings and the traditional tale of the overthrow of the monarchy was crucial in Roman culture. The last king of Rome is said to have been Lucius Tarquinius Superbus dated to c.509 BC. His son, Sextus, rapes a noblewoman called Lucretia. This is the last straw after the murder of his predecessor, years of corruption and tyrannical behaviour and the murder of senators. The nobles rise up, and led by Lucius Junius Brutus, overthrow Tarquinius and establish a republic. One of Brutus's first acts is to get the people to swear an oath that Rome would never again be ruled by a king: 'First of all, by swearing an oath that they would suffer no man to rule Rome, it forced the people, desirous of a new liberty, not to be thereafter swayed by the entreaties or bribes of kings.'

This could of course all be legend, but it demonstrates an attempt by the Romans to legitimise their idea of the republic, an idea that extended into imperial rule even though the republic, in practice, was dead. We do have archaeological evidence showing the presence of a small village as far back as 1000 BC.[3] An inscription referring to 'RECEI', an early Latin form of rex was found under the forum in Rome in AD 1899, leading some to believe there may be elements of truth in the tales.[4] Brutus decreed that Rome was to be ruled by two consuls, appointed each year, and 300 senators. The first two consuls were Brutus himself and Collatinus, the husband of Lucretia – who had committed suicide after the rape by Sextus.

The consuls performed some of the same tasks as a king but crucially they were voted by the people, held office for a year and presided over the election of their successors. This balance of power did not eventually last; however, it is important in understanding Roman thinking. It also contributed to one of the concepts in the film attributed to Marcus Aurelius. Richard Harris has his emperor yearning for a restoration of the republic.

It has to be said it is unlikely the emperor intended to restore the republic, but it is worth noting the emperors made the pretence of never calling themselves king.

We now come to a point in history that may have inspired the idea in the film of a general saving the republic before stepping down from power. Around 458 BC the Aequi, a tribe to the east of Rome, broke their treaty and Rome sent out two armies. The first was annihilated and the second besieged. Panicking senators appointed Lucius Quinctius Cincinnatus as dictator to deal with the emergency. After his victory at the battle of Mount Algidus, Lucius disbanded the army and stepped down, just fifteen days after his appointment. Twenty years later he is said to have accepted the post of dictator once more, this time for twenty-one days. He was thus revered for his virtue, service and civic duty. The Society of Cincinnati was formed in the United States and France in the eighteenth century and he gave his name to the city in Ohio. To the Romans he demonstrated an ideal which many emperors would later attempt to ape. He stepped up when needed, did his duty, but then was willing to step aside and away from power. The film has Maximus portraying the same adherence to duty and reluctance to abuse power.

While much of this cannot be proven, what is clear is the concept of the republic and an aversion to kings was prominent in the Roman mind. The letters SPQR stand for '*Senatus Populusque Romanus*', 'the Senate and People of Rome', and this phrase embodies the ideal, if not the reality, of Roman government. Interestingly, when trying to raise money for his extravagant games, Commodus reversed the word order, '*Populus Senatusque*', putting the people before the senate – which no doubt antagonised them.

If one accepts the accounts at face value, the republic lasted several hundred years. During that time it expanded its territory and influence considerably. It came into conflict with Carthage, waging three wars before destroying the city completely in 146 BC. It is the second of these wars that featured the famous Hannibal, who led elephants across the Alps into Italy and won several famous victories, most notably at Cannae in 216 BC. He was defeated at the battle of Zama in North Africa in 202 BC by Publius Cornelius Scipio, one of the few Roman survivors of Cannae. It is this battle that is re-enacted in the Colosseum in the film. We will cover the accuracy of the scene in more detail later. The defeat of Carthage allowed Rome control of the western Mediterranean.

The exact date for the change to empire is debatable. Some would date it to Caesar's crossing of the Rubicon in 49 BC. For others the following year was more notable. He was appointed consul, dictator and defeated Pompey the Great at Pharsalus. The following year he was appointed dictator, again albeit temporarily. Julius Caesar was a very different man compared to Lucius Quinctius Cincinnatus four centuries before. In 46 BC he was appointed dictator for ten years. Perhaps the most appropriate date was not a time of conflict, however, but when three powerful men made an alliance several years before. In 60 BC Pompey, Crassus and Julius Caesar took control behind the scenes and dominated the appointment of consuls, military commands and key decisions.[5]

The beginning of empire

The death of Julius Caesar resulted in civil wars that culminated in the death of Mark Antony and Cleopatra. The subsequent reign of Augustus, formally Gaius Julius Caesar or Octavious, 27 BC to AD 14, saw a number of reforms.[6] Senatorial decrees were given the force of law along with Imperial pronouncements which together formed the basis of Roman legislation. The difference between senators and equestrians was formally separated with wealth qualifications of 1 million sesterces and 400,000 respectively. Senatorial status was made hereditary for three generations with no obligation of taking office. Senators though became an arm of the state and subordinate to the emperor. Another tradition to be dropped was the ability of a general to celebrate a triumph. The last was in 19 BC, after which only emperors enjoyed the privilege.

Edward Gibbons, writing the *History of the Decline and Fall of the Roman Empire* in the eighteenth century, describes the following emperors thus: 'the dark unrelenting Tiberius, the furious Caligula, the feeble Claudius, the profligate and cruel Nero and the timid inhuman Domitian'. In contrast, he states those reigning between Domitian and up to Commodus as 'the good emperors'. He describes this period in history as the one when the human race was 'most happy and prosperous'. However, this may just reflect the bias of the sources. In reality some of the worst examples may not have been quite so bad, and some of those with a better reputation may not have been quite so good, as we shall see. In fact, senators were executed or forced to commit suicide under all the emperors.[7]

Having said that, in terms of stability the second century was arguably less murderous, at least for emperors. The table below shows the causes of deaths between Augustus and Commodus. We can see the murder and suicide rate subsided, with the emperors from Trajan to Marcus Aurelius enjoying relatively long and murder-free reigns. It is worth noting this pattern reverses after Commodus, who is immediately followed by the 'year the the five emperors'. In the 220 years between Augustus and Commodus six emperors are murdered. In the 283 years after Commodus, thirty-three were murdered – more than half. Tiberius Claudius Pompeianus may have been born into a relatively stable political world but he lived to see the return of political upheaval and civil war.

Table 1: Roman Emperors 31 BC – AD 192

Emperor	Reign	Length of reign	Cause of death
Augustus	31 BC – AD 14	41 years	Fever
Tiberius	AD 14–37	23 years	Fever
Caligula	AD 37–41	4 years	Murdered
Claudius	AD 41–54	13 years	Poisoned
Nero	AD 54–68	14 years	Suicide
Galba	AD 68–69	7 months	Murdered
Otho	AD 69	2 months	Suicide
Vitellius	AD 69	8 months	Murdered
Vespasian	AD 69–79	10 years	Fever
Titus	AD 79–81	2 years	Fever
Domitian	AD 81–96	15 years	Murdered
Nerva	AD 96–98	2 years	Fever
Trajan	AD 98–117	19 years	Stroke
Hadrian	AD 117–138	21 years	Protracted illness
Antonius Pius	AD 138–161	23 years	Vomiting and fever
Marcus Aurelius	AD 161–180	19 years	Lung disease and fever
Lucius Verus	AD 161–169 (co-emperor)	8 years	Stroke
Commodus	AD 177–180 (co-emperor) AD 180–192 (sole emperor)	13 years	Murdered

Trajan has been called the greatest and most renowned of the emperors.[8] He pushed the empire to its furthest extent from northern Britain, north of the Danube, the East and north Africa. He was noted for his good governance and public welfare.[9] One example is his introduction of lament from Imperial funds for the upkeep of the poor and especially children. His wars against the Dacians extended the borders and are commemorated on Trajan's column, depicting soldiers from both sides and scenes from the conflict. Completed during his reign, it gives us a contemporary and accurate portrayal of Roman arms and armour. To celebrate the victory he held a series of extravagant games in Rome in which 10,000 gladiators are said to have fought and 11,000 animals were killed.[10] Three years before his death he defeated the Parthians in the East, annexing Armenia. We can see the extent of the empire at the time of Trajan's death on the map below.

Trajan was succeeded by Hadrian in AD 117. Both Marcus Aurelius and Tiberius Claudius Pompeianus were born during his reign. It is interesting to note that he was the first emperor depicted with a beard, and this trend was continued for the next century.[11] He was characterised as a man of culture and the arts. He gave Rome twenty years of stable government and strengthened the frontiers most notably Hadrian's Wall in Britain. However, Cassius Dio gives a more nuanced picture. He 'hated by the people' despite his 'generally excellent' reign. Cassius cites the main reason as the significant number of murders 'especially at the start and end of his reign'.

Map 1: Roman Empire c. AD 117 (Wikimedia Commons)

However he adds Hadrian did not have 'a bloodthirsty disposition' and on occasions he felt it sufficient merely to put his displeasure in writing. He also often reduced punishment in proportion to the number for children the offender had.[12]

One example of Hadrian's later behaviour was his treatment of Lucius Servianus and his grandson.[13] Lucius was married to Hadrian's sister and was suspected of plotting against the emperor. He was also a respected senator who had governed several provinces and served as consul three times. At the age of 90 he was no threat, but despite protestations of innocence both Lucius and his grandson were forced to commit suicide. Just before his death we hear that he gave orders 'that very many others who were guilty of slight offences should be put to death; these, however, were spared by Antoninus'.[14]

It may be that Hadrian already viewed Marcus Aurelius as the best choice but, being in his teenage years, he was still very young. This may be why a double adoption took place. Hadrian adopted the 51-year-old Antoninus Pius, and at the same time Antoninus adopted the 17-year-old Marcus Aurelius and the 7-year-old Lucius Ceionius Commodus. Hadrian had adopted the latter's father, also named Lucius Ceionius Commodus, in AD 136, renaming him Lucius Aelius Caesar. Unfortunately he died of a haemorrhage in AD 138 and Hadrian was forced to look elsewhere. He had already mentored Marcus Annius Verus, later Marcus Aurelius, but he also was seen as too young. Antoninus seemed a reasonable stop-gap – childless and relatively old. Hadrian, now 62 years old, adopted his slightly younger colleague on the proviso he in turn adopted both children, who took the names Marcus Aurelius and Lucius Verus respectively.

Perhaps unexpectedly, Antoninus reigned for twenty-three years. Under his rule there were no major wars, although unrest continued at the borders. Later historians described him as having steady and sound morals.[15] Marcus Aurelius gives a glowing tribute, describing him as long-sighted and prudent, and placed sensible government above superstition or popularity. He introduced protections for slaves against cruelty and undue abuse and was seen as a benign and moderate ruler.[16] His only surviving child, Faustina, married Marcus Aurelius and so the succession on his death was a peaceful one.

The senate viewed Hadrian and Antoninus very differently. Cassius Dio and the *Historia Augusta* records how the senators wished to withhold divine honours from Hadrian and were shamed into doing so by Antoninus. The new emperor threatened to resign stating his very position as Emperor was due to his adoption by Hadrian, who the senate now wished to insult.

In contrast, on the death of Antonius we see an eagerness to honour him. The *Historia Augusta* records that he was 'deified by the senate, while all men vied with one another to give him honour'. He was praised for his 'devoutness, his mercy, his intelligence, and his righteousness'. He was said to have been, unlike other emperors, 'unstained by the blood of either citizen or foe so far as was in his power'.[17]

The empire of Marcus Aurelius

What sort of empire did Marcus inherit? First, it had a deeply hierarchical social structure with clear boundaries and class distinctions. At the top were the patricians who were the rich aristocratic elite. From this group were appointed senators. Next came the equestrians or Roman knights. Thirdly came the plebeians who formed the bulk of the population. Beneath them came freedmen, and lastly slaves. For the period at which we are looking it is important to note the changes to social and political influence. Importantly, equestrians gained more influence throughout the second century. This was necessary as the empire expanded and more posts were needed and created. However, this caused some friction with senators. One can imagine the feeling of some of the aristocratic families when Commodus placed even freedmen in positions of great power.

It is estimated that in the year Marcus Aurelius became emperor, one fifth of the world's population lived under Roman rule.[18] Of this, 7 to 10 million were slaves. In the city of Rome, up to half of the estimated 1 million people were slaves and one in six of the empire's population. Most of the empire's 70 to 80 million population lived in rural areas, but up to 20 per cent were urban, with over 400 towns or cities in the Italian peninsula alone. Poverty was rife and economic growth estimated at a low 0.1 per cent.[19]

There were high levels of inequality and a rigidly stratified social hierarchy based on property ownership and wealth.[20] The property qualification for the first two ranks were as follows: senator, 1 million sesterces; equestrian 400,000 sesterces.[21] In the first century AD Augustus had reduced the number of senators from 900 to 600. From these men were appointed governors of provinces and legates, commanders of legions. There were approximately 30,000 equestrians throughout the empire with around 2,000 in Rome. From this group were appointed tribunes or procurators to assist governors. Prefects of the Praetorian Guard in Rome were always equestrians.

The next level was set at 200,000 sesterces, allowing rich landowners to serve as jurors. Municipal councillors required approximately 100,000 sesterces. Next came salaried workers such as doctors, teachers, municipal workers and shop owners. Below these came the mass of free people working a hand-to-mouth existence. Last came the slaves. Meritocracy was virtually non-existent and the army was one of the few avenues of mobility for an ambitious and talented man. However, only one in many thousands of recruits could reach the heights of proconsul.

Appointments came with a level of salary per year: senatorial governor, 400,000 sesterces; equestrian procurator, 60,000–300,000 sesterces; whereas a legionary soldier could expect 1,200 sesterces. In comparison, an unskilled slave cost 1,000–2,000 sesterces, and a gladiator between 3,000–15,000. We can compare this to the 500 sesterces estimated to feed a peasant family for a year. Thus even the poorest senator earned several hundred times more than even the average soldier or plebeian worker, let alone peasants and freedmen. Some senators were immensely wealthy and earned many times more than their peers. Average wages was just four sesterces a day (less than 1,500 a year), compared to Cicero who reportedly earned 555,555 sesterces for his legal work alone.[22] A moderately wealthy man had an income 714 times greater than a pauper, while for the very rich it was over 10,000 times. This meant innovation was low as the economy had a supply of very cheap labour through low wages or slavery. Private property was exempt from taxation and death duties set at 5 per cent.[23]

Average life expectancy was as low as 22 for men and 20 for women,[24] although the high infant mortality skewed the figures – a third of the population died before the age of 3 and nearly half by the age of 8. The senatorial class might live a little longer to 30, but there were also many examples of people living into their seventies and later. For those joining the army at age 20, 78 per cent would reach the age of 35, and just 60 per cent would reach 45. Disease and poor nutrition were the main culprits for civilians and soldiers alike. Even in peacetime only two thirds would survive the twenty-five year career to reach retirement.

On average, women bore around six children in a time when infant and maternal mortality rates were relatively high;[25] haemorrhaging and sepsis contributed to 2½ per cent of women dying in childbirth. Stillbirths and miscarriages occurred in a fifth of pregnancies. When Marcus married Faustina, there was a 25 per cent chance that one or both would be dead within five years.[26] When Commodus was born there was no guarantee he would reach adulthood at all.

Rome

To control Rome emperors often used 'bread and circuses', as the first century Roman satirist Juvenal quipped. Supplying free grain to the population of Rome is estimated to have cost 135 million sesterces, or 15 per cent of the empire's revenue. This demonstrates how fearful emperors were of the mob.[27] Adult males also got cheap wine and free theatrical shows, chariot races and gladiatorial games. The height of gladiatorial display was in the first and second century.

To protect Rome there were three urban cohorts, nine praetorian cohorts and seven cohorts of vigils (night watch). There were normally two praetorian prefects, both equestrian, whereas the urban prefect was of senatorial rank. Prefect of the night watch was an equestrian. Provinces were divided by those directly ruled by the emperor and those by the senate. Senatorial, or proconsul, provinces were supposed to be more stable and peaceful. Proconsuls to these provinces were chosen annually by lot and assisted by a quaestor and a legate. Legions tended to be posted only to Imperial provinces, reporting direct to the emperor. Imperial provinces were divided into consular, praetorian and equestrian provinces. These were

Map 2: Imperial and Senatorial provinces AD 117 (Wikimedia Commons)

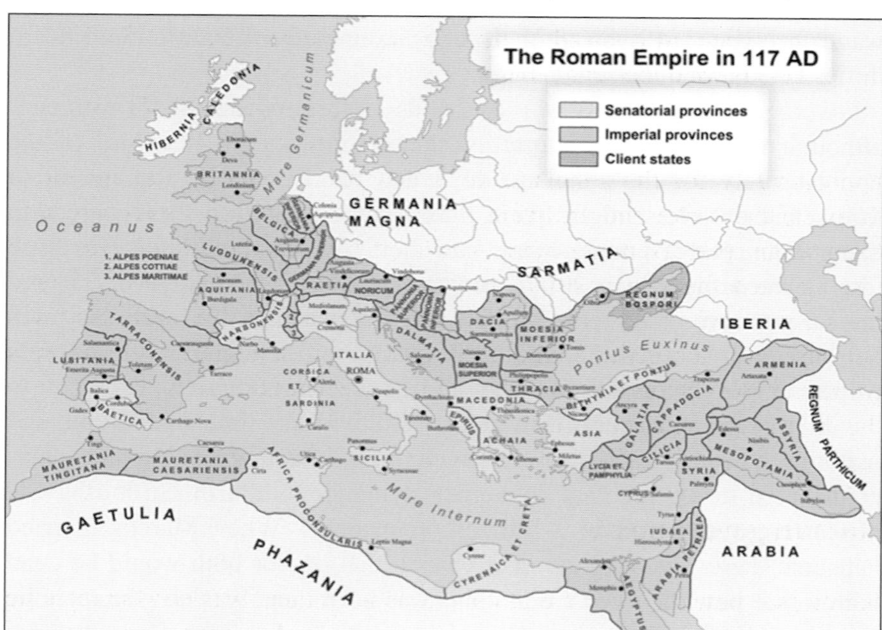

also assisted in financial affairs by equestrian procurators. Map two shows the Imperial and Senatorial provinces in AD 117.

In general, power moved away from the senate over time and towards successive emperors. In turn, later emperors elevated equestrians and freedmen into positions of greater influence. Under Marcus Aurelius the number of proconsul or senatorial provinces declined to just five. The senate was mostly Italian-born in the time of Augustus, by the time of Marcus Aurelius it was down to 50 per cent. Under Marcus, talented soldiers found promotion and social mobility slightly easier. Examples include Pertinax and Valerius Maximianus. We can see an example of Marcus's approach in his appointment of Domitius Marsianus to procurator of Gallia Narbonensis on a salary of 200,000 sesterces. A previous emperor might have selected a man based on birth alone. Here, Marcus stated that he required a man of good character, conscientiousness and experience.[28]

Having said that, Marcus was deeply conservative and played out the pretence that the senate retained the same power as in the republic. This was a fiction, but perhaps necessary. Commodus, though, took a different approach which angered some senators. It was precisely this attitude that contributed to the first assassination attempt. The failure of the plot caused Commodus to distrust the senate even more, especially as the would-be killer had made plain that the senate wanted him dead.

> thrusting out a sword in the narrow entrance, he said: 'See! This is what the senate has sent you.'
>
> Cassius Dio book 73.4.4

Unfortunately for the assailant, his cry gave Commodus a split second to evade the strike and his guards time to respond and apprehend him. Commodus, perhaps understandably, placed his trust more in his freedmen and elevated them to positions of great influence. This in turn angered the senators even more. Perhaps the greatest example of meritocracy was Pertinax, who succeeded Commodus as emperor; he had been the son of a freedman. Serving under Marcus Aurelius as an equestrian he had risen to the senate serving as consul.

Roman government

We can see how the structure of government changed between the republic and empire below. This is important for a number of reasons. First, it shows what type of system *Gladiator* claimed the emperor was trying to revert to. It also highlights why the senatorial class in the second century began to feel aggrieved. Power had increasingly shifted to the emperor since Augustus. The senate became more of a ceremonial institution whose function was to rubber stamp imperial edicts. Additionally, as the empire grew the number of provincial senators increased. Then to make matters worse, equestrians and even persons from lower social ranks began to have more influence, not just within society but in government. Emperors such as Antoninus and Marcus Aurelius maintained the pretence of equality and respect for the institutions. Perhaps for this reason they were seen to govern well and died in their beds.

The first figure gives the structure under the republic, and the second that under the empire. It is worth noting how legislation now derived from the emperor or his council. More positions were now imperial nominations and thus members of the emperor's inner circle had enormous influence.

The evolution of the social hierarchy is also very important. Traditionally the distinction between patricians and plebeians was very important in Roman society. In the early republic most of the power resided in a few aristocratic

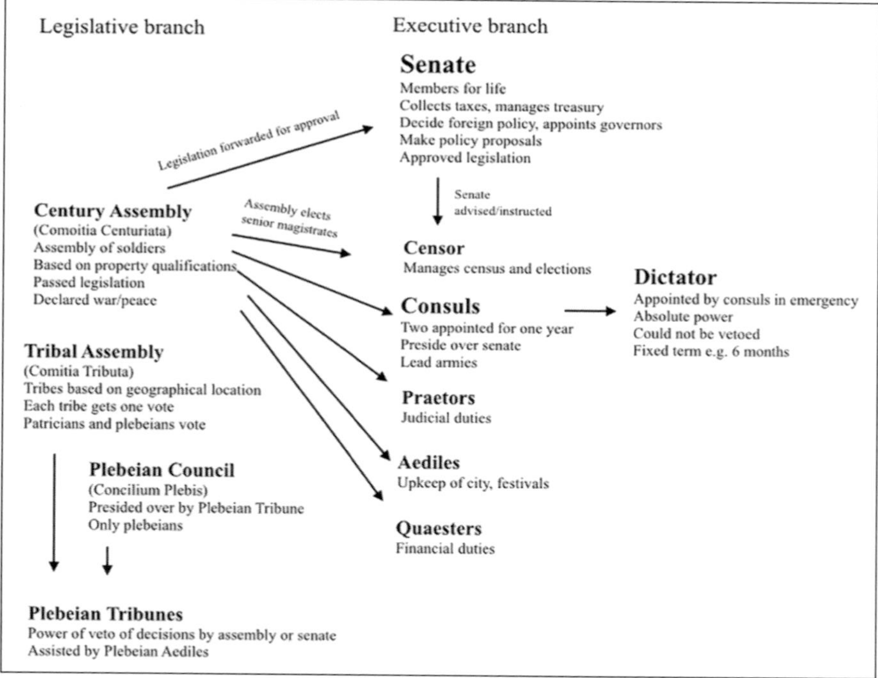

Figure 1: Governmental structure under the Roman Republic

families. The Plebeian Council was a direct result of political and social upheaval known as the 'conflict of orders', which lasted roughly from 500–287 BC. One result of this was the 'Laws of the Twelve Tables', which was displayed in the forum and laid out the rights and duties of all Roman citizens. The governmental structure seen above shows how the republic evolved to produce a balance and separation of powers. This was all very well for a city state but as it expanded and acquired provinces, tensions between competing groups and power bases caused civil unrest and wars. Below we can see how the emperor effectively took the role of dictator from the republican era. Indeed, Julius Caesar was officially appointed dictator. It was partly the fear of this becoming a monarchy that drove his assassins. Future emperors were keen to avoid the accusation of acting like a king and so we get the pretence of titles such as *princeps*, awarded to Augustus, meaning first senator or first among equals. The reality can be seen in the governmental structure below.

As we shall see, the idea that Marcus Aurelius wished to turn back the clock is fanciful. He made several deliberate steps to ensure Commodus succeeded him. Additionally, the idea that a restoration of republic government in Rome meant democracy throughout the empire is also unlikely. There were far too many powerful forces both inside and outside Rome ready to fill any power vacuum. Within the city there was the senate itself but also the Praetorian Guard, which was instrumental in the reign of Commodus and the murder and appointment of succeeding emperors. Outside Rome there were provincial governors and legates of legions with power bases in the city.

Another point to bear in mind is the changes to the social hierarchy. While it was rare in the republic some plebeians, such as Tribunes, did rise

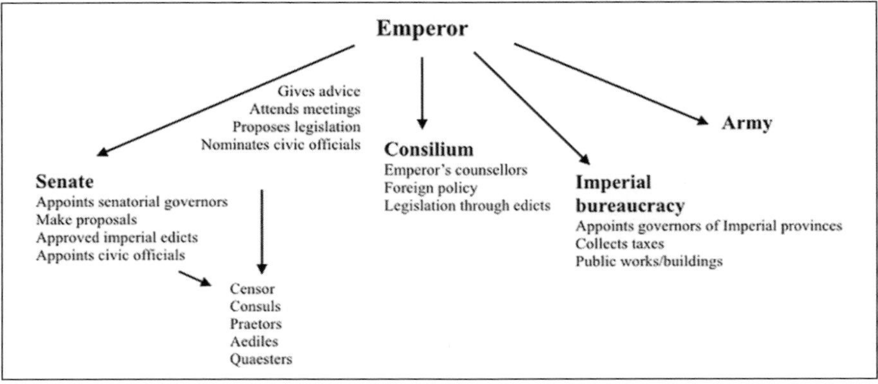

Figure 2: Governmental structure under the Roman Empire

to the senate. The cursus honorum, or 'ladder of offices', shows a likely career path for those of senatorial rank. Similarly the tres militiae gives the three military posts equestrians expected to rise through after which some progressed to procurator to a provincial governor or praetorian prefect in Rome.

The definition of patrician became blurred and it might be more useful to see a stratified upper class of wealthy aristocrats, senators and equestrians. As the empire expanded so provincials were awarded equestrian status and also elevated to the senate. At the same time plebeians could also rise to equestrian status. What was different in the second century was the level and rapidity of social mobility during the reign of Marcus Aurelius. Several important figures rose through the ranks to be appointed to the senate. Marcus was careful to keep the senate on side. Commodus, however, side-lined the senate, relied increasingly on his consilium and placed freedmen in positions of power. It was one thing to have little power and be flattered by the emperor while still able to obtain rank and privilege, quite another to have little power, your access to the emperor blocked, coveted positions go to non-Romans and to see people from a lower social standing

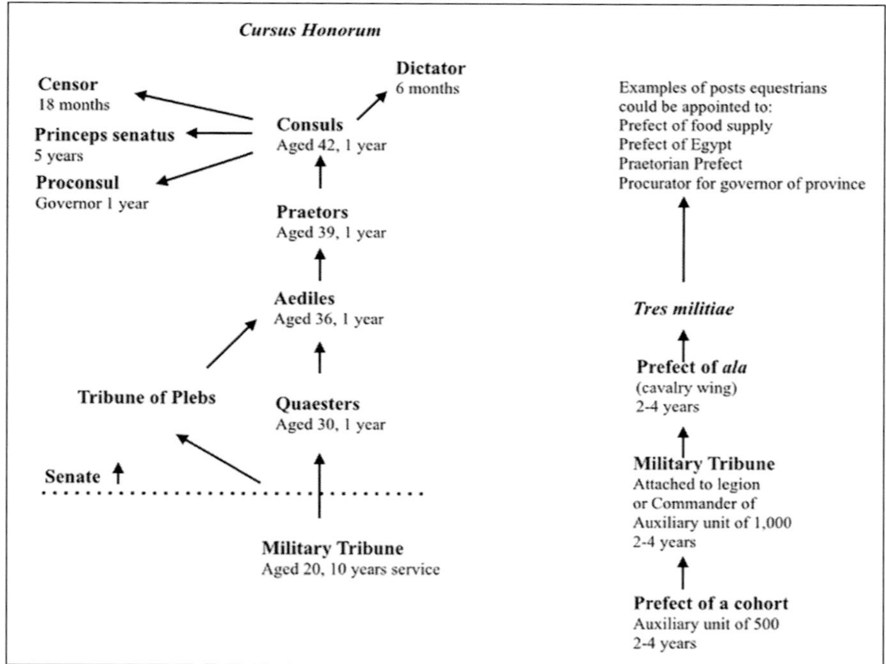

Figure 3: Career paths

rise above you. Even worse if you are forced to kowtow to a mere freedman and have to bribe him for access or appointments.

We will finish this chapter with a map of the Roman Empire under Marcus Aurelius. Hadrian had pulled back from some of the areas conquered by Trajan, most notably Parthia in the East. I have included the main locations mentioned in the film. Firstly Vindobona, modern Vienna, located on the Danube, along which much of the fighting in the Marcomannic Wars took place. It is here Maximus is portrayed winning the final battle. We see Trujillo in modern Spain where Maximus races back in his vain attempts to save his family. He is taken to Zucchabar in North Africa where he trains as a gladiator before the action turns to the Colosseum in Rome. From a historical perspective it is worth noting the importance of the rivers Danube and Rhine for the northern border. In the East we see the importance of the Rivers Euphrates and Tigris in access and trade routes to the Parthian Empire. Armenia was thus a key strategy gateway giving access to Mesopotamia. It avoided a long journey across miles of desert to the east of Syria.

Map 3: Roman Empire under Marcus Aurelius

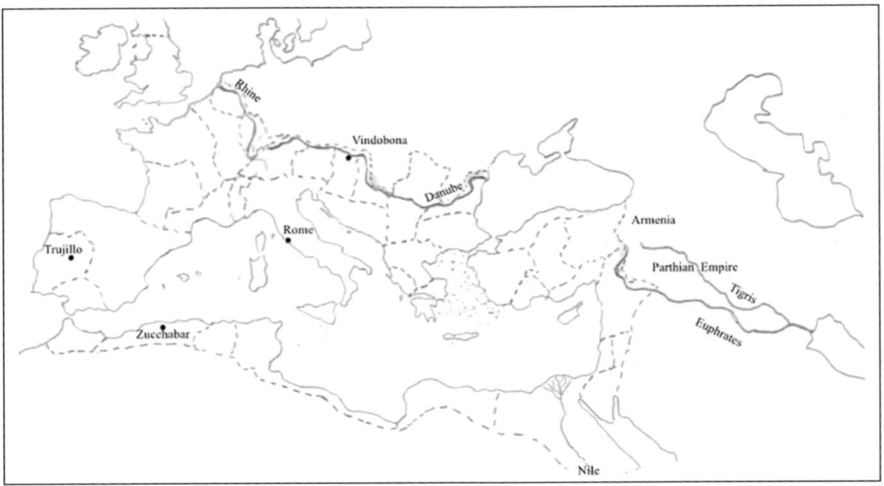

Chapter 2

The initial battle and historical context

Films are of course for entertainment and one shouldn't be too pedantic about slight historical inaccuracies. There are, however, quite a number of YouTube channels devoted to pointing these out, some of which I will list in the bibliography. One rather tongue-in-cheek example pulls apart the very first scene of Maximus dreaming of standing in a wheat field at his farm in Spain: modern wheat is apparently a foot shorter than the Roman variety. Leather wrist straps are an anachronism of Hollywood much used from Romans to Vikings. The road winding down to his farm had grass growing down the middle as one might get from the passage of modern cars. In reality a single horse or ox pulling a cart would wear it down. Additionally, roads used for the transport of livestock between villages would likely be fenced to contain the sheep or cattle when driving them to their destination. The reader may be pleased that I don't intend to go through the film frame by frame pulling apart each scene.

However, it is worth looking at the first battle scene to point out a number of issues. Then we will look at the structure and tactics of the Roman army in the second century before investigating in depth the wars this scene is supposed to depict. We recall it is set in the winter of AD 180 and just before the death of the emperor. In reality, Marcus Aurelius died in March AD 180. The speech Maximus gives about being at home for the harvest in three weeks time is thus impossible. Harvest time was August to September depending on the crop, such as the wheat which features in Maximus's dreams. Some crops can be harvested as early as June, but in March or April a Roman farmer would be sowing, weeding and ploughing.

Fire arrows

The advantage of the bow is it can fire a projectile a long distance and the arrow can penetrate flesh and light clothing sufficiently to injure, if not kill, an advancing warrior. A massed volley of many hundreds, at sufficient frequency, could deliver thousands of arrows in a single minute. A fire arrow requires a small 'cage' to hold lighted material and this makes the arrow heavier, requiring a thicker shaft to prevent the arrow simply breaking from the force. This reduces the range considerably. The fact the arrows are also visible to the approaching warriors gives no advantage and indeed might allow them vital seconds to prepare their shields in defence. It is also quite difficult to maintain a flame as the speed of the arrow is likely to cause the flame to be extinguished in flight. Thus fire arrows tended to be used in sieges and over relatively short distances to attack buildings. Even in the Second World War during the Blitz there were examples of incendiary bombs failing to ignite or fires being extinguished quickly. Thus an attacking army might deploy massed volleys of such arrows hoping to overwhelm the defenders' attempts to extinguish the fires. In cities with predominantly stone and tiled buildings it might not have been practical.

We know the Romans were aware of the concept of using fire as Vegetius, writing in the fourth century, mentions it in relation to naval warfare.

> Arrows wrapped in burning oil, tow, sulphur and bitumen are planted blazing by catapults in the bellies of hostile ships and soon set light to the planking payed with wax, pitch and resin, so much kindling for fires.
>
> Vegetius Book 4.44

There is also have a reference from from Ammianus Marcellinus, also from the fourth century.[1] He describes 'fire-darts (a kind of missile)'. Concerning the construction: 'the shaft is of reed, and between this and the point is a covering of bands of iron'. It is hollowed out with 'many openings' and filled with 'fire and some inflammable matter'. It must be shot from a 'loose bow (for it is extinguished by too swift a flight)'. Once it hits it's target 'it burns persistently, and water poured upon it rouses the fire to still greater heat; and there is no way of extinguishing it except by sprinkling it with dust'.

Firing with a loose bow would mean the range was drastically reduced but nevertheless it is possible the Romans used fire arrows in the second century. However, there is no reference to conventional troops or their use in open battle. In fact, the first reference to fire arrows being used on the battlefield come from China in the tenth century AD at the siege of Yuzhang.

Vegetius suggests a quarter to a third of recruits should be trained to use the bow on foot or from horseback. He suggests there should be picked archers in all centuries. The whole point of this would be to deliver missiles en masse, at distance and with a reasonable frequency to either dull an attack or affect the movement. Arrows directed on the flanks, for example, might force troops to bunch together in the centre. Arrows fired at a high trajectory would force infantry to raise their shields above their heads. If arrows were directed horizontally at the same time this could prove decisive. Using fire arrows in this situation would add no utility and would quite likely significantly reduce the distance they travelled. Using arrows en masse in a wooded area in any context would seem a waste of effort and arrows.

Despite Vegetius's comments, archers tended to be auxiliary troops and it was good to see a realistic portrayal of their armour which would more likely have been ring mail rather than the lorica segmentata of the legionaries. We will discuss arrows in more detail later. Briefly we can say a Roman archer could fire an arrow approximately 200 metres. However, there is a balance between weight, power, accuracy, distance and potential damage. What a defender would want is for an attacking force to enter a 'killing zone'. This could be marked by stakes or stones whitewashed one side at say 50, 100 and 150 metres. If the attacking force was large and you wanted to keep them away you might pepper them with light arrows at distance. If you wished the enemy to advance you might delay your first discharge of arrows. If the attacker wore armour, an archer would wish to use a bodkin type arrow with a heavy shaft. These might be more effective at a closer range.

We have to conclude that fire arrows in open battle, fired into a wooded area in the second century is unlikely and counter productive. Given the scenario in the film, I would suggest it would be better for the defenders to hold fire until the attackers were in the open. The distance between the fortifications and the woods appears to be about 200m. A warrior carrying a shield running over uneven ground might take a minute to cover 100m. In which time experienced archers could deliver several volleys whether the attackers retreated from the first volley or continued their attack. You would not want them to be able to take cover in woodland quickly.

Onagers, catapults

There appear to be two types of artillery depicted in the opening scene and it's worth remarking first on the sense in firing artillery into a wooded area. The trees would likely provide significant protection and make such action a waste of effort. The main heavy type seen appears to be a type of onager, which consisted of a single throwing arm held under tension which could deliver a stone some considerable distance. Also known as a scorpio in the early empire, they could throw stones weighing 25 kg 440 metres. Artillery stones found in the north of Britain weigh up to 50 kg.

Armour provided little protection to these powerful weapons and we hear gruesome details from the sources.[2] One example has a man's head being ripped off and thrown hundreds of yards away. Another has a pregnant woman being 'torn apart' and the unborn child tossed some distance away. While artillery was primarily an anti-personnel weapon, they tended to be used in sieges either to attack or defend the walls. They might be capable of

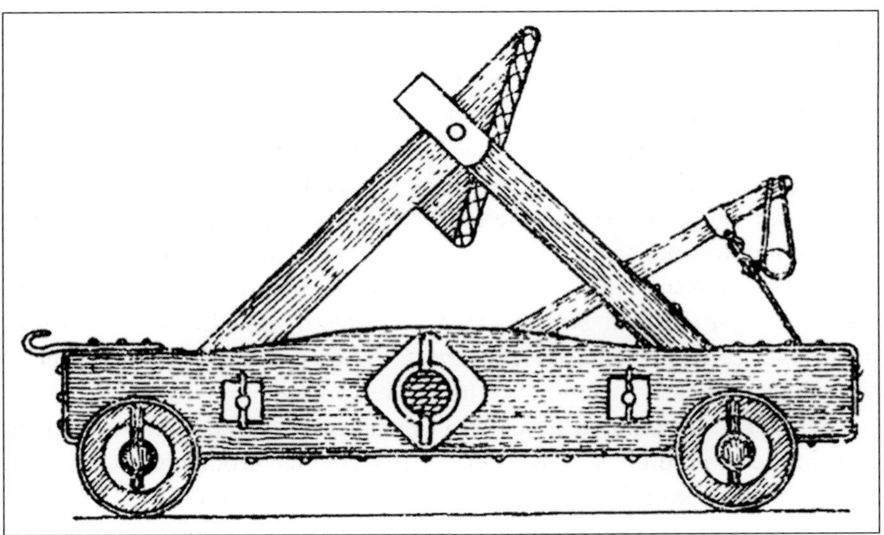

Picture 1: Roman onager (Wikimedia Commons)

Picture 2: Roman ballista (Wikimedia Commons)

Picture 3: Roman sling bullet from a scorpion (Wikimedia Commons)

damaging a thin parapet wall or temporary structure. What they could not do is knock down a substantial, or well-built stone wall or earthwork.

Being very heavy and difficult to manoeuvre, they were not easy to use on an open battlefield. They were either left in situ inside a fortification or, if attacking, transported to, or constructed on, site. In the film they are behind defensive earthworks and one could argue they are static defensive pieces. We see examples of such at Bremenium, High Rochester, north of Hadrian's Wall. Stone platforms 7.5 m by 10 m built behind the wall dated to the third century. Vegetius describes how each legion had ten *onagri*, one for each cohort, transported on wagons by oxen. But one must question the practicality of that when on campaign. A legion could travel twenty miles or more in a day and a cavalry unit much further, but a heavy carriage drawn by oxen would be lucky to travel ten miles in a day.

Nevertheless, the Romans did use some light artillery on the battlefield. One example was the ballista, which could fire either stones or bolts. An example found in Spain is estimated to have had a range of 300 metres.[3] Examples of carro-ballistae can be seen on Trajan's column where the pieces are mounted on carts. Bolts were 23–30 cm long. Ammianus describes one example as follows:[4] Between two posts a long iron bar is fixed which projects out 'like a great ruler'. To this is attached a squared staff 'hollowed out along its length with a narrow groove'. In this groove the gunner places a long wooden arrow tipped with 'a great iron point'. The arrow, 'driven by the power within, flies from the ballista… before the weapon is seen, the pain of a mortal wound makes itself felt.' He goes on to describe the scorpion or 'wild-ass'. A wooden arm, capable of holding a large stone, rises vertically (looking like a scorpion's sting) but can be pulled horizontally using iron hooks with tension supplied via the twisting of ropes. When released the arm returns to the vertical with a violent kick (like an ass) and the wooden beam strikes a 'soft hair-cloth' cushion. Another name he gives is an 'onager'.

While such machines were common, we don't have reports of fire being utilised outside the description of naval warfare by Vegetius. We do have an account of it being used against Roman forces in 52 BC at the siege of Bourges in Gaul.[5] Warriors of the Bituriges attempted to destroy the towers and ramps of the attacking Romans led by Julius Caesar, using pitch and lumps of grease. More warriors attempted to add to the fire and one was killed instantly by a dart from a scorpion. Caesar noted the bravery as one after another stepped forward as each was killed. The attempt to destroy the siege equipment failed but in the event Caesar had to break the siege as his supply line was threatened.

Camp

The opening credits state 'Just one final stronghold stands in the way.' Yet the scene starts at a Roman camp, supposedly Vindobona by the Danube River on the Limes Germanica, border. A civilian town grew around it and a Germanic settlement and market was present on the opposite bank of the Danube. As such it would have looked far more substantial than the film suggests. The provincial capital at Carnuntum was nearly forty kilometres to the south east. The legionary fortress would have covered twenty hectares and housed one of the four legions in Panonnia, approximately 6,000 men. Roman armies were capable of building much smaller, marching forts in a few short hours. The scene we are presented with looks nothing like a second-century Roman camp.

By the end of the fourth century Vegetius complains that building forts, along with the skills required, had been forgotten in his day.[6] Camps should be built near a good supply of water, firewood and fodder, avoiding swampy areas and those overlooked by higher ground. He describes three types:[7]

1. Where there's no immediate danger or for one night: a 3ft deep fosse or ditch is cut 5ft wide with the turves stacked up on the inside edge.
2. A 'stationary camp': a temporary fosse 9ft wide and 7ft deep.
3. When more serious forces threaten, a 12 to 17ft wide and 9ft deep fosse is built. Then inside an embankment 4ft high overlooks the fosse making it 13ft deep.

The bank is lined with sharpened stakes which the soldiers carried with them. Ramparts can be reinforced with logs and battlements and turrets constructed like a wall. If a threat was imminent the cavalry and half the infantry would stand ready as the remainder completed the camp. A legion could march up to twenty-four miles in five hours and then complete a camp by the evening.[8] Temporary marching camps could then be dismantled the next day. So even a small marching camp would likely have some sort of palisade. At the siege of Alesia in 52 BC, Julius Caesar had his men build ten miles of fortifications surrounding Vercingetorix and 80,000 Gauls in the hill fort. This took only three weeks. Realising a relief force of 240,000 was on its way, he then constructed an outer ring fourteen miles long.

We get a more accurate picture of a camp from this time from *De Munitionibus Castrorum*, 'Concerning the fortifications of a military camp', which was written just before the time in which *Gladiator* is set. This gives detailed descriptions of the layout of a typical camp from the first and second centuries. From this and archaeological records we can create a typical layout. This was usually of a square or rectangular 'playing card' shape. Each side had a gate from which two main roads converged on the principia, at the centre of the camp. The principia contained the commander's headquarters and an open courtyard or forum. It would also have contained a raised platform to address the troops and offices for day-to-day business. It also contained an aedes, or shrine, where the legion or unit's standards were kept, under which a strongroom was dug to keep the fort's cash reserves safe; armouries; armamentaria; and even rooms for officer recreation, scholae. Established camps would have had baths, granaries and even shops with local settlements growing up around them. A marching camp in enemy territory though would have no such luxuries.

It would certainly have at least one outer ditch or fossae, about 6ft deep and 5ft wide. Much of this would have be used to build up the rampart which was 6ft high and 8ft wide, to provide a fighting platform. On top of this would be placed a palisade. The legionaries carried 6ft hardened stakes, but these could be supplemented from local woods. This meant an attacker would be faced with a 6ft ditch, followed by a 6ft rampart topped with a 6ft wooden palisade. The gates were quite wide at 40ft, but this allowed rapid deployment and they were often protected by two towers. Inside the wall was the via sagularis, a road running round the perimeter of the camp. This allowed easy access to the ramparts from any part of the camp. Camps differed due to number and nature of units as well as terrain. A cavalry ala of 500 in the north of Britain might have a different layout to a full legion on the Danube. However the consistency between surviving examples from Hadrian's Wall to across the empire is striking.

It is also worth noting they were designed to be defended. Setting up a strong defensive position in enemy territory and provoking an attack can be a good strategy. If an enemy were to appear outside it would be better to allow them to attempt to attack the ramparts. Having gone to the trouble of building a fort, it is not clear why one would throw away such an asset by leaving it straight away.

In the film we don't see a traditional fort, what we see instead is earthworks with sharpened stakes on top. Even so, having taken that position one would be reluctant to leave it to fight on open ground. Far better to let the enemy attempt to attack. Of course it is possible a force might sally out of a camp or fort to counter attack, and we will see examples of that later when we look at contemporary battles.

Map 4: Roman camp layout

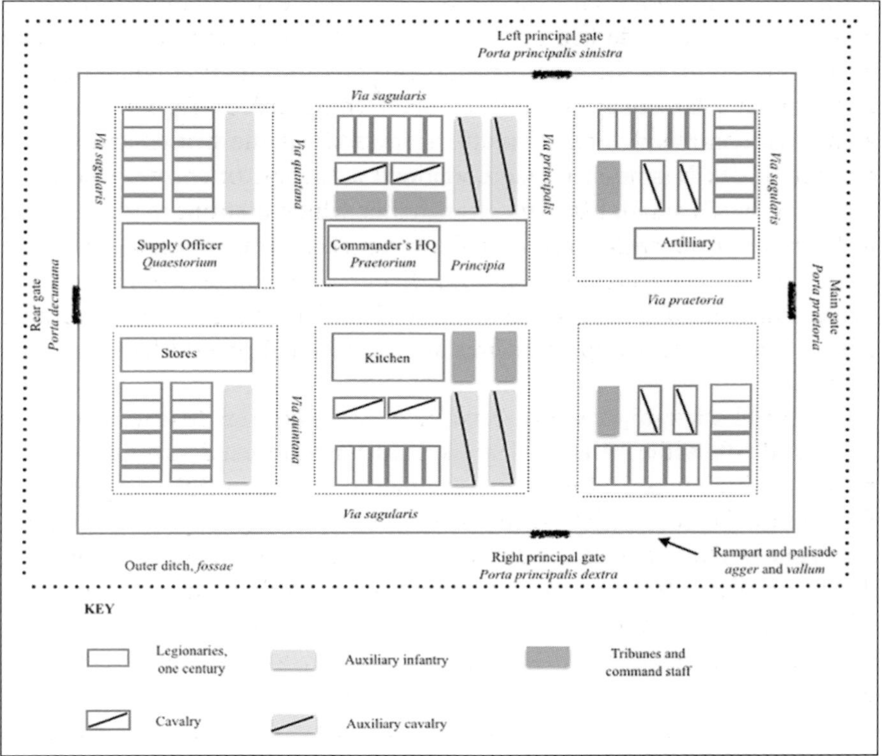

Infantry attack

We will cover the Roman army, tactics and contemporary accounts of battles in greater detail later. Briefly the Romans tended to advance first with light troops. These were often auxiliaries and would have been armed with javelins and light spears. But archers and slingers were also utilised and they would have been lightly armoured, or if auxiliaries, more likely worn chainmail rather than the loricia segmentata of the heavier legionaries. Should an enemy break then they could be pursued by cavalry on the flanks. If the enemy advanced then they would retreat behind the cohorts which, if one legion, were laid out in two lines of five cohorts, in a chequer-board pattern. Each cohort would consist of 480 men consisting of six centuries of eighty men. It was preferable to maintain some depth in the formation rather than several lines each with a depth of two or three as depicted.

The excellent HBO series *Rome* gives a far more realistic scenario. Here, a formation several men deep face the enemy. Each man holds the belt of the man in front. In this way a century of eighty men could, as an example, form a front of ten men wide by eight men deep. On a signal, the first line would form a loose shield wall with a small gap between each column. Every couple of minutes the centurion blows a whistle, the second line releases their grip on the man in front and the first line retreats down the gap between the columns to rest at the rear. The second line now take their place at the front. This allowed the men to rest as well as maintain formation or to advance or retreat in order.

Another feature of the main infantry was that each legionnaire carried two pila. At 2 metres long with an iron head of 60cm, it became accurate at about 30 metres. If it struck a shield it would often become embedded and the shape and length of the head made it impossible to remove, rendering the shield unusable. Thus a legion advancing with five cohorts would have over 2,700 men (the first cohort had five double centuries, giving it 800 men). We can thus imagine the effect of 5,400 pila on an advancing enemy. Especially if archers, slingers and light troops are continuing their barrage from the rear. Do you raise your shield to protect arrows from above

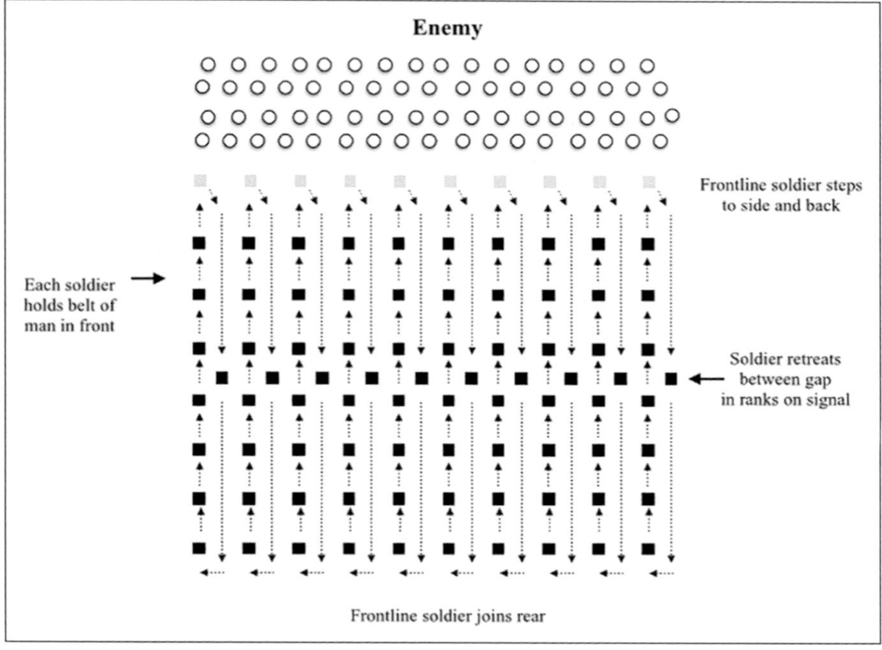

Figure 4: Roman century attacks in close formation

or hold in front to protect from javelins? Even if just the front ranks of the advancing cohorts deliver their missiles, then we are still looking at several hundred iron tipped spears hitting home.

In the battle scene, as dramatic and entertaining as it is, we get none of this. No light troops and no initial throwing of javelins. Instead, the Roman legionaries form a testudo. This formation presented a body of men with locked shields to front, back, sides and above resembling a tortoise or even a modern armoured vehicle. This would indeed protect the soldiers from arrows and javelins. However, it tended to be used in siege situations rather than open battle. It was used at Carrhae in 53 BC, but it restricted the legionaries' ability to fight and they were eventually cut to pieces by heavy cavalry and horse archers. The strength of an advancing legion was its organisation and the testudo disrupted the offensive capabilities. The historical situation was the end of the Marcomannic Wars, which means the final battle would not have been on Roman territory or anywhere near Vindobona. It would far more likely have been north of the Danube, either in an open battle or with the Romans besieging the Marcomanni.

Cavalry charge

The Roman army of the second century had cavalry units attached to each legion, seviri equitum Romanorum. The average strength was 120 men consisting of four turmae of thirty men.[9]

Cavalry were generally used for scouting, skirmishing and flanking. They were also ideal for chasing down a retreating army. The Romans used auxiliary and mercenary troops to supplement their forces. There were three main kinds of auxiliary forces: the cavalry alae; the infantry cohortes; and a mixed force of infantry and cavalry, the cohortes equitatae.

The ala consisted of 500 or 512 troops depending on the source, divided into turmae of thirty or thirty-two men each. Some units had a strength of 1,000 and these were divided into twenty four turmae suggesting a unit with about forty-two men in each. A praefectus commanded the cavalry 'wing' or infantry cohort and he would normally be of equestrian rank. The large scale use of auxiliary cavalry evolved from Caesar's campaigns and initially Gallic cavalry dominated. They used their own chiefs and internal organisms at first but this changed over time. Mixed units of cohortes equitum numbered 1,000 men, which included eight turmae of cavalry totalling 240 men.

It is thus quite possible to have a large-scale cavalry charge with a substantial force, although they would likely be an auxiliary force of Gallic or Germanic cavalry. However, a charge through woodland is unlikely. Aside from the obstruction of the trees, hidden holes and other obstacles would cause leg injuries and thrown riders. Additionally, what is not possible is the type of massed heavy cavalry charge seen in the middle ages with mounted armoured knights. First, stirrups did not appear in western Europe for another 400 years. They were introduced in the late sixth century by the Avars. However, it is not the stirrups but the saddle that enables a 'crashing shock charge' with a lance.[10] Specifically, a supporting saddle with high back and front panels makes this possible and we don't see this for many centuries.

The Normans were among the first to utilise this type of saddle. However, even as late as 1066 at Hastings, cavalry were used predominantly as a mobile missile platform from which to throw javelins. They had no ability to break through a solid shield wall. The Gallic saddle used by the Romans did give a firm platform, but they did not use a long lance until the adoption of the contus, a 4-metre long lance used by the Sarmatians and Parthians from the first century.

The later stirrup allowed a rider to strike downwards, left and right in a mêlée, and thus the longer spatha sword was ideal for such combat. A rider, or more likely a horse, would be vulnerable to a spear thrust however. One interesting tactic is described by Vegetius: when outnumbered, cavalry is mixed with light infantry, velites, with light shields and javelins and he claims this 'cannot be matched' by an opposing cavalry force.[11] Another way to defend against cavalry was with caltrops, made from metal with four spikes. Three rest on the ground with the remaining one sticking up. In general cavalry will not charge into massed infantry and are likely to pull up, especially if there's a solid shield wall protected by spears.

Having said that, there were examples of cavalry charges tipping the balance. At Cannae in 216 BC for example, Hannibal's cavalry returned to the battlefield after routing the Roman cavalry. They attacked the Roman rear, closing the 'box' Hannibal had created by flanking spearmen and the Romans were destroyed. Fourteen years later at Zama, Scipio gained revenge and defeated Hannibal. In this case the two armies fought a closely contested battle that went back and forth. Scipio's cavalry had a numerical advantage and drove off their opponents on both wings. It was their return and rear attack that broke the Carthaginian army. However, both these cases were in open country and involved a rear attack at a pivotal point in the battle.

A cavalry charge through woodland would be hazardous in the extreme. A rear or flank attack by an auxiliary force on open ground is quite possible. But this would not be a medieval heavy cavalry charge. With no stirrups or appropriate saddle they would more likely be throwing javelins or attacking exposed individuals with spear or spatha sword in a mêlée. They would come into their own if the enemy routed and they could chase down fleeing warriors. They would have been an auxiliary force, led by an equestrian praefectus. As a general, Maximus would have been more likely have been positioned to the rear with his command staff.

It is, however, not an impossible scenario. Caesar at the siege of Alesia personally led a counter attack, although as the author he may have embellished the account. We see here another example of a rear attack by cavalry. Caesar was apparently 'known by the colour of his cloak'. As they attacked from the rear they were noticed by the Roman troops on the ramparts besieging the Gallic camp. Then 'the enemy joined battle: a shout was raised on both sides, and taken up by an answering shout from the rampart and the whole of the entrenchments'. The infantry discarded their pikes and got to work with their swords'. As the defenders of the rampart stacked so the cavalry appeared to the rear. The Gauls fled but 'the cavalry met them in flight, and a great slaughter ensued'.[12]

In AD 172 the legionary legate Marcus Valerius Maximianus personally killed the chieftain of the Germanic tribe Naristi. For this act he received a stallion from the emperor as a reward. He led the legio II Adiutrix pia fidelis in the Marcomannic Wars and is one of the possible candidates for our hero in the film. He commanded the army at the final battle of the war at Laugaricio in AD 179/180. To summarise, the concept of a general leading a cavalry charge is not implausible. The scene depicted is, however, most unlikely.

Germanic tribes

Germanic peoples had migrated south from northern Europe and evolved into a myriad of tribes east of the Rhine and north of the Danube. The Roman expansion into what they called Germania was halted abruptly by the devastating defeat in AD 9 in the Teutoburg forest. Three legions were lured into a trap by a Roman auxiliary commander, and chief of the Cherusci, Arminius. Later campaigns by Germanicus achieved some revenge, but the disaster at Teutoburg demonstrates the Germanic tribes were a formidable and dangerous enemy. We can see below the main

Germanic tribes bordering the Danube and Rhine frontiers, as well as Dacians and Sarmatians to the east.

Germanic infantry was usually part time and armed with spears and iron swords, longer than the Roman gladius. In the first century Tacitus recording the wars of Germanicus in the early first century, describes the Germanic warriors as having ‘huge shields’ and ‘enormous spears’. Tacitus claims these were not as manageable as the Roman weapons and armour, especially in forested areas. They carried ‘neither corselet nor headpiece’ and did not protect their shields with metal or hide. The tactic was ‘to strike thick and fast, and to direct the point to the face’. Only the first line carried spears, ‘the remainder had only darts, fire-pointed or too short’. Tacitus had a poor opinion of their fighting spirit describing them as lacking stamina and being ‘faint-hearted in adversary’.[13]

It is important to remember the Germans were not a homogenous group. Tactics and equipment would have differed from tribe to tribe. By the second century shields and helmets were common but only the chiefs and elites wore armour, which tended to be chainmail hauberks.[14] By the fourth century the Roman army had adopted the ‘barritus’, or Germanic war cry.[15] This could be a result of the significant presence of Germanic troops. It suggests it was a feature of Germanic warfare and is a reasonable portrayal in the film. In AD 70, a combined Gallic and Germanic force attacked a Roman camp outside the town of Treverorum near modern

Map 5: Barbarian tribes and Roman provinces, second century (Wikimedia Commons)

Trier. In this instance, a massed night assault breached the defences before being pushed back. So we see here that while the Germans may have had less training and discipline, they were not foolish. There is little point in advancing out of the cover of a forest and standing within range of missile attack from bows or artillery and advertising your presence. If they had intended to attack a fortification, they would more likely have used the element of surprise. It might have made sense if they intended to lure the infantry out of the fort and into the wooded area in order to ambush them. Indeed, many of the successes came from ambushes. Cassius Dio describes how the Sugambri, Usipetes, and Tencteri had 'first seized in their own territory some of the Romans and had crucified them'. They then crossed the Rhine and raided Germania and Gaul. The Romans sent a cavalry force against them but the raiders 'surprised them from ambush'. The Romans fled and were met by Lollius, the governor of the province, presumably with a relief force. But the raiders had followed the Romans and fell upon both groups wining that battle too.[16]

In terms of armour, by the second century many more warriors would have served as auxiliaries or inherited stolen armour from past battles. The German warriors, therefore, would have been far better armed and protected than the film portrays. The army is exclusively infantry and indeed, later heroic poetry of the Dark Ages almost always describes fighting on foot.[17] While they became proficient on horseback after coming into contact with Eastern warfare, the Franks and Anglo-Saxons still fought mainly on foot in the fifth and sixth centuries.[18] Procopius describing a Gothic army in AD 539 states there were few horsemen and they were mainly infantry with swords, axes and shields. The battle began with a volley of axes before they charged with swords and spears.

Although these examples are much later, they are perhaps instructive. A sixth-century manual of war, *Strategicon*, states the Franks and Lombards dismount to fight with shields, lances and swords: 'they fight according to families and not in regular troops … they charge swiftly with much spirit. They do not obey their leaders well. Headstrong, despising strategy, precaution of foresight, they show contempt for every tactical command especially cavalry.'[19]

A different source describes the Franks: 'sword, shield, double-headed axe and barbed spear. With few wearing helmets, mail or having horses. The chiefs had long swords and fought on foot for which they are 'extremely well practised'.'[20] On the other hand, Procopius describes Goths and Vandals using cavalry – not as a mobile missile platform however, but rather to use the spear as a thrusting weapon.[21] The late arrival of

Gothic cavalry at the battle of Adrianople in AD 378 is seen as pivotal in the Roman defeat. The Sarmatian Iazyges used cavalry extensively. Many were armoured with horn scales and the nobility often had chainmail. Their main weapons were the bow and a contos, a 4-metre lance wielded with two hands.

Nevertheless, a Germanic army of Marcomanni or Quadi warriors in the second century would likely be mostly infantry. Shields would have been round, rectangular or sexagonal, with a large boss and iron edging. In the first century, about one in ten warriors would have had swords.[22] This ratio would have likely increased by AD 180, but the spear would still be the dominant weapon. Axes were prominent in later centuries, especially throwing axes such as the francisca of the Franks. Given how common axes were as a tool, there's no reason why it wouldn't have been used in battle. The film does rather well in showing most of the warriors carrying spears. The initial archery volley is also realistic. It is noticeable that there are women present and Cassius does indeed mention this: 'Among the corpses of the barbarians there were found even women's bodies in armour.' (Cassius Dio book 61.3)

In summary, the battle scene is very entertaining and dramatic. The weapons and armour are fairly realistic and there are several nice authentic touches. The archers appear to be auxiliaries correctly wearing chain mail rather than the segmented plate armour of the legionnaires. However, some of the tactics are implausible. Fire arrows, artillery and cavalry charges in woods are perhaps the most glaring.

Marcomannic Wars

We will now turn our attention to the war depicted in the film. Trajan's reign had pushed the borders of the empire to its further extent. Most of the forts on the frontier along the Danube were built during this period. In Trajan's time the Danube became one of the most important routes in the empire.[23] His successors, Hadrian and Antoninus Pius, had experienced a period of relative stability. This ended on the accession of Marcus Aurelius and his co-emperor and adoptive brother, Lucius Verus, in AD 161. War broke out with the Parthians almost immediately, which resulted in a Roman victory by AD 166. At the same time unrest increased in the tribes along the Danube border; Germanic tribes such as the Marcomanni, Juthungi and Quadi in the unconquered Germania Magna, and the Sarmatian Iazyges to the south (roughly modern Hungary).

There had been peace with the Sarmatians Iazyges east of the Danube for five decades. The same could not be said for the Germanic tribes to the north however. A period of instability and insecurity is marked by an increase in the distribution of coin hoards.[24] However, the *Historia Augusta*, possibly from the fourth century, suggests the war did break out unexpectedly: 'While the Parthian War was still in progress the Marcomannic Wars broke out but was skilfully postponed by the men on the spot so that the eastern conflict could be finished first.'[25]

The 'men on the spot' were likely the governors of the bordering provinces: Pannonia, Dacia and Noricum. Events were clearly unexpected because in AD 161 Marcus had redeployed one of his best legions, legio II Adiutrix, to the East. Indeed, vexillations, units temporarily assigned, were taken from nearly all the legions from the Danube to assist Lucius Verus in the war against Parthia. There is some indication that Marcus may have been considering establishing new provinces north and east of the Danube.[26] If true, subsequent events must have put paid to that.

It has been suggested that some of the tribes along the border were actually offering armed help in exchange for permission to settle.[27] There is, therefore, the possibility that some groups might have welcomed coming under Roman protection. This was influenced by the pressure from the expansion of other tribes further east. It is perhaps telling that the initial problems came not from the Quadi or Marcomanni, but from tribes further north and east. Minor incursions began between AD 162 and 165, taking advantage of Rome's distraction in the East. Raids into Germania Superior and Raetia across the Rhine and Danube by the Germanic Chatti and Chauci caused significant disruption before being repulsed. In AD 166, a major invasion of 6,000 Langobard and Lacringli warriors crossed the Danube into Pannonia Superior. These were defeated and driven out after a battle near the River Ister (Danube). Cassius Dio records that it was the cavalry led by Vindex and the infantry commanded by Candidus.[28] The raiders were 'completely routed'. They were thrown into such 'consternation' they sent envoys.

These envoys went to the governor of Pannonia Superior, Iallius Bassus, using Ballomar, king of the Marcomanni, and the kings of ten other tribes. The kings made oaths, peace was agreed and the barbarians returned home. Later that year the Sarmatian Iazyges, with Vandal allies, invaded Dacia. This proved more dangerous; the frontier was overrun and the governor, Calpurnius Proculus, was killed together with the forces he managed to scratch together. The emperor was forced to dispatch the experienced legio IV Macedonia from Moesia Inferior, which drove the invaders out and stabilised the area.

In AD 167 a plague swept across the empire. Likely brought back from Parthia by returning troops, history remembers this as the Antonine plague. The weakened state of the empire may have prompted the tribes north of the Danube to take advantage of the situation. There is some debate whether the following event occurred in AD 167 or 170. The Marcommanic king, Ballamor, broke the treaty and invaded, attacking at Carnuntum. Against them was the legio XIV Gemina Martia Victrix and 14,000 auxiliaries. Rome suffered its worse defeat in a hundred years, losing 20,000 men. Ballamor split his army in two. One group went west to pillage the province of Noricum; the second headed south and reached Italy, sacking Opitergium and besieging Aquileia, on the Adriatic coast.

Manpower was so short that the army was forced to recruit gladiators, bandits and Germanic warriors to their ranks. Marcus Aurelius recruited two new legions, legio II Italica and legio III Italica. In early AD 168, Marcus ordered a praetorian prefect, Titus Furius Victorinus, to lead a force north. He perished with his force in another defeat for the Romans.

Marcus sent his general Tiberius Claudius Pompeianus to drive them off and also turned to Pertinax, the future emperor after Commodus. Marcus Aurelius and Lucius Verus established their base at Aquileia and planned their campaign. In late AD 168, the Romans advanced towards the legionary fortress at Carnuntum causing the Germans to withdraw and give assurances of peace. Having been appointed procurator of Dacia and Moesia Superior, Pertinax spent some time stabilising the area and economy, strengthening the border and fortifications. This allowed the recruitment of much-needed men. Marcus then redeployed legions from the border and appointed the experienced Pompeianus commander in chief. Pertinax also spent some time as aide to Pompeianus before being promoted to senator, allowing him to take command of *legio I Adiutrix pia fidelis* in Pannonia Superior. Pompeianus bolstered the fleet on the Danube and fortifications in Italy before relieving Aquileia. The Marcomanni and Quadi were defeated and driven out with heavy losses. Pertinax led his men West and destroyed the other Germanic force in Noricum. Aurelius spent some time rebuilding the defences along the Danube and seeking treaties with the Quadi and Iazyges.

The emperors returned to winter at Aquileia and plan for the following year. Unfortunately, Lucius Verus died in January AD 169. We know Marcus was in Aquileia in AD 168 and back on the frontier in AD 169, and that he ordered increased fortifications on the border. These facts all suggest the main invasion had passed. Marcus Aurelius, now the sole emperor, returned to Rome to plan for the funeral. By the autumn he was back at the frontier and on the offensive. His target was the Sarmatians, but they struck first towards the goldmines of Alburnum in Dacia.[29] The governor of Moesia Inferior, Claudius Fronto, led a force to defeat and was killed. At the same time, the Costoboci tribe attacked the Roman province of Thracia and advanced as far south as Athens before being repulsed by vexillations led by the local procurator.

By late AD 170 it seems the situation had stabilised. In AD 171, the Romans went on the offensive and in the spring of AD 172, the legions crossed the Danube from Pannonia Superior and Noricum. The target was the Marcomanni, and any other Germanic or Sarmatian tribes allied to them. A quick victory followed, the Marcomanni agreed peace terms and Aurelius took the title Germanicus. There is one battle worthy of note on the frozen River Danube in AD 172 against a Sarmatian Iazyges force. The Romans were pursuing the Iazyges as they crossed the river and the Sarmatians, thinking they might have a tactical advantage on the ice, turned on their pursuers. Some charged directly at the Roman formation, while cavalry swept round the flanks. The Romans, however, formed up into a defensive square. Dio Cassius describes the battle further:[30] The Romans 'formed in a compact body, facing all their foes at once, and most of them laid down their shields and rested one foot upon them, so that they might not slip so much'. They held firm against the enemy's charge and started to seize the bridles of the cavalry and 'the shields and spearshafts of their assailants'.

A close conflict mêlée ensued and Sarmatian men and horses were pulled down by the legionaries. While many of the Romans also fell, they used wrestling techniques to throw their opponents over their heads using their feet. If the Sarmatians fell on top, we get a vivid picture of how the Romans would seize his opponent 'with his teeth'. Cassius then described how the barbarians, 'being unused to a contest of this sort, and having lighter equipment, were unable to resist'. Pertinax led the legio I Adiutrix pia fidelis in the campaign. Another general that rose to fame was Marcus Valerius Maximianus, who led the legio II Adiutrix pia fidelis against the Germanic tribes further north. Notably, he killed the chieftain of the Naristi in single combat and received a stallion from the emperor as a reward.[31]

In AD 173 the Quadi again broke the treaty. They were quickly defeated and the campaign was marked by the 'miracle of the rain'. Other sources describe it as 'The Battle of the Thundering Legion'.[32] A Roman legion was trapped by a much larger force. Thirst and heat led them to the point of surrender when they were saved by a sudden downpour. A lightening strike on the Quadi camp caused them to flee in fear. A fourth-century Roman Christian historian, Paulus Orosius, claimed this miracle was due to a 'division' of Christians in the Roman ranks who prayed to god for a miracle. Cassius Dio, however, attributes the miracle to 'Arnuphis, an Egyptian magician, who was a companion of Marcus, [and] invoked by means of enchantments various deities and in particular Mercury, the god of the air.'

In the same year, the Chauci crossed the lower Rhine and broke through the frontier defences raiding deep into modern Belgium. The governor of Gallia Belgica, Didius Julianus, was another future emperor in AD 193 – the year of the five emperors. In AD 173 he recruited a local force which drove the raiders back across the Rhine before refortifying the border and English Channel. In the following two years Aurelius exacted revenge. Crossing the Danube in the spring of AD 174, he subjugated the Quadi, took hostages, deposed the king, imposed a new ruler and posted garrisons throughout the territory.

The following year the Romans crossed the Danube again and attacked deep into the land of the Sarmatian Iazyges. Troops from both Pannonia Inferior and Dacia advanced deep into modern Hungary, aiming towards the River Tizsa area. A number of victories resulted in the surrender of King Zanticus. Roman prisoners were returned, allegedly numbering 100,000, and the Iazyges were forced to supply 8,000 auxiliary cavalry. A large proportion, 5,500, were sent to northern Britain near Hadrian's Wall. Aurelius received the title Sarmaticus, and this ended the first Marcommanic war. It was during this period that Marcus Aurelius wrote his philosophical tract, Meditations, to himself. We will look at this in more detail later.

Within two years the emperor was forced to fight again. In early AD 177 the Quadi once more revolted. Soon the whole upper Danube was affected by incursions from Germanic raiders. Marcus arrived at Carmuntum in Pannonia Superior and put Marcus Valerius Maximianus in charge of his army. A punitive strike followed the raiders back across the Danube to ravage much of their homeland. From there they attacked the Quadi and comprehensively destroyed their forces at the battle of Laugaricio in modern Slovakia. Maximianus's legio II Adiutrix pia fidelis performed particularly well. The war effectively ended when the emperor died in March AD 180. The last major battle was therefore at Laugaricio in AD 179.

The battle was near Trenčín, Slovakia, near the Czech border. This is about 143 kilometres north-west of Vienna on the River Danube. It is also 123 kilometres directly north of the Danube and the border with modern Hungary – deep inside enemy territory and far away from Vindobona. It would have been more accurate to have had the Germans attack a Roman marching camp. The Romans would have taken about four or five days to cover the eighty-eight miles from Vindobona, and would have constructed marching camps along the way, which would have been garrisoned or dismantled as they went. Perhaps more realistically, the last battle would have been a Roman assault on a last refuge, or a barbarian assault on a marching camp.

We will cover the succession in more depth later. For now it's enough to state that Marcus had raised Commodus to be emperor. There is no indication he had any intention to restore Rome to the republic. Joaquin Phoenix, who played Commodus, was 26 when the film was released. The real Commodus was 18 at the time of his father's death. Nor is there any truth in the scene where he murders his father. Most sources support the fact he died from disease. Galen, the famous Roman physician, was present and recorded his symptoms, which are indicative of smallpox. As he lingered on his deathbed he summoned his counsellors, including Pompeianus – by now his son-in-law after marrying Lucilla. Contrary to the film, she hated her new husband because of his relative old age and low birth. The emperor recommended Commodus to his generals, who in turn presented him to the army.

Marcus was the first emperor in seventy years to have a son and heir succeed him. Commodus showed little interest in continuing his father's campaign. He quickly agreed peace treaties with both the Marcomanni and Quadi, against the advice of his military commanders.[33] The terms included the supply of 20,000 warriors to serve as auxiliaries, spread widely across units throughout the empire. Those remaining were disarmed and the northern bank of the Danube cleared of settlements. They were also forbidden to attack their neighbours, the Iazyges or Vandals. On 22 October AD 180, Commodus celebrated the end of the second Marcommanic War with what was described as 'the Peace of Commodus'.[34]

Within two years trouble broke out again, this time it was the Iazyges and the Buri, a Germanic tribe to the north of the Marcomanni. Commodus ordered his legions north and Maximianus once more led them to victory. Also in command roles were the senators Clodius Albinus and Pescennius Niger, both of whom were to be emperors after the death of Commodus in AD 193, the 'Year of the Five Emperors'. By AD 182 Commodus was able to hail himself Germanicus Maximus, and there followed a long period of relative stability on the Danube frontier. However, the increased influence of Germanic troops and settlement within the empire proved pivotal for later developments, such as the 'Crisis of the third century'.

While there is some debate about the exact timing and sequence of events, it is possible to simplify the Marcomanni wars as follows: an initial period of unrest and incursions between AD 162 and 165 was stabilised by the governor of Pannonia with the Marcomanni king, Ballomar. However, between AD 166 and 170, several major invasions of Roman territory occurred. The Romans suffered a heavy defeat at Carnuntum by the Marcomanni, and Aquileia in northern Italy was besieged. The Sarmatians invaded twice, killing the governors of Dacia and Moesia. In AD 171 the Romans went on the offensive, and by AD 175 had achieved victory. In AD 177 the Second Marcomanni War was confined to the Quadi and Marcomanni, and by AD 180 the Romans were again victorious. The Third Marcomanni War appears to have been a continuation of the war by Commodus. This time, however, it was directed against the Sarmatians, Buri and Dacians. By AD 182 Commodus had claimed victory. The maps below show the main campaigns.

Map 6: First Marcomannic War (Wikimedia Commons)

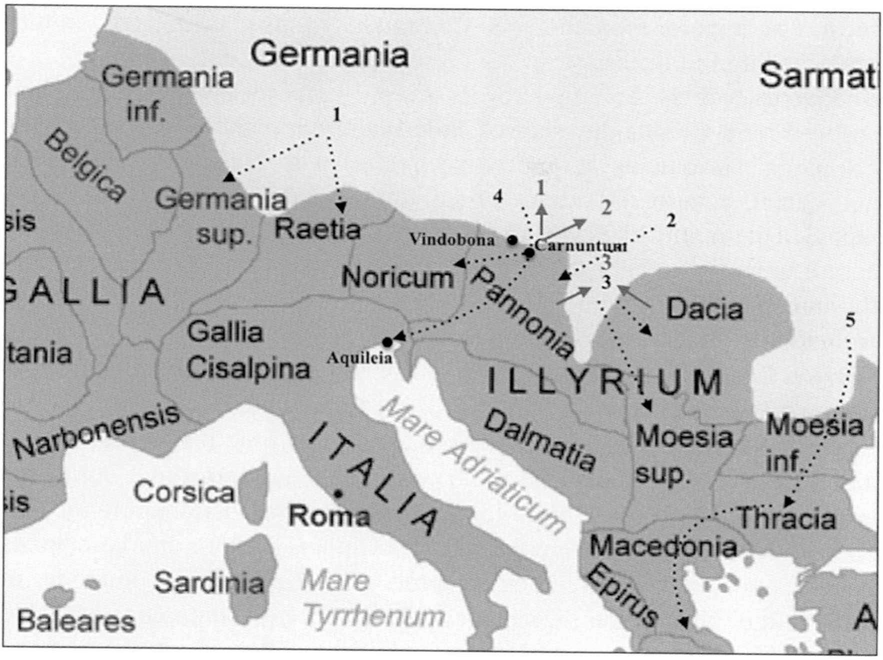

Key
1. c. 162–5 Chatti and Chauci
2. c 166/7 Langobard nd Lancringi
3. 167 and 169 Sarmtians
4. c167/8 marcomanni
5. c 170 Costobocci

Roman counter offensivies
1. c. 172 Marcomanni
2. c. 174 Quadi
3. c.175 Sarmatians

Map 7: Second and Third Marcomannic wars (Wikimedia Commons)

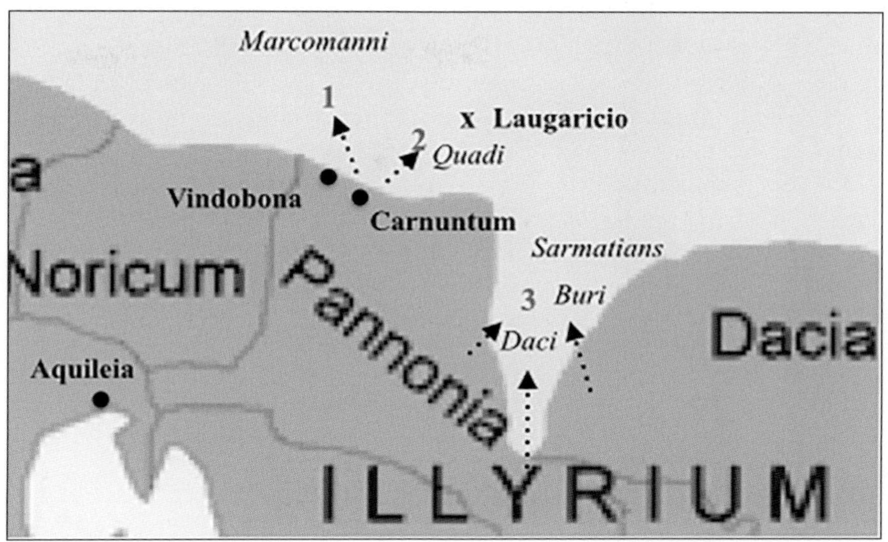

Key

2nd Marcomanni War
1. 178 Marcomanni
2. 179/80 Quadi

3rd Marcomanni War
3. 180–2 Sarmatians, Buri and Daci

The Column of Marcus Aurelius

The column of Marcus Aurelius in the Campus Martius in Rome was erected to commemorate his victories in the Germanic wars in from AD 166 to his death. It depicts scenes from his campaigns in the Danube region and was started after his death in AD 180. An inscription nearby suggests it was completed in AD 193. It is one of the best preserved monuments to have survived. There is some debate about its purpose, but Iain Ferris in *Hate and War, The Column of Marcus Aurelius*, suggests it have have been both a funerary and a triumphal monument.[35] It was the most labour intensive building project for several decades and demonstrates Commodus's wish to honour his father. The whole monument is nearly 52 metres in height and the column itself nearly 30 metres, containing twenty-six 'drums' of marble. The base has a doorway leading to a spiral staircase of 200 steps to a viewing platform on top. Thirty-nine narrow window slits allow some light into the interior.

The scenes cannot be read as a literal or chronological narrative. The column can be distinguished from Trajan's column due to the more defensive nature of the scenes and the greater number of battle scenes. Picture five

Picture 4: The Column of Marcus Aurelius (Wikimedia Commons)

Picture 5: Detail from The Column of Marcus Aurelius (Wikimedia Commons)

shows a number of interesting scenes; first, at the base is a pontoon bridge over which the army crosses. The emperor addresses his troops on the next level. The carroballista directly above can be seen more clearly in picture six.

Picture 6: Roman carroballista (Wikimedia Commons)

Picture 7: 'The miracle of the Rain' scene xvi (Wikimedia Commons)

Two scenes are worth noting. Two weather scenes: the 'Miracle of the Thunderbolt' and the 'Miracle of the Rain'. Both are depicted quite low down in scenes eleven and sixteen. The first scene shows a Roman fort besieged, with Marcus Aurelius to one side surrounded by legionnaires. The dramatic moment a wooden siege tower is destroyed by lightening is followed by the emperor sacrificing to the gods to give thanks. The second scene attempts to depict the famous battle, where a Roman army is on the point of collapse from thirst, heat and hunger. The column has a huge rain god type figure with wings outstretched, bringing salvation, and rain, to the beleaguered army.

One section shows Germanic warriors bound and awaiting execution. One figure lies with his severed head next to his body. The final stages of the Second Marcomannic War was in fact a bloody war of attrition that resulted in the destruction of vast swathes of Germanic territory. Much of it, and certainly the last stages and final battles, was fought north and east of the Danubian frontier. No doubt tens of thousands of people from various tribes were killed, maimed, or taken into slavery. Examples of Roman soldiers in different types of armour can be seen in pictures eight and nine.

There are scenes of bound, captured soldiers being executed; decapitated bodies litter the floor. Villages are depicted as sacked and burnt. Picture ten shows one of the more harrowing scenes. Captured women and children are driven away, presumably into captivity by Roman soldiers. In the centre a woman is being pulled by her hair as she tries to maintain her dignity with her left arm across her falling dress. Just ahead a small child, perhaps hers, is pushed away.

Picture 8: Soldiers wearing lorica segmentata (Wikimedia Commons)

Picture 9: Soldiers wearing lorica squamata and lorica hamata (Wikimedia Commons)

Picture 10: Captured woman scene (Wikimedia Commons)

What we see in the column is the full horror of warfare. Many of these scenes, if taken as pictures today, could be used as evidence in a war crimes trial. Prisoners executed, civilians targeted and women and children taken into slavery. It is tantalising to wonder if Tiberius Claudius Pompeianus and Marcus Valerius Maximianus were depicted anywhere. The artists certainly showed the emperor in several scenes. It is to these two figures we will turn to next.

Tiberius Claudius Pompeianus

Pompeianus was born in Antioch in Syria in c.AD 125. His family came from the equestrian order and gained Roman citizenship during the reign of Claudius. He was the first member of his family to be made a senator and thus was sometimes patronisingly called a novus homo, or 'new man'. During the Parthian War of AD 161–166 he served under Lucius Verus, the co-emperor, as a legionary commander. He was elevated to senator and appointed a 'suffect' consul in AD 162. Usually consuls were appointed for a year, but if one died or retired in post a temporary, or suffect, consul was appointed to serve out the term.

Sometime later, c.AD 164, he was appointed military governor of Pannonia Inferior. He was thus in place when the Langobardi and Lacringi invaded in AD 166 with a force of 6,000. He was also in post when two other senior officers were killed. The first, Calpurnius Proculus, governor of Dacia was killed with his men trying to stop the Sarmatian Iazyges and Vandals. The second, in AD 169, was the governor of Moesia Inferior, Claudius Fronto, who led a force to defeat, again against the Sarmatians. Being a governor or military commander in the Roman Empire of the second century was not a risk-free office job.

In AD 169 the co-emperor Lucius Verus died, leaving Marcus Aurelius's daughter Lucilla a widow at around 19 years old. The emperor arranged the marriage of Lucilla to Pompeianus, making Tiberius part of the Imperial family, the Nerva Antonine dynasty. Lucilla and her mother, Faustina, both opposed the match. Not only was Pompeianus 'old' at nearly 44, but more importantly he came from equestrian stock. Lucilla, having been married to a co-emperor, considered herself far above such a person. It is possible that Marcus did not want his daughter to marry a potential high-ranking rival and have a future claim; whatever the case, he over ruled the objections of both his wife and daughter.

It was at this point that Marcus allegedly offered to name his new son-in-law as Caesar, making him his heir. Commodus was about eight years old at this point and perhaps Marcus was conscious of his own health and wanted someone to protect his son's future. The Emperor Hadrian had had a similar dilemma three decades before; he nominated the obscure and relative elderly Antoninus on condition he in turn adopt the future Marcus Aurelius and Lucius Verus, both of whom were too young to succeed. Whatever the case, Pompeianus declined and was promoted to overall command in the continuing Marcomannic War. Having served with Pertinax in the previous Parthian War they were well acquainted, so it was perhaps natural that Pertinax was posted to Pompeianus's command staff. Further military successes led to a second consulship in AD 173.

Pompeianus continued military operations on the Danube frontier until the death of the emperor in AD 180. He tried to encourage his brother-in-law Commodus, the new 18-year-old emperor, to continue the campaign. Although records claim that Commodus returned to Rome and agreed peace with the Germanic tribes, it would appear he did in fact stay on the northern frontier for a year or two to conduct the Third Marcomannic War, returning to Rome only for his father's funeral. In AD 182 Lucilla was implicated in a plot to kill Commodus; this cost her her life, along with other members of the family. Surprisingly, Pompeianus was not implicated and survived the reprisals. Following this he, perhaps understandably, retreated from public life citing old age and an ailment of the eyes.

Following the murder of Commodus in AD 193, Pertinax – now Urban Prefect of Rome – offered Pompeianus, his old mentor and friend, the throne for a second time. He declined, perhaps sensibly, as Pertinax, having taken the throne himself, was murdered just eighty-seven days later. The year of the five emperors soon claimed another life. The senator Didius Julianus had bribed the Praetorian Guards to take the throne but soon realised he lacked support. Lacking support was often a fatal condition and so Julianus asked Pompeianus to be co-emperor. For a third and final time he declined and the new emperor lasted just sixty-six days. Again, he cited age and eye problems so perhaps this was a genuine reason. The new emperor was Septimius Severus, who ruled until AD 211. Pompeianus appears to have died in AD 193 but his children survived and even prospered, suggesting he hadn't fallen from grace.

There is of course no real connection with the hero of the film. He was arguably Marcus's favoured general and there was a relationship with Lucilla, but that is about where the similarities end. As we shall see later, he may have been in on the plot that finally killed Commodus. At the very least, it was odd he just happened to be in Rome on the night in question. However, there is no evidence he fell out of favour at any point and he certainly never fought as a gladiator.

Marcus Valerius Maximianus

Maximianus fought in both the Parthian and Marcomannic Wars. He is believed to have been born in Poetovia, modern Ptuj in Slovenia. His father, of the same name was a local magistrate and priest. Unfortunately we know very little of his life, but it is estimated he was born c. AD 130. His military career began as prefect of a cavalry cohort and he worked his way up through various posts (listed below). In AD 172 Maximianus led an *ala*, an auxiliary cavalry unit, in the campaign against the Marcomanni, Sarmatian Iazyges and their allies. It was here he killed Valao, chieftain of Naristi, in single combat and received a stallion from the emperor as a reward. In AD 175, he led the cavalry to Syria to help defeat the revolt of Avidius Cassius. He was then appointed procurator of Moesia Inferior. This was a financial administrative post open to equestrians. He must have been reasonably successful as he went on to procuratorships in Moesia Superior and Dacia.

In around AD 178–9 he was elected to the senate, the first native of Panonnia to have achieved this honour. This allowed access to higher positions and he was given command of a legion. As a legatus he commanded the following legions: Legio I Adiutrix, Legio II Adiutrix, Legio V Macedonia, Legio VIII Gemina and Legio III Augusta. He was in charge of the winter quarters at Laugaricio in Slovakia for the final battle of the war in AD 180. There exists an inscription for him in Laugaricio from AD 179:

> To the victory of emperors, dedicated by 855 soldiers of the Second Legion of the army stationed in Laugaricio. Made to order of Marcus Valerius Maximianus, legate of the Second Adiutrix legion

Unlike in Gladiator and his near namesake, Maximianus was decorated by Commodus and he went on to govern the province of Numidia. His last known appointment was as suffect consul in AD 186. His fate is unknown. The fact that such a famous and well connected general is not mentioned by any of the sources might suggest he died before the 'year of the five Emperors' in AD 193. Pompeianus, his contemporary and colleague, remained influential. Certainly if he was born c. AD 130, then he would be in his late fifties when we last hear of him, in an age where life expectancy was relatively short. What we can say is that his life bears little resemblance to the fictional Maximus beyond involvement in the last battle of the Marcomannic War. Having said that, in his early career, as commander of an *ala*, he would indeed have led cavalry charges – although probably not through a dense forest.

A second inscription at Diana Veteranorum, Numidia (Zana, Algeria) gives an extensive and detailed list of his achievements and career, creating a vivid picture of a military and civilian career in the second century. His first military post is as praefectus of the first cohort of Thracians, followed by command of the coastline of Pontus Polemonianus. He was decorated by Marcus Aurelius in the Parthian War of AD 161–6. He was then tasked with bringing food by boat down the river Danube to supply the armies in Pannonia and subsequently served with the Misenum, Ravenna and British fleets. He then returned to dry land, leading African and Moorish cavalry in Pannonia and as praefectus of the first ala of Aravacans. It was during the Germanic Wars he was praised by the emperor for killing Valao, chief of the Naristi, with his own hand. For this he received a horse, decorations and weapons. He then became praefectus of the ala of lance-bearers and was decorated in the Marcommanic and Sarmatian War. All this must have occurred before AD 175 because we then read he was placed in charge of the cavalry of the Marcomanni, Naristi and Quadi and sent to the east to fight the rebellion of Avidius. The next posts listed are procuratorships: Lower Moesia; Upper Moesia, and Dacia Porolissensis, During this time he leads detachments to drive out a band of Brisean brigands on the borders of Macedonia and Thrace. We then read he was admitted to the senate, allowing him a series of posts as legion commander: Legate of Legio I Adiutrix; Legio II Adiutrix; Legio V Macedonica; Legio I Italica; Legio XIII Gemina; and Legio III Augusta, this last one with propraetorian power, meaning he was governor. He was decorated by Commodus during the second Marcomannic War.

A couple of points are worth noting from the long detailed inscription. First, we see how quickly the Romans were to incorporate recently defeated peoples into their auxiliary units. Soon after defeating the Naristi and killing their chief he is leading them east to fight Avidius. It is with cavalry units and not infantry, suggesting the Germans had significant numbers of quality cavalry. Second, we see an example of a career laid out. First as an equestrian passing through various posts as *praefectus* or tribune, before serving as an equestrian procurator in several provinces. For many that would have been the pinnacle of their career. Maximianus, however, was promoted to the senate and this opened up the opportunity to serve as legate in several legions. The next step was to be a governor and he rose to the consulship. In the film, Maximus is already a general and thus a legate. This marks him as of senatorial rank.

The escape and race to Spain

In *Gladiator*, Maximus Decimus Meridius is arrested and his execution ordered. Taken to the woods, he escapes his guards. At one point, an assailant's sword sticks in his scabbard: 'The frost, sometimes it makes the blade stick,' Maximus says. This can happen if water has got in between the blade and scabbard. What is very unlikely is the subsequent sword stroke from our hero, cutting through an iron helmet. It might well give him concussion and on rare occasions knock someone out, but in general, helmets and the padding underneath offered good protection. Equally unlikely is the spinning sword piercing armour. Even if one could throw a sword in such a way, armour was designed to work. In tests, both lorica segmentata and squamata kept out sword blows, either thrusts or slashes. Only ring mail could be penetrated on occasions with the point of the sword, sometimes breaking a ring, but not enough to prove fatal, and with sufficient padding underneath, may not even have met the skin.

Having escaped, he then heads for his home in Trujillo in the modern province of Caceres, Spain. It is worth looking at how long such a journey might take. The Orbis project at Stamford University has a very useful online calculator that measures travel distances in Roman times.[36] His starting point is the Roman camp at Vindobona, modern Vienna, and his destination western Spain, roughly 2,665 kilometres, or 1,656 miles away. Using this tool we can see travelling on foot would have taken roughly ninety-four days. It is possible to change either the season and even the month, but winter, spring – or the more accurate March or April – gives the same result. Being a soldier, if one ignores his injuries and exhaustion, a 'rapid military march' at sixty kilometres a day would take forty-seven days.

Interestingly, the shortest route is not the fastest. A horse travelling at fifty-six kilometres a day would take fifty days. A 'fast carriage' would take just forty-one days. In contrast, the slowest method, an oxcart, would have taken 235 days. The quickest way would be to take a longer route but travel part of the journey by sea and river. This would take only thirty-three days, travelling first to Aquileia then by boat to Italy, crossing the peninsula by land, then a boat again either hugging the coast or across the Mediterranean. However, there was, in theory, a faster way. The empire had a horse relay system that enabled messages to travel across the empire quickly.

The cursus publicus was a courier system created by the Emperor Augustus. The state and private contractors provided relay stations with horses, equipment, wagon wrights, blacksmiths and anything needed to maintain transportation. A certificate was required to use the system and it was supervised by a praefectus vehiculorum. The one example we know about, Lucius Volusius Maecianus, served under Antoninus Pius, who was also a law tutor to Marcus Aurelius. Using this method, at 250 kilometres a day, according to Orbis, the fastest method of sending a message to Spain would take just over eleven days. This should be viewed as a theoretical minimum timeframe. Examples from the sources suggest longer durations would be more realistic. When Pertinax succeeded Commodus on 1 January AD 193, the news took sixty-three days to reach Egypt and not the fifteen days suggested by the Orbis calculator. This might mean the winter weather restricted travel by sea. Indeed when travel by sea is excluded (except the crossing to Byzantium), the time increases to eighty days. We can thus see a combination of road and sea travel, avoiding periods of bad weather, could equate to sixty-three days in winter time.

If an emperor had decided to eliminate a rival and his family, it is conceivable he could have arranged this several weeks before the arrest so that the offender and his family were executed around the same time. Assuming a spur of the moment decision however, this gives us an idea of the fastest possible time it would take a man to travel over 1,600 miles. Even if he changed horses regularly and did not stop to eat or sleep, we could speculate a shorter time of perhaps eight days at a maximum of 200 miles a day. Some examples are recorded in the sources: after the death of Maximinus Thrax in AD 239, news travelled from Aquileia, on the Adriatic coast, to Rome in four days. The Orbis calculator gives us 2.8 days, so we can see in general travel times were longer in practice than in theory.

The nearest Roman town to Maximus's farm on the online tool is Emerita Augusta, modern day Merida, which is about 100 miles further than Trujillo so we can adjust the travel times by one to three days, but we get the general idea. Once captured he is taken presumably 400 kilometres south to make the crossing to North Africa. There then follows a 700 kilometre journey to Zucchabar, in the Roman province of Mauretania Caesariensis, near Miliana in modern Algeria. The sea journey would have taken about six days, whereas the film shows a long desert journey. A person on foot with good conditions and road surface might travel that distance in three weeks. There was, in fact, a Roman road network in North Africa linking Zucchabar with Carthage in the East, to Tingis on the Atlantic coast near the straits of Gibraltar. Over difficult terrain, as depicted in the film, with an injured man, it could take three months.

We can see from these examples that using ships reduced travel times considerably. The final journey to Rome took about ten days if they boarded ship from the nearest port. A 700 kilometre journey to Carthage before taking ship would add weeks to the journey. Even with an extensive road and communication network, important messages could take days, or even weeks to cross the empire. Travel took even longer and an army or merchant laden with heavy goods might take months. If we take the example of the revolt of AD 175 in Egypt. Marcus intended to transport troops from the Danube to Antioch before advancing down the coast to Egypt. The infantry might take ninety days by the quickest route, but oxcarts carrying stores and equipment would take as many as 223 days. A cavalry unit, or infantry at a forced march, could achieve it in fifty days at the most. In contrast, a legion marching at thirty kilometres a day from Alexander could get there in thirty-seven days, or as little as eighteen days if using cavalry or a forced march.

We must also add that in winter time, both travel and campaigning became all but impossible in some areas. If the Parthians attacked in the East, then the message might take a couple of weeks to reach the emperor. A message from Nisbis to Rome using the horse relay system would take sixteen days. Of course, in that time conditions on the ground might have changed again. It would take time to inform and organise troops and resources. It would then take over a hundred days to transport troops from the Danube to the East. It would be very difficult to make a response in the same campaigning season. We see this in both the Marcomannic and Parthian Wars where an initial invasion or defeat was followed up a year or two later by the Roman response.

Map 8: Roman road network, second century (Wikimedia Commons)

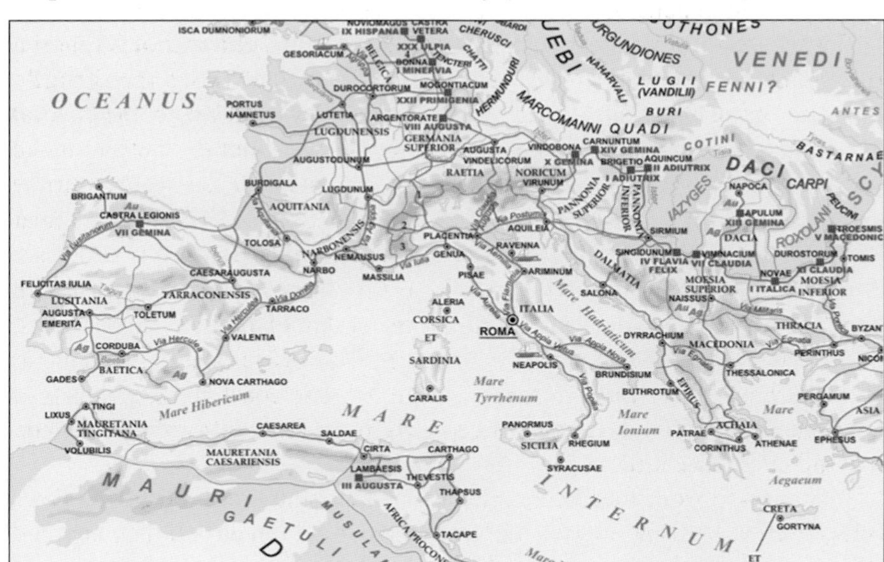

Map 9: Maximus's Journey

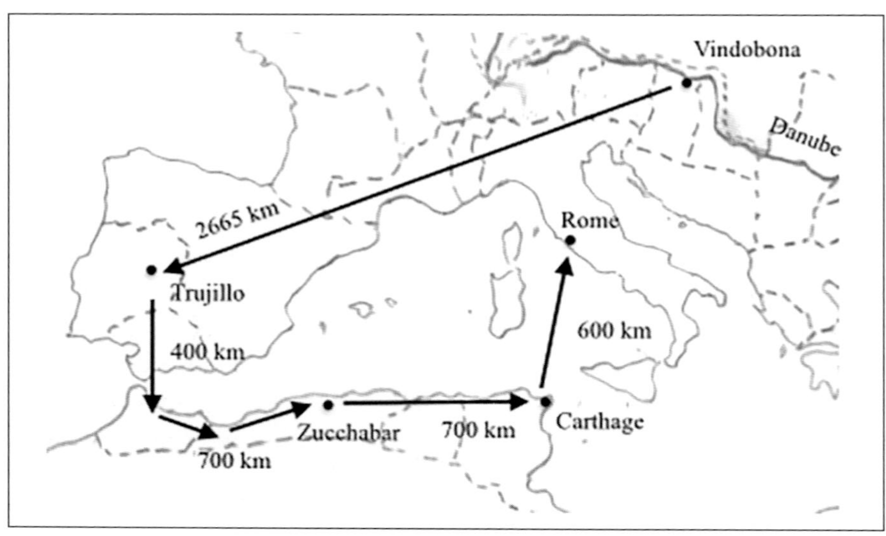

Chapter 3

The Roman army

The Roman army evolved considerably from the republic period. Under Augustus a legion consisted of approximately 5,000 heavy infantry recruited from Roman citizens. His reforms created a mixed volunteer and conscript army with soldiers serving for about ten years. Later this was extended to twenty-five years, and by the end of the first century the army was largely made up of professional volunteers. The first cohort was doubled in size resulting in legions numbering roughly 5,500 men.

Auxiliary troops were raised mainly from the provinces and organised into cohorts of infantry, cavalry or mixed units, each numbering 500 or 1,000 and called cohortes, alae or cohortes equitatae respectively. By the start of the second century the auxilia were also mainly a volunteer force. After twenty-five years they obtained Roman citizenship. In AD 212 the edict of Caracalla granted citizenship to all across the empire, making the distinction between the legions and the auxilia academic. But in the time of Marcus Aurelius and Commodus the difference remained. In addition to these units the empire hired mercenary barbarian units called numen. These would have been led by their own native leaders.

Between the emperors Augustus and Caracalla, the army increased in size from 250,000 to around 400,000. We can see below that the percentage of auxiliary units increased over time to more than half. An inscription in Rome lists twenty-eight legions in the reign of Marcus Aurelius.[1]

Table 2: Legions and auxiliary units first to second century

	Legions	Number of troops	Auxiliary units	Number of troops
Reign of Augustus	25	125,000	250	125,000
Reign of Caracalla	33	181,500	400	200,000

The legion commander reported to the provincial governor the legatus Augusti pro praetore. In a province with only one legion, the legion commander could also serve as the governor. We have seen how during the Marcomannic Wars governors took command of the local forces to defend the province. The legion commander was titled Legatus Legionis. He was usually of senatorial rank and appointed by the emperor. Often serving for three or four years, he generally had experience as a tribune or second in command. This man was called a Tribunus Laticlavius and was also appointed by the emperor or senate. He was often young and inexperienced and of senatorial rank.

The legates was advised by five military tribunes, Tribuni Angusticlavii. These we're normally experienced, battle-hardened men of equestrian class.

The third in command was the Praefectus Castrorum, or camp commander. Usually a long serving veteran promoted through the ranks and who served as a Primus Plus, the senior centurion of the legion. He was normally of 50 to 60 years of age and usually this post would have been his last.[2] A man of equestrian rank and of exceptional ability, experience or patronage could go further and become a provincial procurator or praefectus of the Praetorian Guard for example. We saw how figures such as Pompeianus, Maximianus and Pertinax exceeded even this rare accomplishment, eventually being appointed to the senate. Next in line came the primus pilus, or 'first spear'. This man was the senior centurion in the whole legion and would have led the first century, centuria, of the first cohort. He obtained equestrian class on retirement.

The legion was made up of ten cohorts. Cohorts two to ten each consisted of 480 men divided into six centuries of eighty men. The exception was the first cohort of five double centuries of 160 men. Thus legions had fifty-nine centurions with the lead centurion in cohorts two to ten titled Pilus Prior. The Aquilifer carried the legion's standard or eagle and was a prestigious position. In addition to the 5,120 infantry, the legion had 120-man alae, cavalry, attached called the Eques Legionis, used as scouts and messengers.

Each century was made up of ten, eight men Contubernium, or tent group. They also shared a mess tent and a mule.[3] Within the century an Optio acted as second in command and stood at the rear of the unit in formation. Each century had a signifier who carried the standard for the century. He was also responsible for the troop's pay and savings. Accompanying him was a cornicen or horn blower, and a imaginifer, carrying an image of the emperor to remind the men of their loyalty.

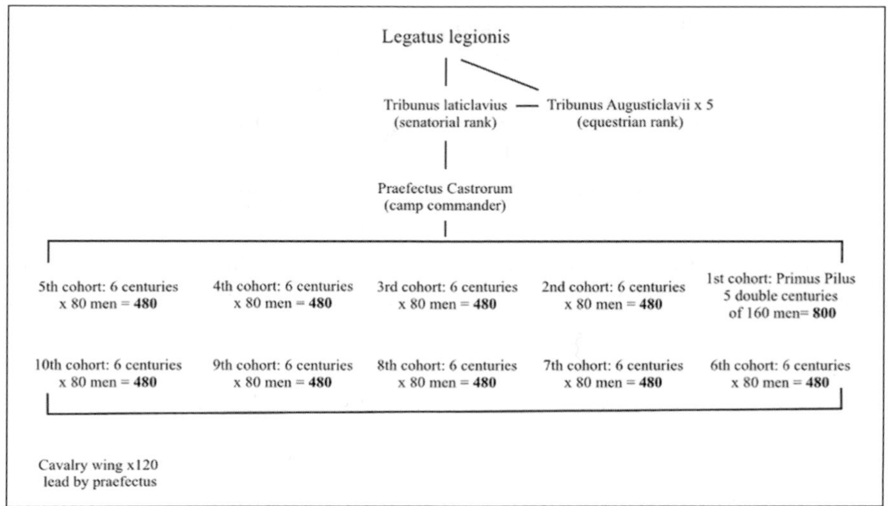

Figure 5: Legion Command Structure

One last point concerns battle standards. Vegetius names three types of military signals: the voiced; the 'semi-voiced', with bugle, horn or trumpet; and the 'mute signals', with eagles, dragons, ensigns and plumes.[4] While the eagle was the standard of the Roman legions, later cohorts had their own 'dragon-bearer'.[5]

We can see below how a cohort might deploy. First, in a loose, line formation and second, in a tighter, close formation similar to the previous example mentioned regarding HBO's *Rome*. We then see how these cohorts might be deployed within the army formation. The first cohort can be seen by the larger black rectangle on the front rank of the formation. The cohorts are then arranged in a chequer board type layout. This was very flexible as flanking or rear units could turn quickly if attacked. At the battle of Zama in 202 BC, we will see how the Romans were able to manoeuvre their units in column to lure the attacking elephants between the gaps, only to form up quickly into a solid line after the threat was neutralised.

The example shown has light troops making the first attack. This task was often carried out by auxiliaries. At the battle of Mons Graupius in AD 84 this was sufficient to defeat the 30,000 Caledonians. Six cohorts of auxiliaries, four of Batavians and two Tungrian, overwhelmed the first lines of warriors. An attempted outflanking movement was itself outflanked by Roman cavalry. Tacitus claims 10,000 were killed against 360 auxiliary troops and the legions played no part in the battle. We can see from this

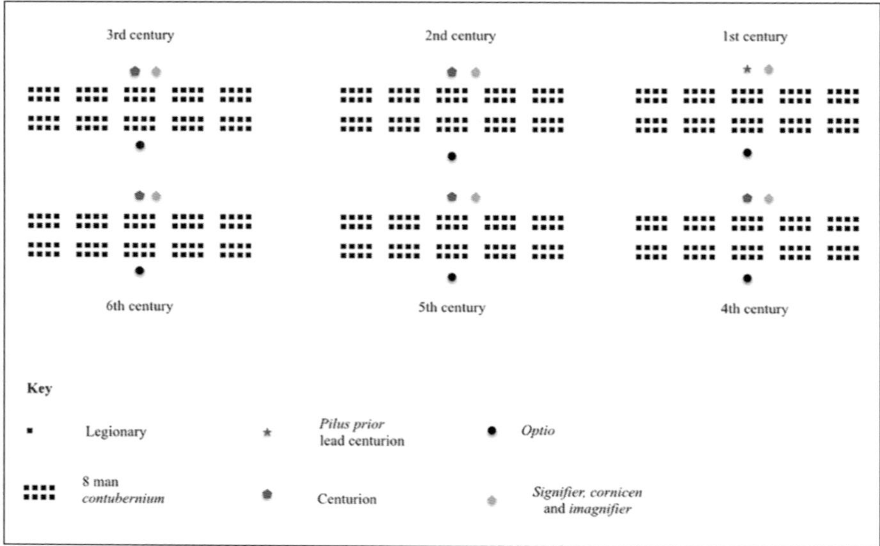

Figure 6: Roman cohort line formation

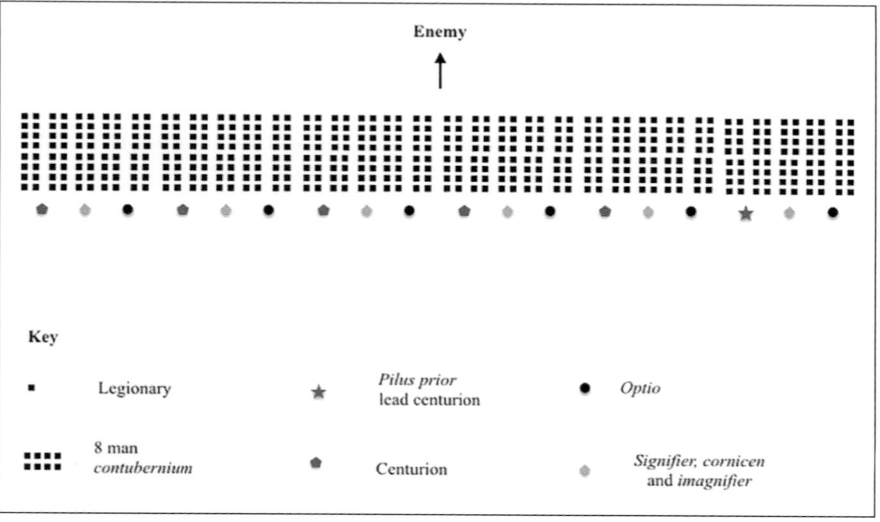

Figure 7: Roman cohort close formation

that auxiliary troops were often a vital part of a Roman army. This was especially true for cavalry. The legionary cavalry force of 120 was in no way sufficient, but a cohort or more of 500 each could be decisive. It is to auxiliary units we will now turn.

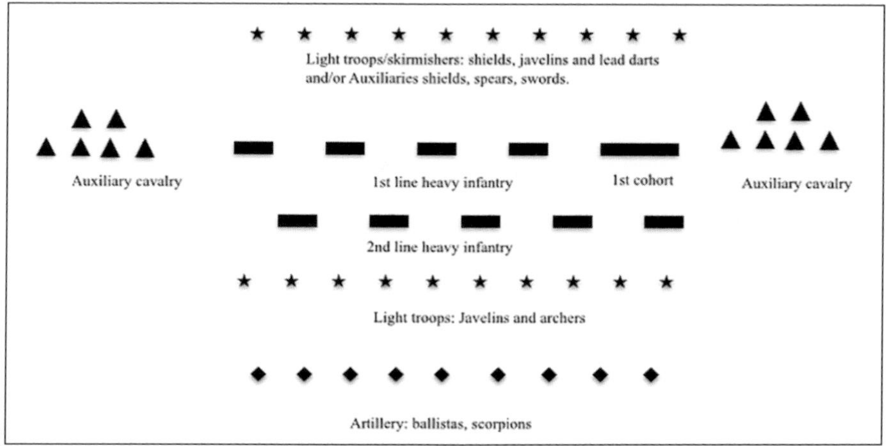

Figure 8: A typical Roman legion formation second century AD

Auxiliaries

By the second century auxiliary troops were a vital part of Rome's military force. Under Marcus Aurelius there were 440 auxiliary regiments scattered across the empire, half of which were stationed along the Danube provinces.[6] Auxiliary forces were generally divided into three types; first, a cavalry alae consisting of sixteen units (turmae), of approximately thirty men each; second, an infantry cohortes of a similar size to a legion cohort; and a mixed force of infantry and cavalry, the cohortes equitatae. Thus units of around 500 (quingenaria) were standard. Double sized units of 1,000 (miliaria) are also recorded. Some examples have twenty-four cavalry turmae suggesting forty-two man units. Other examples of cohortes equitum included eight turmae of cavalry, totalling 240 men and 760 infantry.

The commander of an ala or cohortes was a praefectus. These would initially have been tribal chiefs leading their own men. In the second century, praefectus of an ala was one of the steps on the military career of equestrians. Another was one of the five tribuni angusticlavii attached to a legion advising the legatus. The period of service as praefectus was not fixed, but usually around two to four years. A primus pilus automatically qualified for equestrian status and in the early principate could move on to command an auxiliary unit. However, by the second century nearly all auxiliary commanders came from the established equestrian class, often beginning their careers as magistrates in Italian, and later provincial, municipal cities.[7]

In a cavalry ala, each turmae of thirty was commanded by a decurio. The praefectus alae was senior to an auxiliary infantry commander, praefectus cohortis. Similar to legionary cohorts these were organised into centuries led by a centurion with an optio and signifier. There is some debate from archaeology regarding size of barracks which indicate centuries could have held sixty or eighty men. These numbers no doubt fluctuated and units were often not at full strength.

Two other kinds of units are worth mentioning.[8] First, numeri was a term used for a body of irregular troops. One example is of a unit of Britons posted to the German frontier manning a series of watchtowers. Another example is a numerus of bargemen from the Tigris at South Shields on the Tyne in northern Britain. Second, cunei appears to be specifically a Germanic irregular unit. Literally meaning 'wedge', Tacitus refers to the Germanic tactic of attack and applies it to the Batavii in the civil war of AD 69.

Some auxiliary units specialised as slingers or archers. Heavy infantry units used the scutum shield, while for many the oval shield was more common. Others were trained in specific native tactics; fighting in forested areas might have been one example. We see how one group of auxiliaries were instrumental in the invasion of Britain in AD 43. The description by Cassius Dio likely refers to the River Medway in Kent.[9] The Britons thought that Romans would not be able to cross it without a bridge, and 'consequently bivouacked in rather careless fashion on the opposite bank'. The Romans sent a unit of Germans, 'who were accustomed to swim easily in full armour across the most turbulent streams'. This seems to have been a commando-like operation as we read, 'instead of shooting at any of the men they confined themselves to wounding the horses that drew their chariots'. The Britons retreated to the river Thames where it met the ocean and at flood-tide formed a lake. The Britons were able to cross as they knew where the firm ground was. The Romans were unable to follow but the Germans swam across again and others used a bridge up-stream and attacked from several sides at once, cutting down many warriors.

Cavalry sometimes were armoured. Horses were protected from the front and back and the riders by body-mail and leg guards. Lighter cavalry had no such protection, although images of Gallic cavalry show mail cuirass and leather jerkins. Weapons could be spears, pikes or lances, or missile weapons such as bows or javelins. Examples of shields used by auxiliary units include oval Gallic type, oblong examples from Armenia, or no shields at all as depicted by some Sarmatian cavalry. Arrian, writing in the second century AD, describes a great variety of different types of cavalry units: heavily armoured cataphractarii and unarmoured light cavalry.

> some carry oblong shields, others fight without shields, merely spears and pikes … some with missiles, some use javelins, others bows and arrows … their long flat-bladed sword hangs from their shoulder and they carry oblong shields and iron helmets, breastplates and small greaves.. they also carry small axes.[10]

An example is confirmed by a depiction on a tombstone at Housesteads on Hadrian's Wall with a soldier carrying a bow in his left hand and axe in the right. Trajan's column shows light Gallic horsemen wearing a mail cuirass and leather jerkin, carrying an oval shield. Roman cavalrymen wore mail, lorica hamata, or scale, lorica squamata and we can compare this to the Sarmatian enemies who wear a striking scale armour, covering them from head to foot as well as their horses. This may be artistic licence, as an example of horse armour found at Dura-Europos consists simply of a rectangular piece for the back and flanks with a hole for the saddle.

The table on next page shows the auxiliary units listed as posted to the Western provinces affected by the Marcomannic Wars of the second century.[11] This doesn't gives us a full picture, or include the many temporary troop movements. It does, however, give us a snapshot of the military situation when we come to the distribution of legions later.

Picture 11: Roman and Sarmatian cavalry (Wikimedia Commons)

Table 3: Auxiliary units of northern frontier

Province	Units
Pannonia Superior	Ala I Hispanorum Aravacorum Ala I Caninafatium Ala I Contaforium Ala I Ituraeorum Ala II Pannoniorum
Pannonia Inferior	Cohors II Dacorum Aurelia
Noricum	Cohors I Aelia Brittonum milliaria Cohors I Dacorum Brittonum milliaria
Germania Superior (Upper)	Brittones Aurelianensis Cohors I Septima Belgarum Cohors III Aquitanorum equitata CR
Germania Inferior (Lower)	Cohors IV Tungorum milliaria Ara Colonia Ulpia Traiana Ala Noricorum
Galla Lugdunensis	Cohors IV Gallorum Ala Asturum
Dalmatia	Cohors I Dardanorum Aurelia Cohors I Sacorum Aurelia Nova Cohors I Ulpia Traiana Campestris Voluntariorum

In *Gladiator* we see auxiliary archers depicted accurately in mail armour and archers positioned sensibly at the rear. We have already covered the impracticality of fire arrows in general, and the sense of firing into a wooded area. It would be far more accurate if marker stones had been set out in open ground every fifty yards or so to assist their aim. What we don't see is auxiliary infantry in mail armour (lorica hamata) advancing in the first line of attack. Rather we get legionnaires in lorica segmentata carrying pila but not using them. Auxiliary infantry often carried a short javelin (lancea) or longer 2-metre spear (hasta). The hasta was designed for thrusting rather than throwing. As such, it would be suited to protection from cavalry attack or other spearmen. The cavalry charge we have covered. If it was in open ground then again it would have been auxiliary ala units led by an equestrian praefectus. There is nothing preventing a Roman general leading such a charge but it was not usual practice. While Alexander the Great famously led his company cavalry centuries before, Roman generals tended to position themselves with the bulk of army which usually meant near the heavy infantry of the legions.

The Immunes

Also attached to the legions were a variety of specialists. Some of these tasks were no doubt performed by legionnaires with specific skills who could be let off heavy duties to perform these vital functions. However, there is no doubt non-military personnel accompanied the legions, adding considerably to the numbers. A list of some examples is instructive as to what a camp might have included: surveyors, 'mensores'; medical orderlies, 'medici'; wound dressers, 'capsarii'; veterinaries, 'veterinarii'; master builder, 'architectus'; artillery makers/operators, 'ballistrarii'; craftsmen, 'fabri'; arrow makers, 'sagittarii'; bow makers, 'acuarii'; blacksmiths, 'ferrarii'; bronze-smiths, 'aerarii'; lead makers, 'plumbarii'; carpenters, 'carpentarii'; sword makers, 'gladiatores'; hydraulic engineers, 'aquilices'; stonemasons, 'lapidarii'; hunters, 'venatores'; armourers, 'custodes armorum'; and millers, 'polliones'.

There were also specialist builders such as shipwrights, ship pilots, bridge builders and artillery specialists. Priests were needed to officiate ceremonies, as well as staff to look after sacrificial animals. The various repairs and manufacturers needed officers and managers as well as skilled workers. Added to all this was clerks of various kinds: for the granaries; general book-keeping; and even a clerk for the deceased.

We can see from above how busy an army camp might have been. A cohort in enemy territory would have built a relatively small marching camp. However, an army consisting of one or more legions with a permanent camp would have had the equivalent of a small town accompanying them. Bread ovens, granaries, stables, blacksmiths, doctors, infirmaries, kitchens and buildings for a whole variety of other activities. The camp at Carnuntum on the Danube was home to four legions and covered ten hectares. It became the provincial capital and grew into a city of 50,000 inhabitants.

WEAPONS AND ARMOUR

Gladius

The short Roman gladius was the main sword of the Roman legionary. Recruits were taught to strike with the point rather than the edge; a cut rarely kills because the vitals are protected by armour, whereas 'a stab driven two inches in is fatal'.[12] The gladius was ideally suited to the techniques and formation of the Roman army of the second century. Centuries later the longer spatha sword became more common. This was designed more for a cutting blow than a stab. The spear had greater reach and seemed to be the weapon of choice for most warriors facing the Romans. In later centuries shield walls became more common and often the best way to get to the enemy was over the top of the shield.

The question arises, why use a short sword as opposed to a spear? It is quite difficult to use a spear one handed. In a tight formation a shield wall with spearmen behind is a formidable barrier. However, in a looser mêlée a short stabbing sword is better suited. While the Romans were trained to use it as a stabbing weapon, it could certainly cause devastating injuries as a slashing weapon as Livy's account of the Macedonian Wars shows. He describes Philip's men as being used to fighting Greeks and Illyrians and thus only seeing wounds by javelins, arrows and, in rare cases, lances. When they saw the style of weapon and type of men they were up against a 'shudder of horror' passed through the men, 'they saw bodies dismembered with the Spanish sword, arms cut off from the shoulder, heads struck off from the trunk, bowels exposed and other horrible wounds.' (Livy, book 31.34)

In combination with the large scutum shield and within a formation, the gladius was deadly. In the fourth century, Ammianus Marcellinus describes Gothic swords cutting through the head with such force that 'the severed halves hung down on each shoulder'.[13] Archaeological evidence from later skeletons of later periods shows horrific injuries with blows severing legs, and penetrating and cutting away parts of skulls.[14] However, tests show neither a gladius or spatha sword can cut through an iron helmet. They may well cause a dent and concussion, but in general the shape of the helmet and padding underneath deflected or absorbed most blows. Warriors protected with good quality armour and helmets would have been at a considerable advantage over those without either.

The gladius hispaniensis was used during the republic and had a leaf-shaped blade 60–68 cm long and 5 cm wide, weighing just under a kilogram. Three main kinds have been identified for the period in which Maximus fought: the Mainz gladius, with a shorter but wider blade, 50–55 cm by 7 cm, weighing 800 grams; the Fulham gladius, also at 50 –55 cm, but slightly narrower and lighter at 6 cm and 700 grams respectively; and the Pompeii gladius, the shortest and narrowest blade, at 45–50 cm by 5 cm, also weighing 700 grams. All three swords had handles of 15 cm. In comparison, later Viking and Anglo-Saxon swords were 85–105 cm in total length. The sword found at Sutton Hoo, dated to the early seventh century, measured 85 cm. This is at the maximum range for a *gladius* and in general both the blade and the handle increased in size over time.

In the second century the sword would likely have been about 70 cm in total length and weighing the equivalent of a bag of sugar. During the Marcomannic Wars on the Danube, the scenario in HBO's *Rome* series is very realistic. An infantry force in a well-drilled formation moving forward purposefully. The sword arm is largely hidden behind a large shield that covers most of the body. An enemy warrior attempting to get at the legionary behind the shield risks 2ft of steel punching out from the man in front or the two either side.

Tests on ballistic gel show that it penetrates several inches and would likely cause horrific internal injuries. Armour made from leather, linen or hide offered some protection from slices, but not from a determined sword thrust. Mail armour can sometimes be penetrated by a thrust if a rivet breaks, but the gladius doesn't appear to penetrate deep enough to cause serious injuries. In contrast segmentata or squamata holds up well. One advantage of the longer point on the Mainz gladius may have been as a ring breaker, compared to the shorter point of the Pompeii gladius. A series of tests showed that a gladius had no effect with a slashing blow, but a thrust could penetrate lorica hamata at times.[15] However, the penetration was shallow and an undergarment might prevent any serious injury or, if thick enough, any injury at all.

Picture 12: Roman gladius sword (Wikimedia Commons)

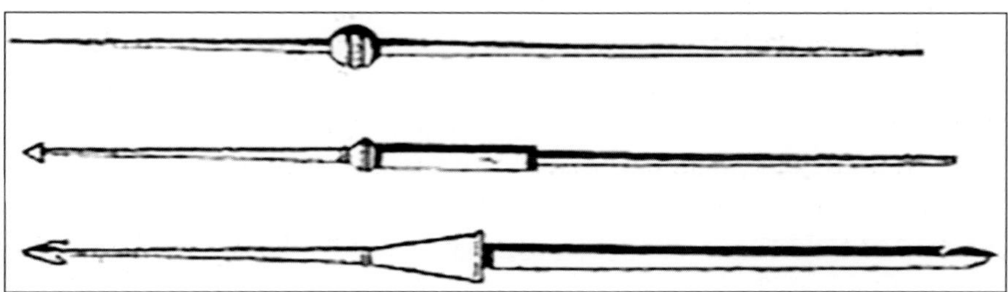

Picture 13: Roman pila (Wikimedia Commons)

Picture 14: Roman plumbatae (Wikimedia Commons)

Spears

The pilum was about 2 metres long, with the top 1 metre being made of iron with a hardened pyramidal-shape head of 5 to 17 cm. Weighing between two and four kilograms, it could be thrown about 33 metres, although it is more effective at 15–20 metres. In Caesar's Gallic Wars he describes how the Gauls were hampered by a single *pilum* piercing two overlapping shields. The heavy shaped point was difficult to remove and weighed the shield down. This caused the enemy to drop their shields and fight unprotected. The Romans held the upper ground and 'easily broke the mass-formation of the enemy by a volley of javelins'. They then drew their swords and charged. The Gauls were encumbered because several of their shields were 'pierced and fastened together by a single javelin-cast; and as the iron became bent, they could not pluck it forth, nor fight handily with the left arm encumbered'. This caused some to cast their shields aside while others struggled on with their shields severely compromised. Eventually they gave ground and retreated.[16]

Shorter javelins were used too, along with lead-weighted darts (plumbatae), five of which could be carried in the rear of a shield. They had a range of 30–60 metres, but these were trained legionaries. An interesting experiment using plumbatae was conducted on a pork joint to simulate human flesh.[17] Dropped from a metre, the barbed head penetrated 4 inches up to the lead weight. They could be thrown 25 metres over head, but they twisted. Thrown like a spear they only reached 18 metres. An underhand throw reached 30 metres. Accuracy was only possible overarm at about 6 metres. However, thrown underarm at a steep angle, would cause a mass throw to 'rain' down on an enemy. Shield and armour would stop them, but any exposed flesh was extremely vulnerable. Vegetius describes infantry men carrying five such darts. We can thus estimate a cohort being able to discharge nearly 2,500 lead darts within a few seconds as the enemy closes in. A similar experiment with slingers and lead shot showed equally impressive results. Interestingly, while a spherical shape might be more aerodynamic, the Roman type was elongated. this made a distinctive noise and one can imagine the sound of hundreds of such missiles. They were able to penetrate 12mm of plywood so may well have gone through shields. Similar to plumbatae, armour seems to have stopped it. However, tests on ballistic gel shows it penetrates flesh and can cause severe injury.

The effective range of the shorter spears or javelins was around 12–15 metres,[18] although re-enactments do demonstrate twice that distance was achievable. Longer spears (hasta) were about 1.8 metres, or 6ft in length.

They lent their name to the hastati, who formed the first line of infantry in the early republic. In the later republic only the rear line, the triarii, carried hastae, with the hastati carrying pila and gladius. In the second century, spears tended to be carried more by auxiliary troops. However, Arrian in the second century describes in detail a war against the Alani in the East. Spearmen are deployed in the front ranks with longer spears behind to counter the heavy cavalry attack. These are backed up by heavy throwing spears followed by lighter javelins and finally archers. We see here that the Roman army was flexible and adapted its tactics and equipment.

Tests using pilum and spears are mixed. In one test, a mail shirt withstood a pilum throw from a few yards.[19] This was solid ring however, which is slightly tougher than riveted mail. Butted mail performs badly, but this method would likely only be for quick repairs. Roman lorica hamata was riveted. In contrast, another tester was able to throw a pilum that punched through 10 inches of shield made from wood and fabric. A test on mail burst a rivet and was able to penetrate a solid wicker target by two inches. A further test was carried out on a mock up of lorica segmentata. The metal used was slightly thicker and better quality and the pilum dented the metal, although on some occasions a small puncture hole was created. It is likely that any shield would have reduced the velocity, meaning the combination of shield and armour, in this case, would have been sufficient. The fact this armour is curved also makes it more likely that blows are deflected away, and only a dead hit at ninety degrees would have chance of penetration.[20]

To visualise the effective range, it is useful to imagine a full size professional football pitch which averages about 110 metres long by 45 metres wide. An attacking force at one goal advances upon a line of infantry standing along the opposite end, from one corner flag to the other. At this range arrows start to have an effect, but become fully effective at the halfway line. At this point, lead darts also rain in. As they pass the centre circle, spears and pilum can reach them. However, as they enter the penalty box they come within effective range and one can imagine the effect of hundreds of pila. It might be difficult for the front ranks to deliver both pila. However, rear ranks could continue a barrage.

Swords vs spears

Various YouTube channels show interesting sparring duels between spear, sword and other weapons.[21] One of particular interest is 'Lindybiege', who focuses on duels between swordsmen and spearmen.[22] In a number of different tests we got the following results: when a spearman faced a swordsman with neither having shields, the spear won 9-3. The longer reach of the spear was decisive. The swordsman had to get past the spearpoint and inside the longer reach to have a chance. If the swordsman was given a small buckler shield, the spearman still won 4-2. The spear also beat a medieval period long sword and great sword. However, if a swordsman had a larger medieval-type shield the results were very even, with the spearman winning 7-6. Interestingly, in six bouts where the spearman also had a shield, the swordsman won every one. It was noted that holding a spear overarm performed very badly. The spear was more effective in a one-on-one in a mêlée when held with both hands underarm. However, we know many warriors used spear and shield combination in antiquity. We can see multiple spearmen did very well in a formation, except when swordsmen were able to outflank or break the formation.

We can thus postulate the following: an infantry force would benefit from shields to ward off missiles and to form a solid shield wall. Spears are excellent in repulsing cavalry or fixing an enemy in place while they are attacked with missiles or flanked. A formation of spearmen could have the front rank(s) with shields, while rear ranks attempt to thrust spears two-handed over the top or through gaps. Once in a mêlée situation, a spearman with a shield would be better off dropping his shield or dropping his spear and drawing a sword or axe. In many of the battles we will look at later we will see the Roman heavy infantry formation was often fronted by auxiliary troops and the spear was a common weapon for those units.

Bows

The Romans used a composite bow and Vegetius suggests a percentage of each cohort were trained in the bow. However, they also employed specialist units of auxiliary with infantry sagittarii units outnumbering horse archers by two to one. In later centuries the majority were deployed in the East, presumably to counter the threat from Parthian and Sassanid horse archers. The maximum range was about 150–200 metres, but with fewer casualties at over 100 metres. They were highly accurate at around 50–60 metres.[23] Archers, whether mounted or on foot, would have carried thirty to forty arrows.[24] According to Vegetius archers trained using targets up to a range 180 metres.[25] Arrow heads had a variety of shapes with narrower bodkin like heads better for piercing armour. However, the plates of the lorica segmentata offered good protection.

Arrow velocity depends upon a number of factors: the draw weight of the bow; the weight of the arrow; the drag on the arrow; and the draw distance (usually around 70 cm). Later medieval long bows were capable of up to 180lbs of pull. Earlier finds from the fourth century suggest bows were less powerful. A pull of 80–100lbs is more likely for a Roman recurve bow. Light 40 gram arrows can travel over 200 metres from a modern 80lb bow, which is about 20 metres further than Vegetius states targets should be set; heavier arrows of say 70 grams might be most efficient at around 50 metres. Although the lighter arrows could reach 200 metres, they had less power for penetration.

Various tests with bows found that segmentata and squamata stop arrows. Riveted mail, however, was penetrated by about 4.5cm; this would certainly cause severe injuries and could prove fatal. However, a more contemporary 45lb Scythian bow failed to penetrate mail, although it did go through padded armour and into ballistic gel by about an inch. Ancient crossbows also failed to penetrate mail.[26] We have noted that Roman bows were probably around 80lbs pulling weight and one source states 40 gram arrows could be fired 200 metres, slighter farther than Vegetius suggests.[27] However, these arrows are relatively light. Heavier arrows would have more power but they lose more velocity than lighter ones, up to 20 per cent over 100 metres.[28] So while they could fire up to 200 metres, their effective range was 50–150 metres.[29]

A series of tests were carried out using a reproduction Scythian recurve bow with a pulling weight of 40lbs.[30] It is likely this is at the lower end of the the range in terms of power. The most common form of Roman arrowheads were tribolate (three bladed) shaped, although bilobate and leaf-shaped were reasonably common. In the East, bodkin type arrows were also prevalent.

Various arrows, targets and distances were used in the tests. At 30ft (nearly 10 metres) all metal tipped arrows went through 3-ply 10mm wooden shields completely. Perhaps surprisingly, tribolate heads performed better than bodkin types on most tests. Padding alone, or unpadded mail, was penetrated 9.4 to 10.7 cm into a piece of pork placed behind. This could prove fatal. However, the thickness of padding made a difference. Lightly padded mail performed not much better, but medium padding reduced penetration by 2 cm. Heavy padding of 18 mm under mail reduced it down to around 3 cm. Thus padding makes all the difference between a potentially fatal and non-fatal wound. At a range of 60ft (just over 18 metres) we see how much the power of the bow is reduced. Shields were penetrated 24 cm. At best, arrows pierced padding, or mail with no padding, by 2.4 cm. Heavy padding under mail reduced it to less than 1 cm. It has to be admitted that some bows were more powerful, but these are interesting findings. Distance and padding were significant determinants in levels of protection.

Some bows may have been far more powerful than the type used, but it is unlikely that archers would be flat-shooting from even 60ft, let alone 30. A rain of arrows would result in firing at an angle and when they fell they would have lost some of their power. We could take a very rough estimate and double our distances to reflect a stronger bow. Doubling the bow strength from 40 to 80lbs does increase the maximum distance from 74 to 148 metres. It may be then that an 80lb bow could penetrate mail over padding by 3cm at 60ft. However, it is likely in a battle scenario that archers were much further away than 20 metres. If the Romans wore thicker padding than 18mm, then protection would increase.

Thus we can imagine a scenario where most arrows are stopped by shields from a distance. However, if the archers move in closer – to less than a football field – and flat-shoot, then shields start to be penetrated. Most armour stops injuries most of the time, but any bare flesh is highly vulnerable. If the archers get close enough, then a bodkin arrow could penetrate through a shield and carry on through mail and padding. Perhaps only an inch or so, but still painful. Without a shield one would be vulnerable, especially if the archer was close. The 40lb bow might be more reasonable for horse archers, so we can imagine the Parthians riding up as close as possible and firing into a massed body of men.

Using the football analogy, on average a Roman bow could deliver an arrow one-and-a-half to two football pitches long. At more than one pitch length however, they were less of a hazard. At about 100 metres an infantry force would need to make a decision. They could attempt to drive the attackers away with their own archers or cavalry. They could retreat out of range. Or they could attack. If they chose the latter, they could use their shields to protect them in something like the Roman testudo formation for example. If they chose to charge however, then they would want to cover the ground quickly. An Olympic sprinter can cover the 100 metres in ten seconds.

A soldier in full armour would be carrying about several kilograms, the lorica segmentata alone was 10kg and the scutum shield weighed the same. He would also need to be able to fight effectively once he got there. Archers could fire over ten arrows a minute, so we can estimate each could fire several volleys before the infantry attack reached the front line. A cohort of 480 archers could fire nearly 5,000 arrows at an advancing enemy, who would then receive several hundred or a thousand pila before they even got to grips with their foe. The question is, how effective would a volley such as this have been? On a poorly armoured infantry with poor or no shields it could be devastating, but good armour could withstand both swords and arrows.

Some sources do give information that is contrary to this however. These might be literary inventions or exaggerations, but it is quite possible the Parthians were able to pierce shields and mail with their arrows at Carrhae. Even if it was only a percentage, 9,000 Parthian horse archers firing several volleys a minute could deliver tens of thousands of arrows in a relatively short space of time. Forty arrows fired at the rate of just five a minute would result in 360,000 arrows in eight minutes, and we are told that they did not run out of arrows. Any bare flesh, damaged mail or badly maintained shield was vulnerable. A close shot with a well-made arrowhead, scoring a direct hit, might penetrate even a well-made shield and mail. If just 1 per cent found a target and penetrated shield/mail, within eight minutes there would be 3,600 casualties – nearly 10 per cent of the force marched by Cassius into Parthia. Yet the Romans held out all day. So we perhaps see here how things worked in practice. The armour and shields held up most of the time, yet it failed on enough occasions to be noted and remembered by the sources.

Armour

There were three main types of armour used by the Roman army. Before we look at them more closely, there is a point worth making again. It was made and worn for a very good reason: armour worked. It offered reasonable protection against cutting or glancing blows.[31] (There are numerous re-enactors demonstrating tests on YouTube and other sites and I have listed some of the better ones in the bibliography.) In general we can make the following rough generalisations: all types of armour withstood strikes and prevented penetration by bows, spears and swords; however, this does not mean a strike from a *pilum*, for example, would not put a man down. It might well break ribs, but it would not pierce the armour and penetrate flesh.

As noted above, any type of padded clothing worn underneath would have given extra protection. The late Roman supermalis was simply two layers stuffed with sheep's wool. The fourth-century *De Rebus Bellicis* describes a thoracomachus to counteract the weight and friction of the armour.[32] It was made from 'thick sheep's wool felt'. Linen or hemp are possible materials, stuffed with sheep's wool. Re-enactors note the necessity of wearing some sort of undergarment, thus some form of under armour would have been essential when wearing metal armour.[33] Even several layers of linen within leather formed a quilted material that could be surprisingly effective. A thicker version covered in rawhide would have been a reasonable alternative for the average warrior who did not possess metal armour. Another alternative is some sort of leather, such as goatskin, as the De Rebus Bellicis mentions 'Libyan Hide'. A battle re-enactor for a later period has found five layers of linen is enough to stop an arrow even at close range.[34] The gambeson quilted leather armour worn centuries later evolved from these earlier types.

The YouTube channel 'Shadiversity' has a very good range of videos, one of which directly concerns the merits of leather and gambeson armour.[35] Another excellent YouTube channel, 'Tod's Workshop', shows a whole range of different tests; he demonstrates that boiled leather armour does indeed offer limited defence. In his attempt to replicate the protection he found five layers of hardened leather restricted arrows, with even a needle bodkin penetrating only 78mm. Although this would still prove fatal we can see that a combination of this, with perhaps a better technique in the manufacturing process, plus a padded undergarment might improve performance. However, even three layers protected one from a stab with a medieval rondel dagger.[36] What is clear is that it does offer some protection from slashing blows.

One notable example of the effectiveness of this can be seen in 1066 at the battle of Stamford Bridge. Harold surprised a Viking army who had no time to don their mail shirts, yet the Vikings were still prepared to stand and fight, indicating that their undershirts offered reasonable protection as well. Deer hide, for example, is nearly as strong as mail, but lighter and more flexible.[37] We can therefore make two important points: first, Germanic warriors, even if they had no mail shirts, might well have had some protection from leather quilted material; second, those with metal armour, whether Romans or Germanic ex-auxiliaries, would have had very good protection from most weapons. Having said that, damaged armour, broken rings or missing plates, would have reduced this. Well made and maintained weapons would have had more chance than blunt or poorly made weapons. No doubt armourers were constantly trying to improve both weapons and armour.

For Roman soldiers, first we have lorica hamata, or chainmail armour. This was constructed using metal rings riveted together. A central ring was riveted to the rows above and below. An example from centuries later at Vimose in Denmark is hip length with sleeves to just above the elbow, which includes 20,000 8mm iron rings weighing about 11kg. In the Roman period, the body and arm length would have been slightly shorter and so we can adjust the weight down. Rings of softer metal or butted (without rivets) could be torn apart by hand. These are seen at re-enactments or in movies, but would not have withstood a blow on the battlefield.

It would take several weeks to produce a good quality mail shirt and thus the price was relatively high compared to other equipment. In AD 500 the cost of a sword and shield was two solidus, a helmet at six and a mail shirt twelve.[38] It was prone to rust and some sources mention them being stored in leather cases when not in use.[39] While they were excellent for defensive purposes, they did have the disadvantage of being heavy and tiring over long distances or prolonged use, hence the Vikings being caught resting after their previous victory in 1066. Tests using a gladius against riveted mail does show a minimal amount of penetration but only by about a centimetre, meaning any padding will protect the body.

A spear thrust from an infantryman performed at least as well as a gladius, and using both hands adds a significant amount of power. One test has a re-enactor using a technique where he uses his right hand to push the bottom of the shaft, allowing the spear to slide through his left while moving forward; this technique did in fact break through several rings of mail armour. The problem for the warrior is he has no shield. In a one-on-one he has a fair chance, but on a battlefield full of enemies with shields one wonders how long a fighter would survive. Repeated stabs to the same spot, or a strike on a damaged part, allows a potentially fatal blow. One can imagine, in close hand-to-hand fighting, several rapid strikes with a dagger might well be sufficient to split the rings and penetrate enough to reach vital organs.

In contrast, a pilum could penetrate mail – although not every time. One test has it bouncing off, while another penetrates several inches, certainly enough to deal a fatal blow. However, the latter was on a static, fixed target. A human being has a certain amount of give and will fall away from a strike. Thus, in summary, one might conclude it is possible that mail might not protect you from every pila or spear. However, in general it was very successful in protecting one from sword thrusts and slices, and bows of this period lacked the power to penetrate mail.

Legionaries of the second century tended to wear lorica segmentata. This consisted of horizontal iron 'hoop' plates, bound together with leather straps to form a flexible, strong protection. The advancing infantry in the first battle scene of the film all seem to be wearing this traditional armour. These are clearly the legionary cohorts. This armour was even better at withstanding strikes and blows than the mail hamata. It appeared in the first century BC and faded from use in the late third century. During the period in which the film is set it was very common and features extensively on both Trajan's Column and the Column of Marcus Aurelius.

A third type of armour is the lorica squamatae, translated as 'scale of feathers', which consisted of overlapping bronze or iron scales This began to replace the iconic lorica segmentata after the second century. At the time of the Marcomannic Wars it was often worn by centurions, officers and cavalry troops. Individual scales were normally iron or bronze and ranged in size from 0.6 x 1.2cm to 5 x 8cm. Thickness was between 0.5 to 0.8mm, yet when overlapping proved very effective. This type is perhaps the quickest and easiest to make. We see similar scale-type armour all over the world from Persia to Japan, made from a variety of material such as bone or leather. It was equally good at defending against slashing and slicing weapons. It did have a slight drawback however; although it was adequate against a downward or straight-on strike from an arrow (for example), when it came to an upward thrust, the point of a weapon could slip under the upper scale. There is a rare type of armour called lorica hamata squamatae, which combines the strengths of both types by attaching the scales to mail armour.

Lastly there was a sculpted cuirass generally worn by officers.[40] By the late Roman period, muscle cuirasses are depicted on monuments as well as lamellar armour and segmented armour for the arms and legs of heavily armoured horsemen.[41] In the early medieval period both chainmail and swords would have been rare for the average warrior.[42] Certainly even in the late Roman army, light units – infantry or cavalry – generally had no armour.[43] Most Germanic fighters would have been armed with a spear and protected by a shield and a leather padded jerkin.

It can be difficult making sense of the different tests and results; weapons, shields and armour were not of consistent quality of manufacture or maintenance. We can, however, make some general statements. Some protection was better than no protection – even fabric or leather armour worked up to a point. Metal armour was better than leather or padded armour. Plate armour was better than chain mail. All armour types provided good protection against slashes or glancing blows and helmets would be the same. Where their performance differs significantly is from thrusts and impact weapons. Metal armour provided good protection against sword or spear thrusts, although chain mail could, on rare occasions, be penetrated. Missile weapons caused the biggest problem. Arrows could penetrate shields and mail armour, although not it seems lorica segmentata. But there was a number of variables in this. The pulling strength of the bow, weight or arrow, type of arrow head and distance were all important factors. At closer distance the pilum was a formidable weapon, being able to punch through shields and mail. Films depicting fighters being easily injured by a sword slash or killed by sword, arrow or even spear strike while wearing armour are not giving an accurate portrayal. In reality a fighter would go for the exposed parts of his opponent. Thrusts to the face, arms and legs would have been common.

The photographs below have been provided with the kind permission of Matthew Parkes of 'Peturia Revisited'. Peturia is the Roman name for Brough in East Yorkshire. The town that grew around the Roman fort was likely the civitas capital of the Paris tribe. It sat on the southern end of the road to York and provided a ferry across the Humber, from which one could travel south to Lincoln. Peturia Revisited are a local community group bringing back to life the ancient Roman settlement. We can see a number of images depicting the various armour and weapons.

Picture 15: *Above left* – Roman legionary wearing lorica segmentata (Matthew Parkes)

Picture 16: *Above middle* – Roman legionary wearing lorica hamata (Matthew Parkes)

Picture 17: *Above right* – Roman centurion with scutum shield and pila (Matthew Parkes)

Picture 18: *Right* – Late Roman soldiers waring lorica squamata (Ross Cronshaw)

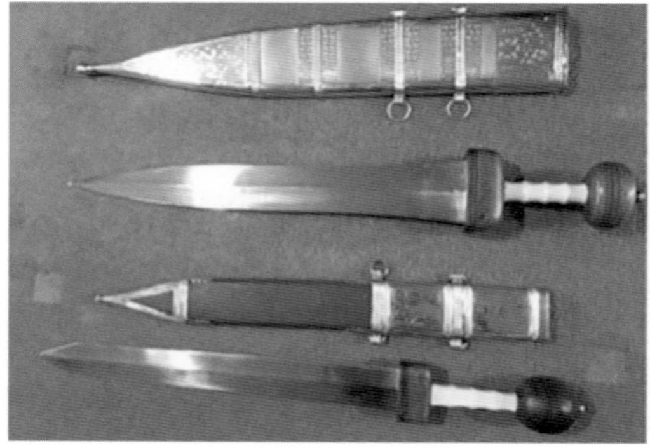

Picture 19: *Above left* – Reproduction Roman gladius sword (Matthew Parkes)

Picture 20: *Above right* – Reproduction Centurion helmet (Matthew Parkes)

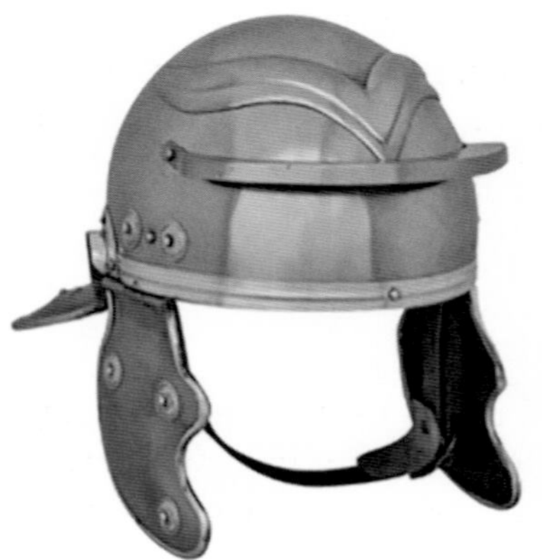

Picture 21: *Above left* – Reproduction Roman legionary 'gallic' helmet (Matthew Parkes)

Picture 22: *Above right* – Roman ballista (Matthew Parkes)

Helmets

They were generally made of bronze with iron trim. A large projecting piece protected the back of the neck and a smaller ridge ran along the front. Hinged cheek pieces projected from the sides and could be tied together by the leather straps attached. The main types in use in the second century were the Imperial Gallic and Italic helmets. Evidence suggests some helmets had a crest holder for plumes of horse hair. Tests have shown replica helmets to withstand arrows, and tests on later Anglo-Saxon-style helmets show good protection against a variety of weapons. However, two points are worth noting. First, the test helmets were better quality steel compared to bronze or iron; second a sword or axe strike may not penetrate the metal, but could still cause severe injury due to the force of the blow through the helmet shaking the brain. Nevertheless, a man with a helmet is at a significant advantage on the battlefield compared to one without. The curved surface would ensure blows glanced off unless it was a direct hit.

During the Republican period, Rome's enemies were often similarly equipped. The campaigns of Julius Caesar and beginnings of empire coincided with increased friction with Germanic tribes. These tribes used different weapons and tactics, including long slashing swords and axes in open formation rather than a solid body of soldiers. Skirmishes, raids and guerrilla-style tactics became more common compared to pitched battles. Fighting often occurred in woodland and hilly areas rather than flat open plains, and this increased chances of attack from above. We see helmets evolving with peaks, ridges and brow bands strengthening specific areas. Rear neck guards and cheek pieces became more pronounced and improved protection. This coincided with the earliest appearance of lorica segmentata from the first century AD.

Shields

The rectangular *scutum* is the iconic shield of the Roman imperial army. It was made of sheets of thin wood glued together with the grain at right angles to the ones both above and below. The edges were bound in iron or bronze. The centre was hollowed out for a hand grip, which was in turn protected by a metal boss. The shield was then covered in leather and when finished, weighed around 10kg; an example from Syria measures 105 x 41cm. Simply put, it would provide cover from the knees to the chin of a 6ft tall man. If that man were also to wear metal greaves and ducked his head a little, only his eyes would be visible (assuming he was wearing a helmet). The curved shape would also give some side protection. Auxiliaries generally had oval shields. Polybius, writing in the second century BC, gives a good description of the shield and general weapons carried.[44] The *scutum* is described as having a curved surface measuring 2½ft in width and 4ft in length. It was made of two planks glued together with the outer surface covered first with canvas and then with calf-skin. The rims were strengthened by iron, protecting it from blows and damage when rested on the ground. The boss was made of iron and could withstand 'the most formidable blows of stones, pikes, and heavy missiles in general'. They also carried a sword, hanging on the right thigh 'called a Spanish sword'. Polybius describes it as 'excellent for thrusting, and both of its edges cut effectually, as the blade is very strong and firm'. In addition the soldiers carried two pila, a brass helmet, and greaves.

The covering of calf skin was important. Shields of bare wood often allowed arrows to penetrate quite deeply, a layer of leather reduced this considerably. The exact type of covering was important enough for King Athelstan in the tenth century to specify what could and could not be used;[45] sheepskin, for example, was not considered appropriate and so was prohibited by Athelstan. Early Germanic shields tended to be hexagonal or oval but would have likely been covered in hide. Lime wood or pine were common material but in reality a variety of wooden boards glued together would suffice. An iron boss protected the hand as with the Roman *scutum*. The rims may also have been edged with iron. Later literary sources depict damage in battle after repeated blows, with one saga describing a sword blow severing a shield in two and embedding itself in the warrior's head.[46]

It is worth noting the use of a shield as an offensive weapon. Tacitus describes auxiliaries using their shield bosses to strike the enemy at the battle of Mons Graupius. Although it may have been a little cumbersome, the edge of the shield was a useful weapon. In later centuries the Anglo-Saxon and Viking round shield was more suited for this tactic, but it is worth describing just how effective it could be. When one holds a round shield with a sword it becomes immediately obvious and natural that one can 'jab' the edge of the shield either horizontally or vertically. The hard edge could easily break a person's nose, either directly or by pushing their own shield into their face.

One very useful technique discovered by re-enactors using round shields is to 'roll' the opponent's shield. If you imagine two right handed fighters, facing each other with their left foot and shield in front. One jabs out their shield holding it vertically and strikes the left edge of their opponents shield. This turns the enemy's shield and by 'rolling' the top of your shield to the left and down this opens up his entire left side. Not only that, but he is now off balance and leaning back, making it harder to strike with his sword. You now have your shield pushing down and away against his, and as you are leaning forward your sword arm is within striking distance of his entire left side. If he is armoured, then you might wish to avoid his torso, but his neck or thigh are easy pickings. Especially if you move fast, strike with shield, roll opponent's shield and then step in quickly to deliver sword thrust.

This technique is ideal for round shields and it demonstrates that techniques and training were important. This could not be so easily done with a Roman shield. The *scutum* could be lifted horizontally and then jabbed forward which knocks the top of the opponents shield. This tilting can open a gap at stomach level allowing a thrust with the *gladius*. Perhaps a more common tactic was simply to keep the sword arm hidden from view. This allowed two likely attacks: first, over the top to the opponent's head and neck; second, a short movement to the left allows the sword arm to jab out at the torso. This can be quickly retracted and the shield covers the body again.

One re-enactor shows how important stance is important, slightly forward with the front foot turned and the head bent forward.[47] If the foot is turned parallel to the bottom edge of the shield, this reduces potential injury to knee, shin and foot. The shield can be lowered quickly to the floor to protect from a spear thrust. Holding the shield slightly away from the body doesn't just protect from the risk of arrows or spears penetrating; by raising it in defence, you produce some distance between the top edge and yourself. This prevents most sword or spear thrusts from reaching home. A turn of the head means that even if a sword or spear thrust does reach, it is more likely to hit the helmet. In fact, the curved surface encourages the blow to slide off.

The shield can be used effectively as an offensive weapon too. Punching out with the bottom edge can produce openings for the gladius either hitting the top, bottom or sides of your opponent's shield. If the enemy had no shield, a strike from a shield rim could easily break your nose. It would obviously deflect a spear out of the way. Most impressive was the way the gladius was hidden by the shield. The strike, when it came, was more like a boxer's right hand than a sword swing, and of course the gladius excelled as a thrusting weapon. The important thing was the shield obscured the first stage of the body movement. The speed at which the sword attack came either over the top towards them face or to the belly would be difficult to counter.

In tests on a combination of shield (15mm poplar wood covered in canvas), mail and pork joint, most arrows were stopped. However, a bodkin arrow punctures through shield and mail to penetrate flesh by an inch. A shield covered in layers of linen stopped arrows but was unable to stop a pilum, which went through the shield, mail and ballistic gel.[48] Comparing a Roman pilum with a Celtic javelin, another tester found that both types were stopped by shields. However, only the pilum punched through mail.[49] Another test found the following: three pila went through completely and eleven stuck in. None bounced off (although some missed). Distances were set at 20–25 metres. In contrast, an experienced javelin thrower achieved distances of 54.5 metres with a light spear and 33 or 34 metres for a heavier type. The tests showed that pilum would have seriously compromised a shield, either through full penetration or through sticking in the shield and making it unwieldy.[50]

So in general we can say the following: most shields gave protection from most missiles most of the time. The pilum, and some arrows, however, were able to punch through a shield to varying depths. The pilum especially could penetrate a shield the full length of the iron head. While scale armour gave good protection, lorica hamata was vulnerable and a percentage of missiles or spear thrusts could break rings and penetrate deep enough to injure or kill.

Legions of the northern frontier

The film depicts a standard with III Felix. However, it was legio IIII Flavia Felix based at Singidinum in modern Belgrade, in the province of Moesia on the Danube, that took part in the war. Its symbol was the lion and we do indeed see lions depicted on standards. Although this possibly refers to the third cohort of that legion. The tables below give details of the legions involved in the Marcomannic War.[51]

Table 4: Legions of the northern frontier provinces in the second century

Province	Legions
Moesia	VII Claudia XI Claudia I Italica IIII Flavia Felix
Pannonia	X Gemina XIV Gemina I Adiutrix II Adiutrix
Noricum	II Italica
Raetia	III Italica
Dacia	V Macedonia XIII Gemina

Table 5: Legions of the northern frontier: Emblems and bases

Legion	Emblems	Main base	Details
VII Claudia	Bull	Viminacium Serbia	Marcomannic War Vexillation sent to Parthian War 161-6 AD
XI Claudia	Neptune	Durostorum Bulgaria	Stationed in lower Moesia throughout Marcomannic War.
I Italica	Boar	Novae Bulgaria	Marcomannic War. Records show many soldiers decorated for bravery. Clodius Albinus, future emperor, officer in the legion.
IIII Flavia Felix	Lion	Singidunum Belgrade	Marcomannic War. Clodius Albinus, future emperor, officer in the legion in 180s.
X Gemina	Bull	Vindobona Vienna	Marcomannic War. Emperor's base. Vexillation sent to Parthian War 161-6 AD.
XIV Gemina	Capricorn, The Eagle	Carnuntum Austria	Marcomannic War. Emperor's base. Vexillation sent to Parthian War 161-6 AD.
I Adiutrix	Capricorn, Pegasus	Brigetio Hungary	Marcomannic War. Part of force led by Petrinax, future emperor, in 170s.
II Adiutrix	Boar, Pegasus	Aquincum Budapest	Fought in both Marcomannic and Parthian Wars.
II Italica	Capricorn, She-wolf, twins	Lauriacum, Austria	Marcomannic War. Possibly used as mobile reserve and part of force led by Petrinax, future emperor.

Legion	Emblems	Main base	Details
III Italica	Stork	Castra Regina, Germany	Marcomannic War. Possibly used as mobile reserve and part of force led by Petrinax, future emperor.
V Macedonia	Bull, Eagle	Potaissa, Romania	Marcomannic War. Vexillation sent to Parthian War 161-6 AD
XIII Gemina	Lion	Apulum Romania	Marcomannic War.

Tactics and formations

Plubius Flavius Vegetius Renatus was a Roman writer of the late fourth century. His book *De re militari* ('Concerning military matters'), is a valuable source of information for Roman equipment, tactics and warfare. It is the only manual of Roman military institutions to have survived intact. It is from Vegetius we get a picture of the formation of the early Roman army. In the republican period, the first five cohorts formed the front line from right to left respectively. Helmets, greaves, shields, swords, five lead-weighted darts slotted into their shields and two javelins. The javelins consisted of a short 4ft type with a 5in tip and a longer 6ft shaft with a 9in iron tip to transfix opposing shields. In the second line were five further cohorts. Early cohorts numbered 555 men with the first cohort on the right wing double in number. A third line consisted of light troops with javelins, slings and archers. The reserve, triarii, were armed similar to the front ranks and cavalry were posted on the wings.

Skirmishers would harass the enemy first and if they ran would be pursued by the light troops and cavalry. If the enemy were provoked to attack, the light troops retreated. The two front ranks then stood like a 'wall of iron'. If victorious, it was again the light troops and cavalry that pursued. The heavy infantry in the cohorts could 'not flee nor pursue easily'.[52] Vegetius also describes a six line formation with the first two lines were heavy infantry.[53] Then came the fast light infantry with javelins and archers, followed by 'light shield bearers' also with javelins and lead darts. The fifth line contained 'carriage ballistas' and 'sling staff men' discharging stones and bolts. Followed by the triarri in reserve.

Tactics, equipment and formations evolved over the centuries taking in a number of important changes. First, the enlargement of the empire required a significant increase in troops. This led to auxiliary units becoming more numerous. Second, cavalry became more important and these were increasingly auxiliary troops. By the time of the Marcomannic Wars auxiliary troops outnumbered legionnaires. A common tactic was to deploy auxiliary infantry in the front line with auxiliary cavalry units on the flanks. Figure 8 showed a typical formation of the second century – which isn't what appears in Gladiator. As previously noted, it would be preferable to let the enemy attack a defensive position. But if they were to sally out to meet them in open battle, one would expect auxiliary infantry cohorts to form the first line of attack.

With that in mind it is worth considering how much space a formation would take up. An infantrymen takes up around 3ft of space. Thus in a mile, just over 1,700 men could form a single line and a legion could form up three lines deep. Between lines, a space of 6ft was usual. Vegetius describes how 10,000 men could take up a position a mile wide and 42ft deep.[54] This would imply six ranks deep with around 7ft between the lines. Of course this assumes a solid front line. In general it's preferable to have depth rather than thinning a line out. Some re-enactors find having a line just two or three ranks deep breaks down quite quickly and descends into skirmishing or mêlée. At the battle of Pharsalus in 48 BC, Pompey is said to have deployed his 45,000 men ten ranks deep.

We get a further picture from Caesar at the battle of Ilerda. He describes holding a ridge, 160 metres wide, with three cohorts. This allows 174 men to line the ridge and three cohorts side by side would leave fifty-eight men in the front rank of each. It follows the depth, assuming 480 in a cohort, would be eight men. If we recall, our earlier examples of formations were also eight deep, as was the example in the opening scenes of HBO's *Rome*. In *Gladiator*'s opening battle scene the troops advance in thin lines and the fight quickly dissolves into close-quarter mêlée. While the Romans were trained for, and were capable of this, their preferred style was to maintain their formation. They were, however, flexible and trained to form a line, a wedge or a circle.[55] Other types of formation evolved over the decades. At the battle of Catalaunian plains against Attila in AD 451, the Romans formed a shield wall, similar to later Saxon or Viking tactics. However, in the second century the most likely scenario would have been to send the auxiliaries in first and, if needed, the legionary cohorts would advance in formation and in depth.

Concerning cavalry we recall the tactic described by Vegetius:[56] when outnumbered, cavalry is mixed with light infantry, velites, with light shields and javelins. Caesar used just this tactic at Pharsalus in 48 BC. A useful defence against cavalry was with the use of caltrops, made of four spikes so that it rests on three on the ground with the remaining one sticking up. These could be scattered quickly to protect part of your line or flank. Another interesting point concerns chariots. Vegetius describes how scythed chariots became a 'laughing stock' on the battle field. Not only did they require flat ground, but they were easy to defend against with caltrops.[57]

Thus, a defensive static line of troops expecting a cavalry attack had a quick and easy defence *if* they had caltrops available. Of course even without these, it would be relatively easy to dig pits and holes if one had time. Even if there was no time for such measures, cavalry of the day would be unlikely to attack a solid infantry formation, especially if they were armed with spears.

We get an interesting account of battle formation against such an attack below. Flavius Arrianus was a military commander and writer in the early second century. While governor of Cappadocia in eastern Turkey, he commanded the army against the Alani. The Alani used both lightly armoured horse archers and heavy cataphract cavalry. Arrianus wrote Ektaxis kata Alanon ('The order of battle against the Alans') and lays out his deployment and tactics.

He describes the Scythians as being 'lightly armed and having unprotected horses'. The deployment of infantry and cavalry archers on the flanks was intended to keep these at a relatively safe distance. However, the formation was designed to withstand a charge from the heavy cataphract cavalry. These were armoured warriors and horses which could deliver a 'shock' charge and potentially break up a formation. These were used with devastating effect by the Parthians at the battle of Carrahe in 53 BC. Crassus formed his army up into a hollow square with twelve cohorts on each side. The Parthians attacked with horse archers. Roman light troops and archers were unable to drive them off and the legionnaires were forced to form a testudo. Plutarch records the Parthian bows were able to penetrate shields, stating: 'the force of the arrows, which fractured armour, and tore their way through every covering alike, whether hard or soft.' Plutarch, The life of Crassus, 24.

This may be poetic licence, as we have seen armour and shields offer reasonable protection. However, if we imagine thousands of arrows a minute raining in, then aside from all the exposed skin a percentage may well have broken through, especially if shields and armour were already damaged. Cassius sent his son, Publius, with 1,300 cavalry, 500 archers and eight cohorts to drive off the enemy. But the Parthians were skilled at feigned retreats and using the bow as they rode. Publius was drawn off then surrounded. We read in Plutarch that the Parthians positioned their mail-clad horsemen in front of the Romans while their light cavalry rode round them 'in loose array'.[58] Publius urged his men to charge the enemy's mail-clad horsemen, but 'they showed him that their hands were riveted to their shields and their feet nailed through and through to the ground'. Publius eventually 'made a vigorous charge' and closed on the enemy. However the struggle is described as 'unequal … both offensively and defensively, for his thrusting was done with small and feeble spears against breastplates of raw hide and steel, whereas the thrusts of the enemy were made with pikes against the lightly equipped and unprotected bodies of the Gauls.' Despite this, the Gallic auxiliary cavalry fought well and 'laid hold of the long spears of the Parthians, and grappling with the men, pushed them from … their horses'. This was difficult owing to the weight of the Parthian's armour. The Gauls even dismounted their horses and 'crawling under those of the enemy, stabbed them in the belly'.

Despite these heroic efforts Publius was killed and his force destroyed. The Parthians then made repeated charges with their cataphract cavalry. We learn a lot from this account: the Gallic cavalry were lightly armoured; the Parthian heavy 'mail clad' cavalry were armed with long spears; they were protected by steel or rawhide armour; and composite bows were perhaps more effective than tests suggest. Crassus still had hope until the Parthians brought up fresh supply of arrows by camels. They then rode up with his son's head on a pike, which dispirited the Romans greatly. The battle went on until nightfall and Crassus retreated to Carrahae leaving 4,000 wounded to be slaughtered by the Parthians. Crassus himself was killed the next day and the Romans lost about 20,000 killed and 10,000 captured. Wars between Parthia and Rome continued and the Emperor Trajan captured the Parthian capital at Ctesiphon, installed a client king and annexed Armenia in AD 117.

Two decades later the Alani invaded the East with similar threats of horse archers and heavy cavalry as the Parthians. Arrianus describes his tactics and formation to counter this threat.[59] The army should deploy in close ordered ranks, eight deep. The front four ranks must be spearmen 'whose spearpoints end in thin iron shanks'. The front rank holds them 'at the ready' so they can 'thrust the iron points of the spears at the breast of the horses'. The second, third an fourth ranks thrust their spears forward. If the horses and their riders escape death or injury, the rider is put 'out of action with the spear stuck in their heavy body armour and the iron point bent because of the softness'. Ranks five to eight are armed with javelins and the ninth rank are archers. This provides a barrage of missile weapons while the enemy is pinned by the front ranks. Artillery pieces are deployed on the flanks. To the rear, the cavalry is placed in eight wings. They are positioned next to the infantry on both flanks, with heavy infantry and archers as a screen. Horse archers form close to the battle line so as to shoot over it. Last, 'javelin-men, spearmen, swordsmen and axe-men must guard both flanks and await the signal'. Arrianus goes on to describe the tactics. If the 'Scythians' got through the missile barrage they were met with a wall of shields. The first three ranks 'locked their shields and pressed their shoulders and receive the charge as strongly as possible in the most closely ordered formation bound together in the strongest manner.' The fourth rank should discharge their javelins overhead, while the first rank stabs up at both riders and horses.

The Roman army had changed considerably in the nearly 200 years since Carrhae. Auxiliary troops were more numerous and better armed and armoured, especially the cavalry. As tactics and weapons evolved some general tactics that remain constant can be described. Vegetius gives us seven general battle tactics below:[60]

1. Rectangular formation with extended front. Should only be used with numerical superiority lest the flanks become enveloped. He describes this as the usual way to do battle in his day.
2. Oblique or angled formation engaging enemies left flank with your stronger right and strongest cavalry to turn flank.
3. Same as 2 but engaging their right flank with your left.
4. Advance to 400–500 paces then spur on both wings having thinned out your own centre.
5. Same as point 4, but place light troops and archers in front of centre to protect from breach.
6. He describes this as the best: a letter 'I' formation, oblique with the right flank attacking first and cavalry and light troops outflanking enemy.
7. Use of terrain: simply by anchoring one flank against mountain, forest or river then placing all light troops and cavalry on the opposite wing.

We can see an example of one of these at the battle of Pharsalus. Pompey had drawn his force up into three lines, ten ranks deep. Caesar, heavily outnumbered, had thinned his three lines to six deep. Pompey also outnumbered Caesar with cavalry, placing the bulk on his left flank, his right being protected by a river. We can see here how Pompey was using

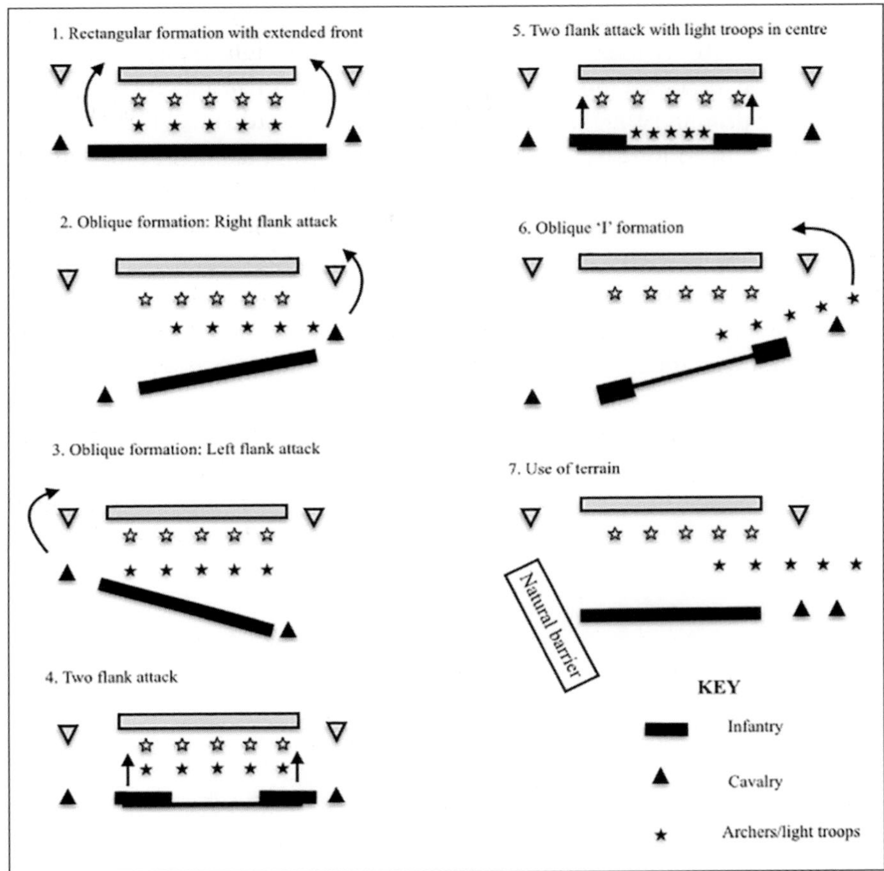

Figure 9: Vegetius: General battle tactics

number seven from the options above. His intention was to drive off a relatively small enemy cavalry force and outflank the smaller infantry force. Unfortunately for Pompey, Caesar deployed something akin to Vegetius's combined cavalry-infantry force. He had thinned out his infantry even more and positioned a fourth line behind his cavalry. This resulted in the routing of Pompey's cavalry, and Caesar wheeling his right around onto the enemy's left flank.

By the time Vegetius was writing in the fourth and fifth centuries, another formation was also common:[61] light units of infantry and cavalry, followed by a line of heavy infantry flanked by heavy cavalry. Archers and slingers behind and a reserve force in the rear. We see from these examples how knowledgeable the Romans were concerning tactics. The Germans on the other hand suffered from a number of drawbacks:[62] they had no siege craft, hence their inability to take Aquileia; they had inferior weapons and armour with fewer swords and missile weapons. They sometimes had little structure or organisation and fought almost as distinct units led by a chief within a mass of mainly infantry. They often relied on a quick mass charge, and one tactic that developed over time was the 'boar's head' or wedge shape, with the best equipped nobles at the tip. There were, however, examples of success, often when united under one leader such as Arminius at the battle of Teutoburg Forest in AD 9. Tacitus states the attacking wedge, or keil, was more like a rectangle with forty warriors in the front line. This developed into a more triangular shape in later Anglo-Saxon and Viking armies a few centuries later. We can see an example in figure 10 below alongside the response by a defending force.

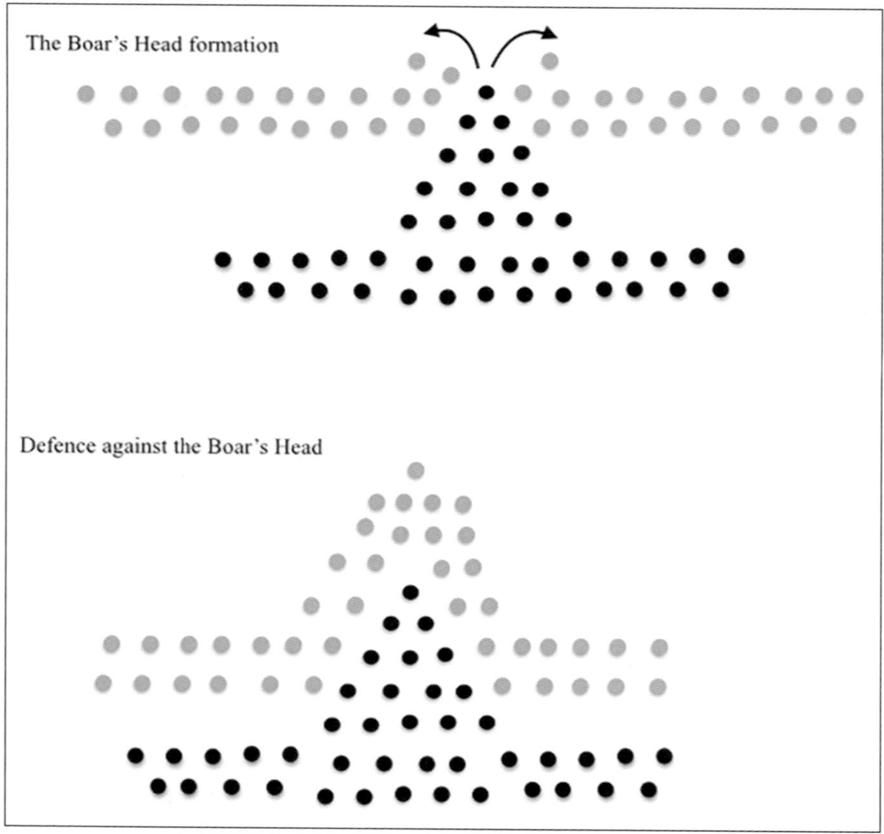

Figure 10: The 'Boar's head' or wedge formation

This was certainly a tactic of which the Germanic tribes and Romans were aware. The Romans applied a similar formation in defeating Boudicca at the Battle of Watling Street. We must remember the Britons had inflicted a series of defeats upon the Romans, showing that they were not invincible. Tacitus records the words of the general Suetonius to his troops, although it's likely he is once again using literary licence.[63] He extolls them to ignore the noise as empty threats and the multitude as 'more women than soldiers … unwarlike and unarmed, they would break immediately'. In a very Shakespearean speech he states it is just a few men who decide the fate of battles and it would be added glory if just a handful of troops gathered the 'laurels of an entire army'. They should keep close order, deploy their pile and then, using 'shield-boss and sword, let them steadily pile up the dead'. But they were to forget the thought of plunder until victory was gained.

Estimates of the size of Boudicca's army vary widely to as high as 230,000. This seems impossibly high, but they clearly outnumbered the Romans, who had about 10,000 men. Tacitus often put words into people's mouths, but this seems rather plausible. A small battle-hardened force faces a disorganised but hugely overwhelming force. One can imagine the commanding officer encouraging his troops. No need to remind them of what defeat would mean to them personally. Rather tell them, 'remember your training, stay together, keep your discipline and stay in formation'. Tacitus goes on to describe the events, including the 'wedge like formation'. The legionaries stood motionless and waited for the Britons to advance before discharging their pila. They then 'dashed forward in a wedge-like formation'. The auxiliaries charged in the same way. The cavalry, 'with lances extended', also charged, breaking through. The Britons fled, but their own wagons to the rear blocked the way. The Romans showed no mercy 'even to the women: the baggage animals themselves had been speared and added to the pile of bodies'. Tacitus claims 80,000 Britons were killed against only 400 Romans. Next we will consider other contemporary accounts of battles which will help give a detailed picture of military tactics.

CONTEMPORARY ACCOUNTS OF BATTLES

Battle of the Teutoburg Forest

A famous victory for the Germans occurred in AD 9 in the battle of the Teutonburg forest. Arminius was a prince of the Cherusci tribe, who were allied to Rome. He served as a Roman officer and achieved equestrian rank.

However, he conspired with other Germanic tribes to lead the Romans into an ambush. He advised General Varus to take legions XVII, XVIII and XIX with six auxiliary cohorts and three cavalry alae, through the forest, with a force of around 20,000. The Romans became stretched out over ten miles. As the army passed along the narrow track they were attacked by volleys of arrows and javelins. The Germanic warriors were then able to attack in force at particular points, with the Romans unable to organise into any kind of formation.

Velleius Paterculus lived through the events of and was active in the Germanic wars of the early first century. He no doubt had access to eye-witness accounts of the battle. His is the oldest surviving description of the battle. He describes the Roman army as 'unexcelled in bravery' and the first 'in discipline, in energy, and in experience'. Its loss he blames on:

> the negligence of its general, the perfidy of the enemy, and the unkindness of fortune was surrounded.... Hemmed in by forests and marshes and ambuscades, it was exterminated almost to a man by the very enemy whom it had always slaughtered like cattle
>
> Paterculus, Roman History, 2.119

We don't need to go into the background of the conflict. The interest here is in the tactics and equipment used. Verus commanded three legions of the province of Germania inferior. The line of march suggested it was towards the Chauci along the River Hasse to the north west. On the first day the Romans entered the forest and Arminius and the other conspirators, having escorted Varus into the forest, left the main body on the pretext of assembling the allied forces to assist the Romans.

On day two, the army approach the narrows between the Kalkriese Hills and the 'Great Bog'. By now it was spread out over about ten miles along a narrow path. Cassius Dio describes the army as crossing through a difficult terrain and having a difficult time felling trees, crossing ravines and bridging places.[64] They had with them many wagons, beasts of burden and 'not a few' women and children. They began to be spread out along the track and then a violent storm made conditions even worse, the track became very slippery and the tops of trees started to fall. Then the Germans attacked. They came 'on all sides at once, coming through the densest thickets, as they were acquainted with the paths.' First they used missile volleys from a distance. Seeing the Romans were not in regular order with many wounded they approached closer. The Romans were 'mixed in helter-skelter with the wagons and the unarmed … unable to form readily anywhere in a body.' The Germans were able to mass their attacks at specific points along the line and overwhelm them.

The strip of land is about 220 metres wide and we can imagine a long, thin line of soldiers, wagons and civilians strung out over several miles. The hill had been fortified with an embankment 700 metres in length and about as tall as a man, topped with a wooden palisade. Archaeological finds support the theory that the Romans attempted to take this but were repulsed. It is unknown exactly which part of the army was attacked, but the implication is that the attack split the army in two. There is no evidence from the sources or material finds that the army retreated. Some finds extend north west towards the intended line of march, and others to the south west where the subsequent line of march went. It could be that the vanguard had already advanced north west and either returned to the main body or were driven into, and lost in, the bog to the north. The survivors of this first attack made it out into open land and made camp. Cassius Dio states the camp was made 'on the spot, after securing a suitable place, so far as that was possible on a wooded mountain'. So perhaps only a little way further on from the narrow path between the hill and bog.

Map 10: Battle of Teutoburg Forest

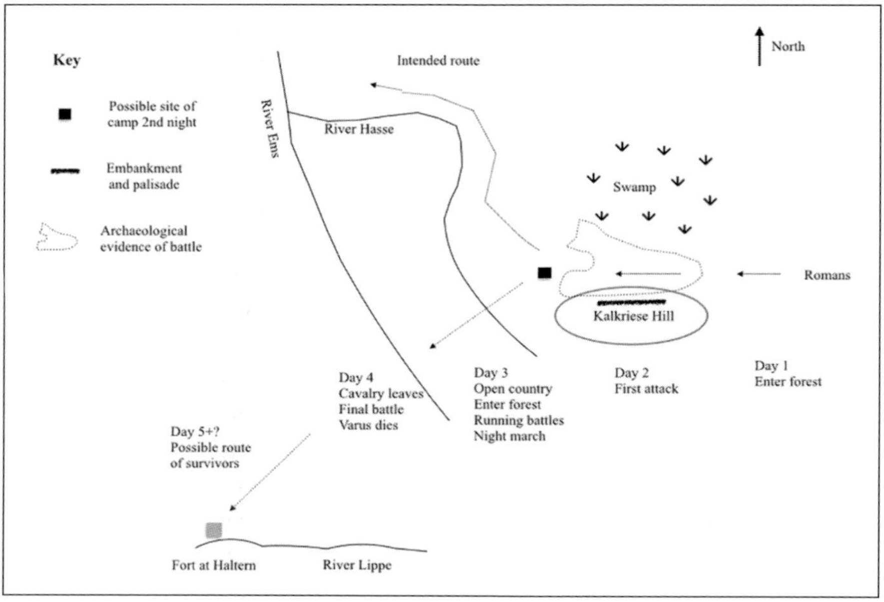

According to the sources, on day three Verus decided to push on, but traceable remains suggest they turned south west towards the River Lippe rather than north west as intended. A large part of the army survived the first attack but the situation was already dire: 'they either burned or abandoned most of their wagons and everything else that was not absolutely necessary to them'. They advanced and reached open country, although 'they did not get off without loss', suggesting running battles and repeated ambushes. During the day they 'plunged into the woods again', but here they suffered further heavy losses. We see here the danger of attempting cavalry manoeuvres in wooded terrain: 'For since they had to form their lines in a narrow space, in order that the cavalry and infantry together might run down the enemy, they collided frequently with one another and with the trees.'

The sources don't mention a camp at the end of the third day but they do imply a night march. Cassius states they 'were still advancing when the fourth day dawned'. It may have been day three or four that part of the Roman cavalry left. The implication is they abandoned the army. Whatever the case, they were caught and slaughtered. Paterculus once again provides details.[65] A certain Numonius, a 'lieutenant of Varus' made a dash for the Rhine with his cavalry. How many he doesn't say, but this left the army unprotected. His gamble ended in failure: 'for he did not survive those whom he had abandoned, but died in the act of deserting them'.

A previous provincial governor had constructed a road between the Ems and Lippe Rivers and it is likely this was the target. But the fourth day proved to be the most fateful for the Romans. Cassius Dio tells us a heavy downpour and a violent wind not only prevented them advancing further but deprived them 'of the use of their weapons'.[66] Their bows became useless and heavy shields were soaked. The Germanic warriors, being lighter in armour and equipment were less effected and were able to manoeuvre more easily. They had also been reinforced as wavering tribes smelled blood, revenge and plunder. The Roman ranks had become thinned and we read it was at this point 'Varus and all the more prominent officers … took their own lives'.

So we see here how on day four they became stuck 'unable to go forward'. They had suffered several days of running battles, had no cavalry, were being attacked by their own auxiliaries led by Arminius as well as German tribes and now the weather was affecting their equipment. The death of their commander no doubt was the last straw for many. Any remaining cohesion and discipline must have disintegrated. Paterculus records disapprovingly that one camp prefect, Ceionius, 'after the greater part of the army had perished, proposed its surrender'. Another, Lucius Eggius, 'furnished a precedent as noble', presumably committing suicide. Cassius Dio records that when news of Varus spread many soldiers either committed suicide or gave up. The Germans 'cut down every man and horse'. Interestingly, they also occupied 'all the strongholds save one'. Paterculus gives us a clue what this means. He tells of how Lucius Caedicius, prefect of the camp, was besieged at Aliso, 'by an immense force of Germans … they watched their chance, and with the sword won their way back to their friends'.[67]

It would appear there were some survivors and the most likely location for the fort is Haltern on the River Lippe. Cassius shows the importance of archers and fortifications in his remarks: The Germans were 'unable to reduce this fort, because they did not understand the conduct of sieges, and because the Romans employed numerous archers, who repeatedly repulsed them and destroyed large numbers of them.' He continues with a little known and rather dramatic scene. The garrison fought off the attackers for some time but were running low on food. They waited for a stormy night and made a run for it. The soldiers 'were but few, the unarmed many', but they managed to slip past two 'enemy outposts'. At the third they were discovered. It would seem they dropped whatever they were carrying because Cassius says the Germans were more concerned with plunder. In addition, a soldier signalled a 'double-quick march' causing the Germans to believe a relief force was closing in and they ceased their pursuit.

Tacitus records the grisly remains discovered by the army of Germanicus six years later. They found Varus's first camp with a wide circumference and the measurements of its central space clearly visible. Further on they found a partially fallen rampart and shallow fosse, then in 'a field were the whitening bones of men, as they had fled, or stood their ground, strewn everywhere or piled in heaps'. Nearby were fragments of weapons and limbs of horses, and human heads, prominently nailed to trunks of trees. In nearby groves they discovered 'the barbarous altars, on which they had immolated tribunes and first-rank centurions'. But we do hear of survivors who escaped the battle, or later, from captivity. They describe the spot where the officers fell and the eagles were captured. They were able to show where Varus committed suicide and where 'Arminius had harangued his army, the number of gibbets for the captives, the pits for the living, and how in his exultation he insulted the standards and eagles'.[68]

We see here that there were indeed survivors both from the battles and captivity. Cassius Dio also confirms this by stating later some of the prisoners were ransomed by their relatives and returned from captivity although they had to stay outside Italy.

Germanicus

A few years later Germanicus led 12,000 men, twenty-six auxiliary cohorts and 8 alae of cavalry across the Rhine where Tacitus states 'for fifty miles around, wasted the country with sword and flame'. The Bructeri, Tubantes, and Usipetes attempted to repeat Arminius's victory as Germanicus passed through the Caesian Forest. The Romans anticipated this and were able to counter attack successfully. In AD 16 at Idistavisus, Germanicus attacked a combined force led by Arminus with eight Roman legions.

The plain of Idisiaviso lay between the River Weser and hills. The Germans placed themselves on 'the level', along the tree line with the Cherusci placed on high ground opposed the river. Germanicus formed his army up as follows:

Line 1	Auxiliary Gauls and Germans
Line 2	Infantry archers
Line 3	Four legions, Germanicus with two praetorian cohorts and the 'flower of the cavalry'
Line 4	The other four legions, light armed troops, mounted archers and the rest of the allied cohorts.

Germanicus ordered his cavalry to attack the flanks and sent a portion around to attack the rear. The infantry advanced at the same time and

Map 11: Battle of Idisiaviso

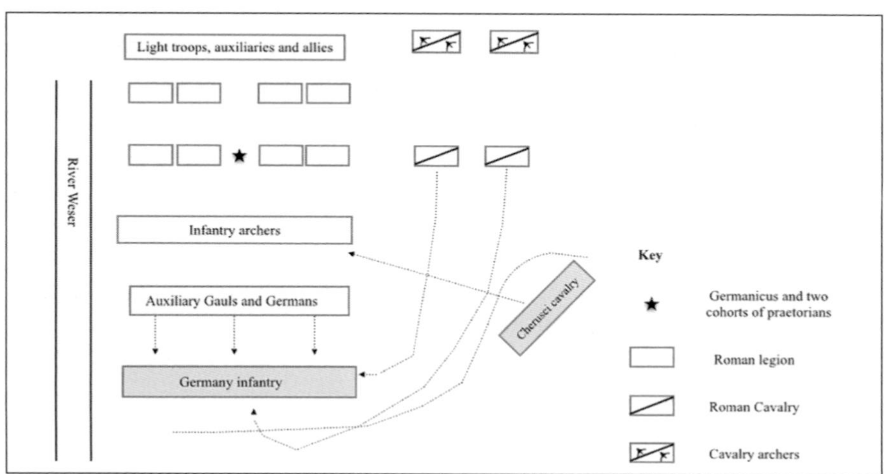

it would seem the Germans broke quickly, retreating into the forest. Arminius led the Cherusci and charged into the archers, nearly breaking through. It would seem while the first line was engaged with the pursuit, Arminius came in from the flank into the Roman second line. He was fought off by German and Gallic cohorts and Tacitus claims that Chauci, serving among the auxiliaries, recognised him and let him pass. The slaughter is said to have lasted from midday to sunset and bodies strewn for ten miles.[69]

Mons Graupius AD 83/4

We get an account of this battle from Tacitus writing about the victory of his father-in-law, the general Agricola. The Caledonians muster a large force under many kings, one of whom is named Calgacus, with over 30,000 men. It is at this point Tacitus records one of the best known lines from antiquity. The Romans are described as 'robbers of the world' and 'rapacious'. They 'lust for dominion.'

> Alone among men they covet with equal eagerness poverty and riches. To robbery, slaughter, plunder, they give the lying name of empire; they make a solitude and call it peace.
>
> Tacitus, *Life of Agricola*, chapters 30-37

Agricola laid out his troops in what would be a familiar formation to Pompeianus a hundred years later. His auxiliary infantry, 8,000 strong, strengthened his centre while 3,000 cavalry were posted on the wings. The legions were drawn up behind the auxiliaries. the Britons posted themselves on high ground with their van on the plain. The rest of the army rose in an arch-like form up the slope of a hill. On the plain below were placed chariots and cavalry. The engagement began with missiles and attacks from the chariots which the Romans repulsed with cavalry and volleys of their own.

The Britons were armed with their 'huge swords and small shields' and delivered 'a dense shower of darts' on the Romans. Agricola ordered three Batavian and two Tungrian cohorts forward to close in with their swords. The swords of the Britons are described as 'unwieldy' and 'not pointed'. They proved no match for the experienced Germnaic troops and they pushed the enemy backwards up the hill, striking them with the 'bosses of their shields and stabbing them in the face.'[70] We can compare this to later tactics where the sword was used more as a cutting weapon and the edge of the shield would be more effective than the boss. The cavalry easily dispersed the chariots and then outflank the enemy and attack the rear. Tacitus estimated 10,000 Caledonians lay dead with Roman loses below 400.

The Batavian revolt AD 69-70

It is worth noting the presence of Batavian auxiliary cohorts at Mons Graupius. These were a Germanic tribe who had been allied to Rome since the time of Caesar. In AD 69, the 3,000 strong legio I Germanica, together with cohorts of Belgian auxilia, tried to stop eight veteran Batavian auxiliary units returning to their homeland. The legion's commander tried to capture the Batavians but was routed and pursued back to their camp. Large numbers of men were killed in the crush or cut down outside trying to reach safety.

The following year, Gauls and Germanic warriors attacked the Roman encampment on the east banks of the Mosel River opposite the town of Augusta Treverorum, Trier, on the west bank. A massed assault was carried out at night from the forested area to the west and breached the outer defences. Auxiliary cavalry stationed nearby were routed and the bridge over the Mosel was captured. This could easily have been a disaster for the Romans.

Map 12: Battle of Augusta Treverorum

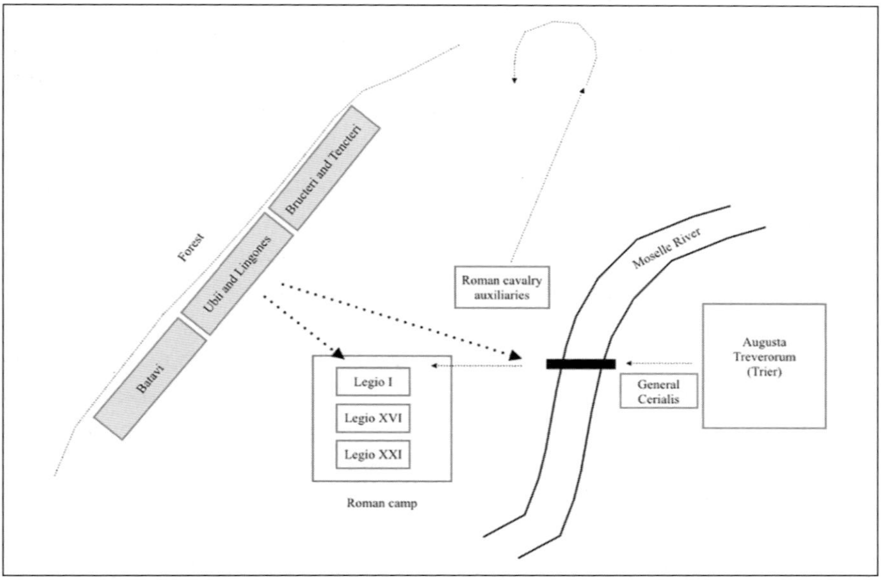

The Roman general Quintus Petilius Cerialis was not in the camp; it is likely he was in the town just across the river. He awoke from his bed to find the cavalry routed, the camp 'had been forced' and the bridge over the river connecting the 'colony' to the camp was held by the Germans. According to Tacitus the general himself led the counterattack, retook the bridge and entered the camp. He found confusion and disorder. Tacitus states the cohorts could not form into line and battle was raging within the entrenchments. The situation seemed 'in favour of the enemy' until legion XXI, 'having more room than the others, formed itself into a compact body, withstood, and soon drove back the assailants'. The Germans also mistook the returning auxiliary units for major reinforcements. A counterattack forced the Germanic and Gallic warriors to flee in some disorder. The Romans came very close to disaster, but once the initial assault faltered the Romans were allowed to organise into cohorts and the attackers eventually broke and ran.

We see here how a Germanic force might actually attempt an attack on a well defended position or fort. They attacked at night and en masse, relying on surprise and ferocity to overcome the defenders. The strategy was the same as that in open battle: a fierce initial charge to break apart the formation upon which the Roman army relied, hence the development of tactics such as the 'boar's head' or wedge.

A decisive battle of the Batavian revolt occurred in AD 70 fought near Castra Vetera on the Rhine. The Romans held their legions in reserve and placed their auxiliary infantry and cavalry in two lines in front. The Batavians launched missiles to provoke an attack across the marshy ground; when this failed, they charged and forced the auxiliaries back. The legions then advanced and while the battle hung in the balance, on a signal two troops of Roman cavalry who had circumvented the marsh attacked from the rear. This simultaneous attack broke the Batavians and they fled towards the Rhine.

A much later battle is instructive as it not only shows a Roman defeat to a Gothic army, but also describes the effects of weapons. In AD 378, Emperor Valens led 30,000 Roman troops against a Gothic force of around 15,000 at Adrianople. Amminaus Macrcellinus described the events: the Romans outnumbered the Goths by about 30,000 to 20,000, but they had marched eight miles in the hot midday sun. The Goths were drawn up in a circular formation on raised ground behind their wagons, although the bulk of their cavalry was not present. Initial negotiations began, but either by accident or design an impulsive volley of arrows from a Roman unit started the battle. The Romans attacked and the cavalry on the left reached the wagons first.

However, the Gothic and allied Alan cavalry returned from foraging just at the right moment and and charged at the right and left flanks. Both wings of Roman cavalry were routed 'with great slaughter', or pushed against the flanks of their infantry. Realising what was happening, the Gothic infantry advanced. Before the armies came together, arrows and javelins flew and the lines pushed backwards and forwards 'like the waves of the sea'. The Roman infantry were then pressed so close together that a man could 'hardly wield a sword or draw back his arm once he had stretched it out'. Nor was it possible to 'see the enemy's missiles in flight and dodge them'. The Goths poured into the battle and the crush made ordered retreat impossible. We get a vivid account of the effects of weapons, with severed limbs and helmets and breast plates being split by battle axes. Spears were shattered and the infantry had to 'make do' with swords. This indicates that for some units at least the spear was the primary weapon. Eventually, the Romans, 'weak from hunger, parched with thirst and weighed down by the burden of their armour', broke. The Romans lost two thirds of their forces, around 20,000 men.[71]

The above example demonstrates how, while a battle can hang in the balance, once one side breaks the slaughter can be enormous. Fleeing men, disorganised and without formation, are easy prey to pursuing cavalry and light troops. By the fourth century the Roman army had recruited a large number of Germanic soldiers and often adopted the 'barritus', a Germanic war cry.[72] This could be to intimidate their Germanic enemies or simply to signify the presence of Germanic soldiers in the ranks; it may be the case that this evolved from earlier centuries. The opening scene of *Gladiator* has the barbarians making such a noise (although it sounds similar to the soundtrack from the 1964 film *Zulu*). Germanic warriors were armed with short spears and iron swords, longer than the Roman gladius. Shields and helmets would have been common; the chiefs and leaders tended to wear armour, mostly chainmail hauberks.[73] The bulk of the army consisted of part-time infantry. However, the Romans utilised Gallic and Germanic cavalry extensively because of its quality.

Later Germanic warriors such as Anglo-Saxons appear to have fought mainly as infantry, with the shield wall a common tactic. Indeed, heroic poetry of the Dark Ages almost always describes fighting on foot.[74] There is more surviving material from later centuries which, while not contemporary, gives an idea of the tactics and formation of many Germanic tribes. In the fifth century the Franks and Anglo-Saxons still fought mainly on foot.[75] The Franks used sword, shield, double-headed axe and barbed spear with few wearing helmets, mail or having horses. The elite alone had long swords and they fought on foot for which they are 'extremely well practised'.[76] Yet the Alamanni were renowned for their 'excellent' cavalry. Procopius describes a Gothic army in AD 539 as consisting of mostly infantry with swords, axes and shields. They advanced quickly to use the spear as a thrusting weapon.[77] Throwing axes were utilised first before an infantry charge with swords. In a sixth-century manual of war, *Strategicon*, the Franks and Lombards are described as dismounting to fight on foot with shields, lances and swords. The following description is worth noting: 'they fight according to families and not in regular troops ... they charge swiftly with much spirit. They do not obey their leaders well. Headstrong, despising strategy, precaution of foresight, they show contempt for every tactical command especially cavalry.'[78]

Conclusion

A fitting way to end this chapter is to lay out the most likely scenarios for an historically accurate battle scene, as opposed to the fictional representation in *Gladiator*. First, the Romans were not invincible. However, they did have the clear advantage in open country where their legions could form up. If the Germans wished to attack a fortified location, it is highly unlikely they would advertise their presence first. Far more likely they would attempt a surprise attack, preferably at night as at the camp opposite the town of Augusta Treverorum. Alternatively, they might attempt an ambush hoping for a another Teutoburg Forest. However, as we saw with Germanicus a few years later, even that did not guarantee success. The best that could be said for the opening scene of *Gladiator* is perhaps that they wished to lure the Romans into the forest – although the presence of Roman cavalry unrealistically charging through dense woods suggests otherwise.

Second, the Romans would be unlikely to leave a fortified place. If they sallied out they would advance with auxiliary or light troops. They used specialist troops extensively and so would no doubt have other Germanic tribesmen enlisted in auxiliary cohorts they could send in. A far more likely scenario would have been a Roman army deep within Marcomannic territory, destroying the remnants of resistance.

Regarding the fighting, the armour and shields would work more often than not. Sword slashes do not penetrate steel armour, whether mail or lorica segmentata. Even thrusts of sword or spear would be unlikely to do so, although the latter especially might break ribs or at least knock the wind out of someone. Shields largely did their job well, especially if covered in hide. Yet pila would penetrate several inches, making them useless. Helmets too would have caused blows to glance off, but a direct hit, especially with an axe, could easily be fatal. Those without any armour would have been horribly exposed. Severed limbs and head injuries would have been common. The Romans would have at least attempted to keep their formation.

I am not sure this would have been any less entertaining. An engagement in open field might have had the Romans in a tight formation with two lines of eight men deep, fronted by auxiliaries. Germanic warriors, many wearing mail, might have attempted a boar's head wedge attack. Breaking through the auxiliaries it might have been met with hail of pila before smashing into a wall of heavy infantry with the men behind holding the belts of those in front.

Chapter 4

Marcus Aurelius

In his famous book, *The History of the Decline and Fall of the Roman Empire*, Edward Gibbon described Marcus Aurelius as the last in the line of 'good emperors'.[1] By implication, Commodus is a 'bad' emperor. This view was certainly shared by his contemporaries. Cassius Dio (born AD 155) was a young boy when Marcus Aurelius became emperor and served in the senate through many more (died AD 235). His description is worth noting: When Marcus died, Rome descended from a 'kingdom of gold to one of iron and rust' (book 72.36).

Early life

Marcus Aurelius was born 26 April, AD 121. His family came from Spain and grew rich from the olive oil trade. His great-grandfather achieved senatorial rank and his grandfather, Marcus Annius Verus, became prefect of Rome three times under Vespasian and consul three times. He married Rupilia Faustina, whose step-sister went on to marry the emperor Hadrian. Marcus Annius Verus and Rupilia Faustina had four children, the eldest, Verus, being the father of Marcus Aurelius. Marcus Aurelius's mother, Domitia Lucillia, had come from another wealthy family. They had two children, Marcus in AD 121, and Anna Cornificia Faustina in AD 123.

At nine days, Marcus would have received the Roman naming ceremony, where babies were lifted from the hearth, ceremonially 'purified' and given their name. Two presents were bestowed, a rattle and a golden amulet worn round the neck until the boy reached manhood. He spent his infancy in his parents' villa in Rome. When Marcus was 3 years old his father died and so his grandfather became influential in his life. Marcus reports later that it was his grandfather who taught him the virtues of good character and self control. Hadrian, having ascended the throne before Marcus was born, took a keen interest in his development and promoted him to an equestrian at the age of 6. Hadrian's nickname for Marcus, '*vertissimus*', or most truthful, could indicate he was teasing him for his earnestness. From a young age he took a keen interest in Greek philosophy and one of his first teachers promoted 'the Greek way of life'.[2] In practice this meant encouraging the intellectual over the more hedonistic pursuits Hadrian enjoyed. Marcus went to the other extreme and embraced austerity and a self denying lifestyle. When he was 12 his mother found him sleeping on the ground in a simple cloak and had to convince him to sleep in his bed.

On his fifteenth birthday Marcus went through the Roman right of passage. His gold amulet and striped toga were replaced by the toga virilis, the white robe of the Roman man. The boy had developed into a 'perfect meld of Greek sophistication and Stoic sensibility'.[3] Hadrian had looked to a Ceionius Commodus as his successor but he was in poor health. As soon as Marcus reached adulthood, Hadrian ordered his betrothal to Commodus's daughter consciously adding more legitimacy to him. As an adolescent, Marcus enjoyed physical sports such as boxing, wrestling, ball games and hunting, but disliked gladiatorial shows and chariot races. He was described as over-serious, gloomy or austere. A complete contrast to the more hedonistic Hadrian.

Hadrian

Three aspects of the emperor Hadrian are worthy of note. First, his policy of stability and peace. There was still constant warfare on the borders, but the expansion of Trajan was stopped. The second was his homosexuality. While Romans generally accepted it when young, once in his twenties a Roman man was expected to be heterosexual and settle down to raise a family. The last aspect of Hadrian was his tireless travels throughout the empire.

In appearance he was tall and well built, bearded and austere looking. He was very active and energetic. He was skilled with weapons and at hunting and one of his favourite party tricks was killing a lion with a javelin.[4] He also put on lavish shows in the arena and was especially keen on lions, once killing a hundred in one show. One important change was with official administrative positions. Previously held by freedmen they now had to be of equestrian rank, which opened up a career path and led to this class dominating the civil service.

The general view of his personality is negative. He could be unpredictable, envious, fickle and cruel. He killed off all his likely successors and once stabbed a slave in the eye with a stylus for a minor offence.[5] Soldiers and freedmen were executed for petty insults and he could be vengeful and vindictive. The Jewish revolt of AD 132–135 resulted in nearly 1,000 villages being razed and according to Cassius Dio, over half-a-million Jews killed in battle. Hadrian adopted Ceionius Commodus as his son and renamed him Aelius Caesar. Unfortunately, Aelius died in AD 138 after returning from the Pannonian border. His son, Lucius Verus, then only six, went to become adoptive brother and co-emperor, of Marcus Aurelius.

In AD 138 Hadrian's health grew worse and he surprised everyone by naming a relatively unknown senator as his successor. Aurelius Antoninus was reluctant, but it was his lack of ambition and relative age that underpinned Hadrian's decision. With no siblings and one surviving daughter, Antoninus was required to adopt the 17-year-old Marcus and the 7-year-old Lucius Verus. Marcus is not reported to have been enthusiastic with these developments. Hadrian's last acts were to make Antoninus consul and Marcus a quaestor, seven years before the usual age limit of 24. The emperor died aged 62, 'hated by all' as the *Historia Augusta* records. In Marcus's later writing he praises Antoninus, but has little to say about the man who enabled him to become emperor.

Picture 23: Hadrian (Wikimedia Commons)

Picture 24: Antoninus Pius (Wikimedia Commons)

Antoninus Pius

At 52, Antoninus was expected to reign just long enough for Marcus and/or Lucius to mature into the role. As it turned out, Antoninus lived another twenty-three years. Antoninus was the polar opposite of Hadrian. Marcus's learning continued under Antoninus and he later listed those who influenced him the most. From Alexander of Cotiaeum he learned how to correct people without angering or humiliating them. Marcus wrote later it was better to reply to mistakes by the use of correct grammar or facts in your answer. While this seems a minor point, the fact Marcus remembered it demonstrates what sort of man he aspired to be. Another tutor with significant influence was Sextus of Chaeronea from whom he learnt logic, how to be a 'true father', live 'according to nature', and to avoid anger and negative emotions.[6] But it was Apollonius of Chalcedon who was one of the people Marcus especially thanked the gods for knowing in his writing. From him he learnt the Stoic doctrine.

Antoninus continued Marcus's education and training. He seems to have genuinely liked Marcus and groomed him for succession. Another man who had a profound influence was Claudius Maximus. Twenty years senior to Marcus he had been the consul in AD 144, and governor in both north Africa and Pannonia. He too was a stoic and taught Marcus a number of lessons, which he took to heart: maintaining a balance and dignity, speaking the truth, be neither rash nor hesitant, refrain from malice, envy and whining and be generous, honest and forgiving.

One of his senatorial friends was Claudius Severus Arabianus. From Claudius he learnt the Aristotelian philosophy of balance and resistance to tyranny. He also taught Marcus the virtues of the republican tradition and ancient Roman liberties. Quintus Junius Rusticus stressed simplicity of style and the need to train and discipline one's character. In many ways he had the teaching and training worthy of a philosopher king, but it does not follow that he ever intended to return the empire to its republican roots as the film portrays.

The appearance of beards on imperial portraits and busts are worth speculating on. No contemporary writer gives a reason. Mary Beard, in *SPQR A History of Ancient Rome*, suggests the emperors from Hadrian onwards may have been trying to emulate their Greek philosopher heroes.[7] Antonius Pius appointed Marcus Cornelius Fronto as tutor to his adopted sons. Fronto later wrote with pride to Marcus, when he was emperor, that his star pupil 'had portraits everywhere, in banks, shops, bars, gables, colonnades, windows everywhere … on public display'.[8]

Antoninus followed Hadrian's non-expansionist policy. Unlike the previous emperor he remained in Rome, citing the wish to avoid the expense. He worked closer with the senate, allowing them some sense of autonomy, if in name only. He was conservative both socially and economically. A tall, good-looking man, contemporaries described him as intelligent, honest, kind, genial, dutiful and hard working.[9] Marcus Aurelius praises him for his compassion and loyalty to his friends. Unlike Hadrian, he did not insist his friends agree with him on everything or accompany him everywhere. Nor did he share his predecessor's envy and spitefulness. Marcus goes on to state he was never rude or lost self control and was both reliable and predictable. Attributes one could never accuse Hadrian of possessing. Perhaps most importantly, he was always willing to listen to experts and be swayed by argument. Antoninus continued to mentor his adoptive son, making him co-consul in AD 140 and later head of the equestrian an order.

The emperor forged even closer links by arranging the marriage of his 14-year-old daughter, Faustina, to the 24-year-old Marcus. They went on to have fifteen children, six of whom reached adulthood. Twin sons died in their first year but their third child, Annia Aurelia Galeria Lucilla, survived and went on to marry Lucius Verus and later Pompeianus. This is the Lucilla portrayed in the film, who in reality was executed by her brother Commodus for plotting to have him assassinated. A girl then a boy both died young. But Annia Aurelia Galeria Faustina survived, followed by a boy who did not. Two more surviving daughters, Fedilla and Cornificia, were born by AD 160. In the 150s Marcus also lost his mother and sister.

In AD 160 Antoninus appointed Marcus and Lucius as joint consuls for the following year. In March AD 161 he fell ill after a meal; he vomited in the early morning and developed a fever high enough to produce a bout of delirium. Antoninus realised the gravity of his situation and summoned Marcus and the imperial council. He formally named Marcus as his successor and left us perhaps a telling anecdote as to the character of Marcus Aurelius. Antoninus wished Marcus would treat the empire as well as he had treated his daughter Faustina. On 7 March AD 161, Antoninus died aged 74, nearly twenty-three years after Hadrian had appointed the reluctant senator to act as an expected stopgap for Marcus. As it turned out, Antoninus was instrumental in providing a long period of good governance and stability. There appears to have been genuine affection and respect from Marcus.

Emperor Marcus Aurelius

Marcus was 40 years old when he became emperor. He was said to have been unconcerned about outward appearance to the point of being careless and wore plane clothes in keeping with his stoic beliefs. His demeanour was 'poker-faced'; he did not enjoy good health and suffered insomnia and frequent pains in the chest and stomach, resulting in his spitting blood. A range of causes have been suggested such as tuberculosis, ulcers or a blood disorder. Another possibility is that he was a hypochondriac, exaggerating the effects of the stress of his responsibilities. At the same time, his stoic beliefs meant he accepted and endured his illnesses rather than take measures to look after himself, such as getting proper sleep. The physician Galen prescribed the drug theriac to relive the pain.[10] Galen added mandrake and poppy juice to the mixture and this has caused some to speculate Marcus became addicted to opium. Others have suggested he suffered from a form of depression. He was described as rather humourless and had a notably prudish attitude to sex and sexuality.

Writing about himself he stated that he was not quick witted and emphasised the importance of plain speaking, integrity and simplicity; the most important thing being the freedom to act in a moral way. Like Antoninus, he was a conservative man who disliked change, but he was also generous with money. Politically, he also followed Antoninus in placing a level of sovereignty in the Senate. His first act was to appoint Lucius Verus as co-emperor and this innovative decision seems to have been his own. Cassius Dio records that Marcus was genuinely reluctant to be emperor, preferring his intellectual studies instead.

Lucius was in many ways the polar opposite of Marcus who, despite this, had a genuine affection for his adoptive brother. Lucius had also been made quaestor and consul before the official age and had received similar training and learning to Marcus. Lucius, however, had little interest in academia and revelled in physical pursuits of all kinds. Unlike his brother, he loved chariot races and was a fanatical supporter of the Greens against the Blues, Reds and Whites.[11] He was described as tall, good looking, vain and unpredictable. It is fair to say that Marcus was more like Antoninus and Lucius like Hadrian. However, Lucius is described by some as weak rather than cruel.

The emperors gifted the Praetorian Guards in Rome 20,000 sesterces, each demonstrating how powerful they had become politically. Funeral games, including chariot, races were organised after Antoninus's ashes were laid to rest in the mausoleum of Hadrian. No doubt Marcus saw this

Picture 25: A young Marcus Aurelius (Wikimedia Commons)

Picture 26: Emperor Marcus Aurelius (Wikimedia Commons)

as a necessary political and cultural event to commemorate his respected predecessor. Lucius would certainly have enjoyed the games more. Hedonistic and charismatic, he was popular with the people. In some ways they were a good team and there seems to have been no rivalry and some genuine affection.

Lucius was 31 when he became co-emperor and it was unusual for a Roman of that age to be unmarried. Whatever the reason, Marcus arranged the betrothal to his then 11-year-old daughter, Lucilla. Later that year Faustina gave Marcus twin sons, Titus Aurelius Fulvus Antoninus and Lucius Aelius Aurelius Commodus. The elder twin died before the age of 5, leaving one of history's 'what ifs?' Perhaps Titus would have been as different from Commodus as their grandfather Antoninus was from Hadrian. But Titus died and Commodus survived, and it was he who became emperor as we shall see later.

It is worth noting a scandalous rumour involving Faustina.[12] It was said she conceived Commodus through an illicit affair with a gladiator. One version has her admitting it to her husband, who then consults a soothsayer. He advises Marcus to kill the gladiator, get Faustina to bathe in his blood and then have sex with her. Having followed these unlikely recommendations, he then raises Commodus as his own. It is likely this tale was promoted to explain Commodus's later fascination with the arena. However, historians are sceptical and it would have been very out of character for Marcus to have behaved in this way.

Given his temperament and upbringing, it is very likely his reign would have been similar to that of his predecessor Antoninus: marked by its stability. Even Hadrian had avoided the expansionist policy of Trajan. Unfortunately, events conspired against him. Cassius describes him as being studious and 'vigorous' in his youth, fighting in armour and hunting wild boar from horseback. But his health and body were frail and this got worse as the years progressed. Cassius states Marcus did not meet with the good fortune that he deserved, 'for he was not strong in body and was involved in a multitude of troubles throughout practically his entire reign'.[13] Yet he admired him all the more for this reason, 'that amid unusual and extraordinary difficulties he both survived himself and preserved the empire'.

By the end of his first year the unlucky Marcus was to suffer three problems in quick succession. In the autumn of AD 161, the Tiber burst its banks and caused a severe flood in Rome, which was followed by an earthquake in Cyzicus in modern Turkey. While both events severely drained treasury funds, it was the outbreak of war with Parthia that caused the biggest headache. Parthia had taken over parts of the Seleucid empire that had evolved from the conquests of Alexander the Great. As Rome expanded east and Parthia west, friction was inevitable. Marcus Crassus had led seven legions to destruction at the battle of Carrhae in 53 BC, but there had been peace for forty years since Trajan's campaign AD 113–117.

Marcus sent Lucius east to lead the campaign with his best legions, such as the Legio V Macedonia from lower Moesia on the Danube, and the use of the Misenum fleet to transport Verus east. En route, at Canusium in southern Italy, Verus fell seriously ill, suffering what is thought to have been a mini stroke. Marcus joined him until he recovered, further evidence that there was a genuine bond between them. Once well again, Lucius continued his journey in the summer of AD 162.

Parthian War

In late AD 161, Vologases IV of Parthia invaded the Roman client state of Armenia and installed his puppet-king, Pacorus. Severianus, governor of Cappadocia in eastern Turkey, led a legion to expel him, but his force was utterly destroyed after being trapped at Elegeia and he committed suicide. Marcus Aurelius sent the governor of Britain, Marcus Statius Priscus, to take the vacant spot in Cappadocia. Meanwhile, the governor of Syria, Lucius Attidius Cornelianus, had led another Roman army to defeat.

Marcus sent a number of legions from the northern frontier: I Minerva, II Adiutrix and V Macedonia, along with vexillations from other legions. Lucius spent much of his time at Antioch and received criticism for his debauchery and lifestyle. The best one can say is that he was a great delegator. He certainly had with him a host of experienced generals who conducted the war for him: Publius Julius Geminius Marcianus, the commander of X Gemina leading the vexillations; the praetorian prefect Titus Furius Victorinus, with a detachment of the guard; and the senator Marcus Pontius Laelianus Larcius Sabinus, former governor of Pannonia and Syria, who was known as a serious, capable man. While Lucius spent his time drinking and gambling, his generals increased training and improved discipline.

By AD 163 the Romans had gone on the offensive. In the north from the province of Cappadocia, Priscus led I Minerva and V Macedonia to victory in Armenia and captured the capital of Artaxata. Verus took credit for this receiving the title Armeniacus, despite never swinging a sword in anger. A new capital, Kaine Polis, was built thirty miles closer to the Roman border and a new king was installed, a Roman senator of Arsacid descent. While Priscus was pushing the Parthians out of Armenia, the Parthians repeated their previous intervention by deposing the Roman client king of Osroene on the eastern border of Syria, with its capital at Edessa. In late AD 163, the Romans moved into the northern Euphrates and prepared to advance into Mesopotamia. In late AD 163 or early 164, Lucius travelled to Ephesus to be married to Marcus's daughter. Lucius was of course only half-brother to Marcus by adoption. Lucilla, now 13, had travelled with her mother Faustina.

In AD 165 Verus and legio V Macedonia recaptured Edessa and reinstated the Roman client king, Mannus; they advanced and captured Nisbis. Further south meanwhile, Avidius Cassius led the III Gallica. By the end of AD 165, Cassius's army had captured the cities of Seleucia and Ctesiphon on the Tigris. The Parthians relied on two main tactics: first, the charge of heavily armoured knights – cataphractarii; second, the heavy use of mounted archers. The destruction of Crassus at Carrhae in BC 53 demonstrated how devastating this could be.

But the Romans had developed counter measures which were successfully used in Trajan's Parthian War. Not only did they utilise slingers and archers to counter the missile attack, they also used heavier cavalry, and the legions were trained to form a square, ringed by pikemen. As long as the infantry stood firm, even heavy massed cavalry would baulk at charging into a wall of spears. In fact, a direct charge of cataphractarii against a legionary square was 'almost certain to be repelled' by the tactical formation used.[14] The first rank held longer spears at an upward angle, the next three ranks threw heavy spears, followed by four ranks of javelin throwers and behind these were the archers. Thus any charge was met with repeated waves of missiles and if they got through that, a wall of men with shields and spears. Mounted archers were kept at bay by Roman archers or chased off by cavalry.

By AD 166 the Parthians were defeated and a triumph was held in Rome on 12 October. Marcus had a 'deep loathing' for games and public spectacles.[15] On this occasion he insisted the gladiators used blunted weapons. Lucius insisted his nephew accompany the emperors, and one wonders what effect this had on the young Commodus. As we will see as an adult, he appears to have been far more similar to his charismatic uncle than to his rather stoic father. Commodus, aged 5, and his 3-year-old brother, Annius Verus, were made Caesar, demonstrating an early indication that Marcus intended he should succeed him.

Marcus continued to take a keen interest in legal matters and spent a significant part of his time conducting his judicial duties. He steered legislation away from cruel and unusual punishments.

His philosophy was based on tolerance and the avoidance of the tyranny of previous emperors.

He was also deeply conservative and fully supportive of the hierarchical nature of Roman society, even as far as supporting differences in nomenclature and dress. One important distinction was to keep senators as legionary commanders and equestrians as praetorian prefects. On the other hand, some form of meritocracy did exist as we see with the rise of Pertinax, son of a former slave, who rose through the ranks of the legions under Marcus.

Unfortunately, Lucius did not only bring back victory from Parthia – a deadly plague had begun to spread; it is thought soldiers returning from the Parthian War in the East carried it with them. Galen described eyewitness accounts of symptoms which included a blistering skin rash and diarrhoea.[16] The most likely explanation is smallpox. Estimates for the extent of fatalities range between 1 and an unlikely 30 per cent of the population.[17] Most of the Praetorian Guard , including its commander, Furius Victorinus, were said to have died. Marcus ensured the state paid for the funerals of all plague victims.

Marcomannic Wars

It was noted previously that war broke out unexpectedly while the Parthian War was still in progress.[18] Minor raids around AD 162-165 took advantage of Rome's distraction in the East.

The Chatti and Chauci crossed the Rhine and Danube causing much damage to the north-western provinces of Raetia and Germania Superior before being repulsed. The more serious incursion occurred in AD 166 when 6,000 Langobard and Lacringli warriors crossed the Danube into Pannonia Superior. These were defeated at a battle near the River Ister.[19]

When the Marcomanni advanced on Aquileia in AD 167, Marcus tried to stem any panic the Romans might be feeling. He suspended imperial debts and, in what may have been more of a public relations move, auctioned off imperial property. He withdraw troops from Britain and spent much of AD 168 building defensive fortifications to protect northern Italy. It was in this period that Pompeianus came to prominence and forced the Marcomanni away from Aquileia, back across the Danube and out of Roman territory. In April of AD 168 Marcus travelled away from Rome and southern Italy for the first time. At 47 he was already reasonably old by the standards of the day. While Antoninus lived to the age of 74, Marcus was not as healthy nor as robust.

He travelled to Aquileia accompanied by his brother, Verus. It may be he didn't trust him enough to leave him at Rome or go on ahead to lead the campaign. The intention was to winter in Aquileia before the campaigning season in AD 169. Events conspired against him once again however. First, Verus insisted he had to return to Rome. On the return journey, accompanied by Marcus, he fell seriously ill again. It would appear he suffered the same stroke-like symptoms he had experienced years earlier en route to the Parthian War. In January AD 169, at Altinum near modern Venice, Lucius Verus died after lingering on for three days. As ever, rumours of murder or poison circulated or were suggested by later writers. However, given Marcus appears to have been genuinely fond of his brother, the simplest explanation is that he died of stroke. He was, after all, of ill health, from a family with a history of early deaths, and in a period where this was common. His history, previous stroke, and the fact the plague was still common, would suggest theories of foul play are the least likely explanation.

Marcus directed the funeral and quickly married Verus's 20-year-old widow Lucilla (his own daughter) to Pompeianus. Lucilla and her mother the empress were reported to be furious as they hated Pompeianus for his low birth,[20] although his age might also have been a factor. When Lucilla had married Verus at the age of 15, her bridegroom was in his early thirties and an emperor; Pompeianus was in his forties – perhaps thirty years older, and a mere equestrian and general. There's no record of what Pompeianus thought of the match, but there was certainly no unrequited love from Lucilla as the film suggests.

After the funeral Marcus headed back to the front in the autumn of AD 169, basing himself in Pannonia. His new son-in-law, Pompeianus, went with him. In AD 170 the Romans were able to go on the offensive; crossing the Danube they attacked the Marcomanni. It is at this point some sources claim they suffered a major defeat. Little is known of the battle but it is thought Roman casualties were 20,000.[21] Again there is evidence that the Germans were a serious threat and a capable enemy. Worse was to come that year. First, the Quadi broke their treaty and gave aid and sanctuary to the Marcomanni; second, the Sarmatian Iazyges assisted them. As noted, it is far more likely this battle occurred two or three years earlier. There is no indication that Marcus was anywhere near the border, or in any danger at the time of the battle. Yet we know he was in Aquileia in AD 168 and moved from there to the border, only returning in the spring of AD 169 on his brother's insistence.

Whatever the case, another problem emerged when two other Sarmatian tribes, the Costoboci and Roxolani, raided the Balkans, reaching as far south as Greece. At the same time in the north west the Chatti raided across the Rhine. Pompeianus was sent to deal with the latter incursion while the threat in Greece was neutralised by legions there. In AD 171 the fortunes of war changed. The future emperor, Pertinax, led an army to clear the provinces of Raetia and Noricum. One of his legion commanders, Maximianus, capped the achievement by defeating the Naristae and killing their king Valao in single combat.

Next, the Romans caught the invaders retreating back across the Danube with their booty. This was Marcus's first battle and resulted in a total victory. It was to be the last time the Marcomanni crossed the Danube in anger. Marcus wintered at Carnuntum then went on the offensive in AD 172, crossing the Danube and invading Marcomanni territory. Another victory followed and the Marcomanni agreed peace terms, returning hostages and agreeing to a ten mile demilitarised zone on the east bank of the Danube. Marcus presented his son Commodus to the troops, giving him the title Germanicus. One is reminded of Caligula a century before, who was presented to the legions by his father, Germanicus.

As AD 173 opened, Marcus turned his attention to the Sarmatian Iazyges. Frustrated with their repeated acts of treachery, he made it known he wanted to exterminate them completely.[22] The Iazyges attacked first but were defeated in Pannonia. The Quadi then broke their treaty again and removed their Roman client king, replacing him with the pro-Sarmatian Ariogaesus. For once the normally unflappable Marcus lost both his temper and usual stricture against capital punishment. He put a price on the king's head and added the Quadi to the list of tribes to be exterminated. Winter fell early and hard in AD 173 and the Romans caught the Iazyges and Quadi as they retreated across the frozen Danube. A total victory followed. The column of Marcus Aurelius displays the nature of this bloody warfare. It displays villages being razed, bound prisoners and captured Germans being decapitated.

In AD 174 Marcus attacked once more against both the Iazyges and Quadi. Pertinax led one army against the Quadi. It is during this campaign we hear of the 'Battle of the Thundering Legion', also known as the 'miracle of the rain'. A trapped legion, surrounded by enemies and suffering from thirst, is saved by a sudden thunderstorm. Marcus personally led the column against the Iazyges. By the beginning of AD 175 the Quadi sued for peace under the same conditions as the Marcomanni. The Iazyges, however, were marked for total extermination as Marcus viewed the nomadic horseman as incapable either of absorption or keeping to their word. By June AD 175 their king, Zanticus, begged for peace. Marcus was on the verge of rejecting their desperate plea and sending the embassy back to Zanticus empty handed. Fortunately for the beaten Sarmatians, events forced Marcus to change his mind.

In the East, Avidius Cassius had proclaimed himself emperor. He apparently had received a message that the emperor was dead. Reports differ as to whether this was a simple misinterpretation, as Marcus was often ill. Some claimed that Faustina had deliberately misled Avidius.[23] The suggestion was that Faustina, seeing that her husband had fallen ill and expecting that he would die at any moment, was afraid that the throne might fall to someone else. Wishing to secure her own place and that of Commodus, she 'secretly induced Cassius to make his preparations so that, if anything should happen to Antoninus, he might obtain both her and the imperial power'. Avidius was considering this proposal when he received a message that Marcus was dead.

Faustina had been at his side for a year and travelled east with him after the rebellion, so it is possible this rumour was false. Avidius claimed he was acting in the interest of the state as Commodus was too young. It is likely he did not wish a rising star such as Pompeianus taking the throne, but once he learnt the truth that Marcus was in fact alive, he likely thought he could not back down.

The emperor granted peace terms to the Sarmatians on the same basis as the Marcomanni and Quadi, except for settlement rights. Perhaps the Romans felt the Germans could be civilised, but that the Sarmatians were irredeemable. Whatever the case hostages were returned, possibly up to 100,000, and a demilitarised zone created north of the Danube. The Sarmatians were forced to supply 8,000 cavalry to serve across the empire in the auxiliaries. Most of the force, 5,500, were sent to northern Britain. The Germanic tribes supplied troops for the expected eastern campaign against Avidius. Valerius Maximianus led some of the newly acquired German troops east as Marcus prepared to follow. Commodus was summoned and received the toga virilis a few months early, meaning he was now officially a man. This act demonstrated that Marcus clearly intended to ensure his son's succession. The emperor sent significant numbers of vexillations to Rome to ensure stability.

Avidius had acquired a reputation of strict discipline and cruelty.[24] One story tells of how his men disobeyed orders and slaughtered 3,000 peaceful Sarmatians, resulting in Avidius crucifying the centurions. Deserters were mutilated and criminals burned or thrown – tied up – into rivers. On the other hand, he had proved a capable commander in the Parthian War. He drilled the troops regularly and improved discipline and training. However, while Egypt declared for him, most of the empire remained loyal to Marcus. Tellingly, Marcus declared that not only would he forgive the rebels, but only banish Avidius rather than execute him. The pretender did not reply to Marcus's overtures. By the summer, the crisis was over; Avidius was slain by a centurion called Antoninus and another officer.

Marcus decided he had to carry out his intentions and travel east anyway. En route in Cappadocia, his wife Faustina died. Again, some suggested foul play while others thought it revenge for her alleged role in the rebellion of Avidius. However, given Marcus's actions and general behaviour and philosophy, it is perhaps more likely she died of natural causes or disease. She was 45, had borne at least fourteen children and was travelling to foreign lands while the Antonine plague was still a menace. Marcus described her as a 'fine woman'.

Marcus reached Antioch and it was here that he banned gladiatorial games and spectacles as a punishment for supporting Avidius, who had made the city his headquarters. *Gladiator* has Proximo, an ex-gladiator, telling Maximus that Marcus had banned gladiatorial contests in Rome; this is not true. He had no love for the spectacle but they were an integral part of Roman culture and Marcus was, above all, deeply conservative and traditional. Marcus wintered in Alexander and then journeyed back in

AD 176. Reaching Rome, via Greece, he gave the 15-year-old Commodus an undeserved triumph and the title imperator. In AD 177 he made him consul and went on to make him a tribune and title him Augustus. Later that year he married Commodus to Brutta Crispina, and Marcus made sure decisions were made not just in his name, but that of his now co-emperor son. All the signs were that he was actively preparing for the succession. Perhaps this was made a greater priority as Marcus suffered an illness the same year.

The drain of the wars and the plague had reduced manpower. One area affected was gladiatorial games, which suffered a shortage of fighters. Despite his dislike of the games Marcus pressed condemned criminals into training and provided money so the mob could be mollified. Many provincial aristocrats found putting on games increasingly expensive. To help, Marcus abolished the tax on the sale of gladiators in AD 177, a move that cost the treasury 20 to 30 million sesterces.[25] He went further, fixing the prices for gladiators.

In the same year, the Marcomanni and Quadi started a guerrilla campaign. Valerius Maximianus had already been dispatched there with vexillations and Pertinax was switched from Moesia to Dacia. Marcus left Rome on 3 August AD 178, but unlike in the film, he took Commodus with him. Commodus was four weeks short of his seventeenth birthday. He also took Claudius Pompeianus. One of his first actions was to negotiate another peace agreement with the Sarmatian Iazyges so he could concentrate on the Marcomanni and Quadi and their Roxolani allies. This time the Germans felt confident enough to meet the Romans in open battle. In AD 179 they were routed with huge casualties and 40,000 were taken prisoner. Marcus Valerius Maximianus led the army and was made a senator and legate of legio I Adiutrix. Pompeianus was present too, although there's no record of either leading a cavalry charge let alone through a dense forest.

Death

In March AD 180, Marcus fell ill in Sirmium in Pannonia. The symptoms match those recorded for the Antonine plague which, as mentioned earlier, is suspected to have been smallpox. Marcus summoned Commodus to his bedside and made it clear he wished the German war to be continued until the threat was entirely neutralised. Reluctantly, Commodus agreed to remain in camp for a few days. Marcus then stopped eating and drinking. On the sixth day of the illness he summoned his leading men, among them Claudius Pompeianus. He reproached them for grieving and urged a more philosophical attitude as well as prioritising the empire's needs. He then brought Commodus in and and formally announced his succession. He asked his advisors to be 'guides' and 'fathers' to Commodus, so that he could become 'an excellent emperor'.[26] This proved to be a forlorn hope. One of Marcus's last acts was to recommend Commodus to the army. His last words on 17 March AD 180 were to a tribune, requesting the day's watchword. He replied: 'Go to the rising son for I am already setting.' As usual, rumours of foul play abounded. Some said Commodus poisoned him but contemporary writers such as Cassius Dio had cause to hate Commodus and looked back on his father with fondness:

> I admire him … that amid unusual and extraordinary difficulties he both survived himself and preserved the empire. Just one thing prevented him from being completely happy, namely, that after rearing and educating his son in the best possible way he was vastly disappointed in him.
>
> Cassius Dio, book 72.36

In summary, I thought Richard Harris displayed the character of Marcus rather well. He comes across as quite conscientious and kind, although Marcus was perhaps a little more sombre and serious.

Lucilla

Lucilla seems to have had a high opinion of herself. She resented the influence her husband's sister, Fabia, had on the co-emperor. When Lucius Verus died in AD 169 Marcus Aurelius quickly arranged a new match for his 20-year-old widowed daughter. One reason might have been that Marcus wanted his daughter married quickly to someone he could trust and who wasn't a threat to Commodus. He chose his close friend and advisor, Claudius Pompeianus, well over twenty years her senior. As noted previously, both Lucilla and her mother were against the match, partly because of the age difference, but mainly because Pompeianus was the son of an equestrian and had been promoted by Marcus. Lucilla is described by Cassius Dio as, 'no more modest or chaste than her brother Commodus, detested her husband.' Nevertheless, she bore a son who was also named Tiberius Claudius Pompeianus Quintinaus. Later sources claim Marcus offered to make Pompeianus his heir by naming him Caesar. A satire by Emperor Julian in the fourth century states Marcus should have as he,

> failed to see that his son was ruining the empire as well as himself, and that though Verus (Aurelius) had an excellent son-in-law who would have administered the state better, and besides would have managed the youth better than he could manage himself.
>
> Julian, *Caesars*, 312

But no other contemporary writers, such as Cassius, corroborate this. If true, one can only imagine what Lucilla would have thought about it. She had been an empress and now was married to a mere general – then he turned down the one thing that would return her to her rightful place. What is forgotten is that Commodus had already been declared Caesar in AD 166 at the age of 5. However, with the plague sweeping across the empire, and high child mortality in general, there was no guarantee Commodus would survive. He was aged only 8 when his sister married, and 14 when Avidius rebelled in Egypt. It is quite possible that Marcus asked his closest friend and son-in-law to perform a similar task to the one Hadrian asked of Antoninus. It would also keep his daughter, Lucilla, safe.

At the end of the *Gladiator*, Commodus and Maximus lie dead in the arena with Lucilla standing over them. In reality, Lucilla was executed in AD 182 by Commodus; Pompeianus survived. He was indeed offered the throne after the death of Commodus by both Pertinax and Julianus, both of

Picture 27: Lucius Verus (Wikimedia Commons)

Picture 28: Lucilla (Wikimedia Commons)

Picture 29: Faustina or Lucilla (Wikimedia Commons)

which he declined. Their son went on to become a consul, suggesting the family retained their standing even after Lucilla's death. He eventually was executed by the Emperor Caracalla in AD 212. At one point he took the name Lucius Aurelius Commodus Pompeianus, but it is unclear when exactly this occurred. It is possible the childless Commodus looked to his young nephew as a potential heir. In the film Lucilla's son is called Lucius Verus, which appears to be a reference to her former husband.

Lucius Verus

Lucius was the son of Lucius Ceionius Commodus and was born on 15 December AD 130. He had two sisters, Ceionia Plautia and Ceionia Fabia. We recall how the Emperor Hadrian had adopted and renamed Marcus Aurelius and Lucius Verus. With similar upbringing, and having lost their fathers at an early age, the adoptive brothers appear to have had a genuine fondness for each other. The *Historia Augusta* paints a poor picture of Verus: idle and pleasure loving. His conduct during the Parthian War caused particular criticism. His priorities were feasting, gambling and drinking rather than the war, which he left to his able generals. On the other hand, one could argue he was a master of delegation who knew his limitations and left the war to the experts, although he was more than happy to take the credit. The *Historia* also admits that while he had few virtues, he did not have so many vices. Importantly, he followed his brother's lead and accepted his seniority. Marcus himself acknowledges this in his meditations.

The *Historia Augusta* paints a picture of someone who had a contempt for learning. He shared many of the tutors that Marcus Aurelius had and received a similar education. Additionally the letters that survive between Lucius and his tutor Fronto suggest something different. It is worth noting what his brother Marcus wrote: 'I thank the gods for giving me such a brother, who is able by his moral character to rouse me to vigilance over myself, and who, at the same time, pleased me by his respect and affection.' (Marcus Aurelius, *Meditations* (1.17))

The reign of Antoninus Pius was one of relative stability and peace. In AD 145 Lucius reached the age of 15 and received the toga virilis. The *Historia* describes him as 'tall and stately in appearance', and busts depict him with a full head of hair and beard. At the age of 23 he was appointed questor, and a year later in AD 154 he held his first consulship. He developed a great love of the arts, but also gladiatorial contests and chariot races in which he favoured the Greens. We have already noted the contrast with his older brother. Later, Marcus's son Commodus would follow his uncle's love of the games.

Antoninus died in March AD 161. Marcus appointed Lucius as his co-emperor. Cassius Dio (71.1.3) remarks, 'Lucius, on the other hand, was a vigorous man of younger years and better suited to military enterprises.' It is noteworthy that Marcus sent Lucius to address the Praetorian Guard. The support of the nine military cohorts based in Rome was crucial to any new emperor and they were offered 20,000 sesterces each. In letters to Fronto, Marcus acknowledges his brother's oratory skills and it is likely he saw Lucius as better suited to this task. However, while both men were titled Imperator Caesar Augustus, it was clear Marcus was the senior of the two. For example, he held the post of *pontifex maximus*, the chief priest of Rome. His nephew Commodus was born a few months later in August of AD 161, and named Lucius. With Antoninus dead the Parthian king, Vlogaeses IV, entered Armenia and ousted the pro-Roman king, Sohaemus, in favour of a pro-Parthian Pacoras.

Rome and Parthia had been at war at various times over the previous two centuries. In 53 BC, Crassus had lost his army and his life at the battle of Carrhae. A key point of conflict was the Kingdom of Armenia between the Roman province of Cappadocia and the Parthian Empire. It was a strategic gateway to Mesopotamia if one wished to avoid crossing the Syrian desert. Zeugma was a crucial crossing point of the Euphrates River which gave access to the Parthian cities of Seleucia and Cresiphon.

The governor of Cappadocia, Severianus, reacted immediately but was besieged in the Armenian city of Elegeia. He took his own life and lost an entire legion. The Parthians then moved into the kingdom of Osrhoene bordering Syria and took the capital of Edessa. Once again a pro-Parthian ruler, Wael, was installed. The Parthians then invaded the Roman province of Syria and defeated the army of Attidius Cornelianus. These two defeats were a shocking blow to Rome and the decision was made to send Lucius Verus to the East. As noted previously, Lucius fell ill en route and was joined by Marcus. The sources blame his over indulgence but recent scholars suggest it could have been a stroke, possibly similar to whatever killed him eight years later.

Once fit enough to travel he continued, arriving in Antioch in AD 162. *The Historia Augusta* is rather scathing of Verus reporting that as the eastern provinces were being devastated he was 'hunting in Apulia, travelling through Athens and Corinth accompanied by orchestras and singers, dallying through all the cities of Asia … notorious for their pleasure resorts.' (*Historia Augusta*, Lucius Verus (6.9))

On the other hand, in *Lucius Verus and the Roman Defence of the East*,[27] Bishop argues that Lucius was actually an able administrator and willing to delegate to experienced commanders. Positioning himself at Antioch placed him almost equidistant between the two main objectives of Armenia and the Parthian capital, as well as maintaining good communication links with the nearest provinces and Rome.

Lucius inspected the troops and found standards rather low, so spent much of the first few months training and in preparation. He also found time to take on a low-born mistress, Panthea. This may have prompted Marcus to bring forward the marriage of his daughter Lucilla to Lucius. In AD 162 she would have been 12 years old, a little young by Roman standards. Lucius would have been 32 – surprisingly old still to be a bachelor, but we have no indication of any previous marriages. In late AD 163 or early 164 Lucius travelled to Ephesus to be married to Marcus's daughter. Lucilla, now 13, had travelled with her mother Faustina.

A number of experienced advisors accompanied Lucius; Furius Victorinus, equestrian and praetorian prefect; and three former legionary commanders, Sabinus, Valerianus and Fronto. His army was split in two: The northern exercitus Cappadocius was led by Statius Priscus into Armenia. He had a distinguished equestrian career before being promoted to the senate and consul in AD 159. Sent to Britain as governor in AD 161 he was promptly recalled to lead the Armenian expedition. The exercitus Syriacus was to take place after Armenia had been subdued; accordingly, the offensive was launched first towards the Armenian capital of Artaxata in AD 163. They likely advanced from legionary bases in Cappadocia at Satala and Melitene, roughly mid-way between Antioch and their objective. The nearly 500 km march would have taken about three weeks and Priscus stormed and captured the city before the end of AD 163. The Roman-backed king, Sohaemus, was reinstated.

The second phase of the war involved Fronto leading an army into Osrhoene. Edessa and Nisbis both quickly fell. Avidius Cassius, who later revolted against Marcus Aurelius, led a third force across the Euphrates and then turned south towards the cities of Ctesiphon and Seleucia on the banks of the Tigris, which were taken in AD 165. Of the enemy, Cassius says, 'The Parthians make no use of shield, but their forces consist of mounted archers and pikemen, mostly in full armour. their infantry is small, made up of weaker men, but even these are all archers.' (Cassius Dio: book 40.15.2-4)

Yet the fact remains, the Parthians were able to inflict heavy defeats on two Roman armies at the beginning of the war. On this occasion, however, the victory for the Romans was total. The map below shows the three main phases of the Roman campaign.

Cassius also records that the withdrawal from the Tigris was ravaged by famine and disease. By AD 166 Lucius was back in Rome and received a triumph on 12 October. He insisted Marcus join him and share the titles Armeniacus, Parthicus, Medicus and pater patriae. He also insisted the two sons of Marcus, including the 5-year-old Commodus accompany them and were proclaimed as Caesar. The plague that followed reached Rome in AD 166 and Aquileia two years later. Galen was in Rome at the time and was able describe symptoms of fever, diarrhoea and pharyngitis, inflammation of the throat. He also describes ulcers:

> a young man broke out in ulcers all over his whole body on the ninth day, just as did almost all the others who were saved. On that day there was also a slight cough. On the following day, immediately after he bathed, he coughed more violently and brought up with the cough what they call a scab.
>
> Galen, *Methodus Medendi*, 5.12

It has been estimated that 2 million may have died and this would have significantly impacted manpower especially in the army. To make matters worse it was at this point 6,000 Langobardi and Obii invaded Pannonia. These were driven off, but in AD 167/8 the Marcomanni and Quadi invaded, reaching as far as Aquileia. Both were driven off and the emperors left Rome together establishing their base at Aquileia. Lucius had not wanted to travel north but Marcus insisted and they travelled to Pannonia. However Lucius soon insisted he wished to return to Rome and Marcus relented, accompanying him around January of AD 169. This was to be their final journey together. Lucius fell ill near Altinum north of Venice He survived for three days, unable to speak before passing away.

Lucius Verus has been much maligned by some of the contemporary sources. Possibly resulting from an exaggerated comparison with his

Map 13: Roman-Parthian campaigns AD 161–166

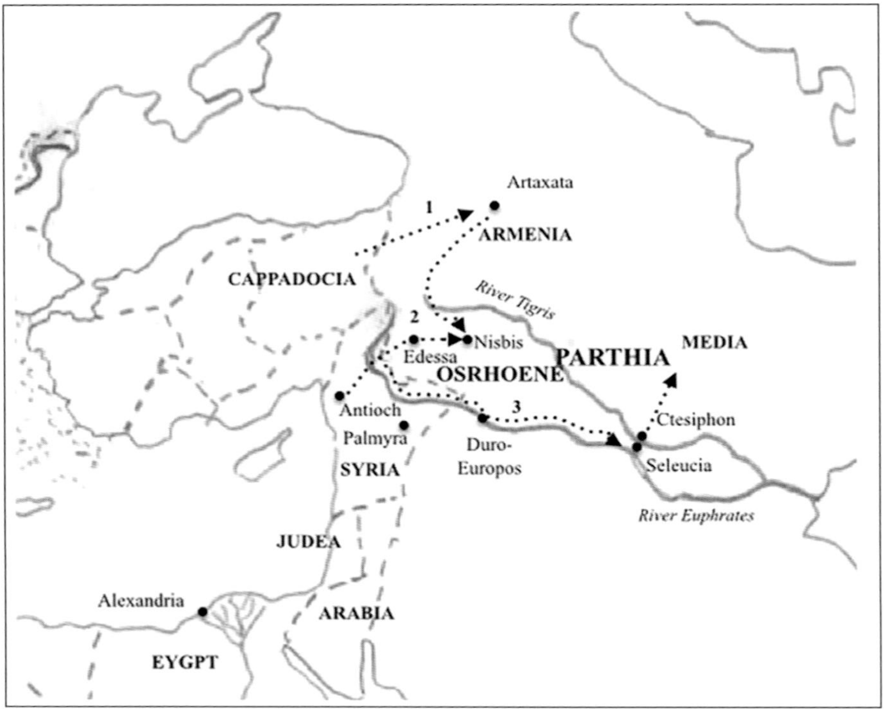

Key
1. Armenian campaign by Priscus 163 AD
2. Campaign of 165 AD captures Edwssa
3. Campaign of Cassius captures Parthian capital 165 AD
4. Cassius crosses Tigris, invades Media 166 AD

famous adoptive brother and co-emperor. Perhaps it was a result of his similarities with his nephew Commodus, who was given an even worse press – although as we shall see, he may have deserved some of it. Yet Lucius was very successful in his Parthian campaign. He showed he was a competent administrator and willing to delegate. Many leaders in history have not been humble or trusting enough to follow this example. Nor was there ever any hint of disloyalty or jealousy from Lucius towards Marcus. No one knew Lucius better than Marcus himself and we recall his own assessment of his younger colleague and adoptive brother. It is perhaps fitting to leave the last word to Bishop: 'There is every indication that he was held in high regard by both his brother and the people of Rome.'[28]

Philosophy

Marcus remarks that his grandfather taught him the virtues of good character and self control. This approach provided fertile ground for later Stoic teachers. One such tutor was Sextus of Chaeronea, a professional teacher of philosophy who had a significant influence on Marcus. He taught him how to be a 'true father' and live according to nature. He learnt how to use logic to make sense of the world and to avoid negative emotions and passions. He was also taught by the Stoic philosopher Sinna Catulus. Marcus named another teacher of philosophy as one of the three men he thanked the gods for knowing. Apollonius of Chalcedon taught that the most important thing to learn was the purity of the stoic doctrine.

Stoicism is a school of thought founded by Zeno of Citium in the third century BC. They taught that behaviour was more important than what one said and that virtue was the goal for anyone wishing to be a good man. Other essential elements include living according to nature and acknowledging the 'oneness' of the universe. It is necessary to overcome one's emotions and use logic to understand the world. Key Stoic thinkers included the Roman philosopher Seneca and the Greek Epictetus, with the latter perhaps influencing Marcus the most. Cicero used the expression summum bonum, which means the highest good or virtue. Virtue is the stoic's answer to 'what is good?' Virtue in turn can be divided into four chief virtues and we hear this echoed in *Gladiator*.

Marcus tells his son he will not be emperor and Commodus replies: 'You wrote to me once listing the four chief virtues: wisdom, justice, fortitude and temperance.' Of course we know Marcus did no such thing. In reality he groomed Commodus to be his successor from an early age and recommended him to his generals from his deathbed. But Commodus's words do accurately reflect the four chief stoic virtues: wisdom, courage, temperance and justice. A stoic accepts that we can't control the world around us, and thus must accept what we cannot change while being in control of our response to that world. Thus, we should have the courage to bear what we must but to change what we can. We get a hint of this in one scene when Maximus is tied up awaiting his final fight in the arena with Commodus himself: 'Nothing happens to anyone that he is not fitted by nature to bear,' Maximus says to the praetorian officer.

Of the four virtues Marcus placed justice above all, as the other three could all be used in self interest. It is this idea of universal justice and oneness with all that can be seen in Cicero's *De Officiis*, 'On Moral Duties. Man should do no harm to another; is not born for himself alone; born not for their own sake but to do good for others; follow nature and contribute to the common good; be steadfast and truthful.' This idea of symptheia or mutual interdependence runs through stoicism. Epictetus stated: 'Seeking the very best in ourselves means actively caring for the welfare of other human beings.' His teacher, Musonius Rufus, describes the 'most honourable lesson' to make 'just people' as follows: 'to honour equality, to want to do good, and for a person, being human, to not want to harm human beings.'

Such men influenced the thinking of Marcus Aurelius. At the same time he was a deeply conservative man who valued the Roman culture and no doubt saw the social hierarchy as the natural order of things. Let us now turn to his own words and try to compare them with how he was portrayed by Richard Harris.

At the start of *Meditations,* Marcus lists the people who influenced him the most and describes what he learnt from each. In so doing he reveals what attributes and behaviours he values. This is very revealing and can be seen in his decision making throughout his reign.
Grandfather: decency and a mild temper.

Mother: piety, generosity avoidance of wrong doing or even the thought of it.

Tutor: Not to support chariot racers or gladiators. Tolerate pain and feel few needs.

Diognetus: avoid empty enthusiasms. Ignore quacks and 'miracle-mongers'.

Rusticus: seek correction and treatment for character.

Apollonius: moral freedom. Prioritise reason and be unchanged regardless of pain or loss.

Sextus: a kindly disposition. Live life according to nature. Be agreeable and tolerant and don't give into anger or passion.

Alexander the grammarian: don't leap on mistakes. Rather lead by example and behaviour.

Fronto: Avoid being suspicious, capricious or hypocritical.

Alexander the Platonist: don't use the excuse of being too busy without good cause.

Catulus: don't spurn a friend's criticism even if unreasonable.

Maximus: self-mastery, immune to any passing whim.

From his adoptive father, Antoninus Pius, gentleness and 'an immovable adherence to decisions made after full consideration'. I lack of vanity or desire for 'so called honours' and no 'superstitious fear of the gods … populism or obsequious courting of the mob. Marcus cited his readiness to defer ungrudgingly to experts and 'those with some special ability'. From Severus he admired the 'love of family, love of truth love of justice'. Here we get some echoes from the film. He highlights the idea of a balanced constitution, 'a commonwealth based on equality and freedom of speech and of a monarchy which values above all the liberty of the subject'.

Book two was written among the Quadi on the River Gran. Sometimes what he criticises is as telling as what he values. He talks of having to deal with the 'meddling, ungrateful, aggressive, treacherous, malicious, unsocial'. He learns not to be angry or harmed by them, by knowing and sticking to what is right and good. Repeatedly he notes that life is 'a mere moment' and so we must give every hour 'vigorous attention'. The one thing that can assist a man is philosophy. This keeps 'the divinity within us inviolate' and maintains truth and integrity independent of others' actions. It seems rather similar to concepts in Eastern religions: 'think good thoughts, say good words, perform good deeds' and do not be swayed from this path by the words and actions of others.

Book three was written in Carnuntum and continues many of the same themes. There is an urgency that should not be wasted on the thoughts of other people. One should prioritise thinking about 'the common good'. Take no action 'unwillingly, selfishly, uncritically, or with conflicting motives'. The key virtues are justice, truth, self-control and courage and he advocates: 'stand straight' and retain 'independence of outside help'. Attempt to be self sufficient of mind and act in accord with reason, while accepting fate that is outside our choice or control.

> Nothing is so conducive to greatness of mind as the ability to subject each element of our experience in life to methodical and truthful examination.
>
> book 3.11.2

Here he goes deeper: The whole earth is a mere point in space; the universe is one living creature, comprising one soul; a huge gulf of time before and infinity ahead. Human life is short, a 'tiny fragment of time' through which one should pass in tune with nature. There is a reference to this in the film, just before Maximus meets Tigris the Gaul in the arena. Proximo tells him: 'We mortals are but shadows and dust.' Marcus consistently advocates being non-judgemental and to avoid allowing oneself to be hurt even is actions or words were intentional.

> Where should a man direct his endeavour? Here only, a right mind, action for the common good, speech incapable of lies, a disposition to welcome all that happens as necessary.
>
> book 4.33

Rather than bemoan bad luck one should be grateful that it can be bore without pain or being crushed.

> Because such a thing could happen to any man but not every man could have borne it without pain.
>
> book 4.49.1

In book five he lists several virtues which are in our power: integrity, dignity, hard work, self denial, contentment, frugality, kindness, independence, simplicity, discretion, magnanimity. One must always do one's duty and look within for truth. Repeatedly he displays a rather modern view, stating all that exists will soon change, scattered into atoms. Despite his role he takes care not to be 'Caesarified' or 'dyed in purple', and states vanity is the greatest seducer of reason. One should keep oneself 'simple, good, pure, serious, unpretentious, a friend to justice, god fearing, kind, full of affection, strong for your proper work'. The goal is 'a godly habit of mind and social action'.

Book seven starts with the statement there is nothing new and all is familiar and short lived. A person's worth is measured by the worth of what he values. Marcus makes clear he does not value pomp or trivial interests. His priority is to 'be a good man'. This battle is an internal one. He constantly encourages one to ignore outside influences, but also to 'erase the print of imagination'. In this section we get some of his most revealing quotes: 'On death. Either dispersal, if we are atoms or, if we are unity extinction or change of home'. Surprisingly open to the concept of no afterlife. We should learn to, 'Love only what falls your way and is fated for you.' Be careful not to behave as the misanthropic do, but rather treat others as we would like to be treated. We recognise the maxim to 'live each day as if it were your last'.

Book eight continues with the theme of inner control. It is not the thing itself that hurts us but our own judgement of it. We have the power to control our emotions. We can choose to let it in and feel pain or we can choose to erase it. He also emphasises that men are born for each other so we should 'teach or tolerate'. The message of tolerance comes up again and again. We see this in his offer to Avidius and other conspirators after the rebellion of AD 175.

He viewed injustice and lying as sins. But so is the pursuit of pleasure and avoidance of pain. Rather, we should be indifferent to these opposites because they will make us act badly. We shouldn't hope for Plato's utopian republic, but be content with small steps forward. We then get a another point linked to the scene in the film described earlier. All that happens in life is within our natural ability to bear it or not. If we are able to bear it, we should do so without complaint. Rather approach it as a duty. If it is something we cannot bear, we should accept our fate equally without complaint.

Towards the end he gives his profession as 'being a good man', which perhaps explains his main motivation. The qualities of a good leader are listed: act in the interests of those one leads; be tolerant of others faults; be mindful of one's own; and don't assume one is in the right. The greatest grief comes from constant anger and pain rather than the initial cause of that pain. Kindness is invincible and one should be even to those being aggressive or insulting.

He finishes the last book stating that we should accept our fate regardless. The nature that brought us in to the world is the same process that takes us out. Another of his quotes is worth noting: 'If it is not right, don't do it: If it is not true don't say it.' (12.17) He finishes with the phrase, 'go then in peace: the god who lets you go is at peace with you.' (12.36.)

In summary Marcus comes across as a deeply conscientious, thoughtful man. He seems genuinely motivated to perform his duties as best he can and to treat those around him with respect and kindness. A more fatalistic phrase is repeated throughout the Meditations and used in *Gladiator*, although in this case it comes from the mouth of Maximus and is directed at Commodus before the final fight in the arena: 'Death smiles at us all. All a man can do is smile back.'

Chapter 5

Gladiators and games

The Roman games, or munus, became an integral part of social and political life in the Roman empire. The gladiators were one part of this, although in some ways they were a relatively minor part of the whole experience. In an example from the third century, in a festival of 176 days, 100 were for theatrical shows, sixty-four for horse and chariot racing and just ten set aside for gladiatorial contests.[1] However, their popularity and cultural significance was much higher than that would suggest.

Gladiatorial contests are thought to have evolved from funeral games. Etruscan tombs depict mural paintings of chariot races and athletic contests. One of the earliest example in Italy is from Naples dated to c.370–340 BC. Chariot races and boxing matches are accompanied by two fighters armed with spears, shields and helmets. Livy, writing at the end of the republic, recorded gladiators fighting after the Samnite war in 327–304 BC. The first record of a gladiatorial contest in Rome dates to 264 BC, where three pairs of gladiators fought at funeral games to honour the deceased.[2] The next recorded example in 216 BC has twenty-two pairs of gladiators. In the Second Punic War, Hannibal is said to have used captured tribesmen to fight for their freedom and entertain his troops.

We learn a little more of the nature of those who fought from Livy, in 206 BC in Spain.[3] They were usually slaves or 'men who sell their blood', but in this case they 'were all volunteers and gave their services gratuitously'. They were sent by their chiefs who wished to demonstrate their ability to their general. For others it was simple rivalry or to settle a score, suggesting one could choose one's adversary. In the second century BC gladiatorial games spread throughout Italy and became a spectacle in their own right, distinct from funeral games. In 165 BC the Roman writer Terence complained that gladiator contests had become more popular than plays and other more highbrow forms of entertainment.[4] By this date they were already using these events to stage public executions. In 167 BC, Aemilius Paullus had ordered deserters to be trampled to death by elephants.[5]

One notable event was the Third Servile War which began in 73 BC, when Spartacus led seventy gladiators to escape from a gladiator school in

Capua. They attracted other runaway slaves and defeated a Roman force of 3,000 sent against them to besiege their camp on Mount Vesuvius, blocking the only route down. We see here the importance of fortifying a camp and underestimating your enemy. During the night Spartacus used ropes to lead his mean down a different way and attack the undefended camp. While the initial victory no doubt was aided by a disproportionate number of gladiators, as his army grew it contained mostly runaway rural slaves. It was eventually defeated in 71 BC.

Julius Caesar owned a gladiator school at Capua, estimated to have trained around 5,000 fighters.[6] In the film the inscription above the entrance of the gladiator school reads LUDUS MAGNUS GLADIATORES, 'Great school gladiators'. A more correct form would be, LUDUS MAGNUS GLADIATORUM, great school of the gladiators. In 65 BC, Caesar paired 320 fighters in honour of his father. As his father had died twenty years earlier, see can see how games gradually became separated from the actual funeral. Games would often last days or weeks and at times were elaborate. In 46 BC Caesar arranged a battle involving 1,000 infantry, third cavalry and twenty war elephants. State financed contests began after Caesar's death in 44 BC.[7] The general Pompey had used twenty elephants, 600 lions and 410 leopards.[8] It is worth noting that the Romans were perfectly capable of simulating an accurate battle of Zama depicted in the film, which in reality involved elephants on the Carthaginian side. This is something we will look at in more detail later.

The average games around the empire might have consisted of twelve pairs in a single day and possibly lasted a week. These examples were dwarfed by the events sponsored by emperors in Rome. Augustus recruited 10,000 fighters in eight great contests or shows, with 1,000 gladiators in each. He also claimed that 3,500 animals were killed. Some emperors, such as Caligula, used the games to show their brutal side and cruelty, throwing prisoners to wild beasts or forcing others to fight to the death. In AD 44 Claudius celebrated the conquest of Britain with a show depicting the assault and sacking of a town. There was a distinction between professional gladiators and criminals or prisoners. In the first century AD, Seneca records the latter having 'no defensive armour … helmet or shield'.[9] In the morning they 'throw men to the lions and the bears'. He records the outcome of every fight was death by 'fire and sword', and this occurred even when the arena was empty. When the Colosseum opened in AD 80, in games lasting over a hundred days, 9,000 'beasts' were killed.[10]

While emperor Hadrian enjoyed the games his successors, Antoninus Pius and Marcus Aurelius, did not. Hadrian is said to have been skilled at combat but the only record we have is of his beast hunts. During his birthday celebrations he is said to have killed 200 lions.[11] Marcus's co-emperor, Lucius Verus, followed Hadrian's example, but Commodus outdid them both with his passion for the games. Commodus took part in over 1,000 gladiatorial fights, a third of them while his father was still alive. His preferred type was a secutor armed with a heavy shield, armour, distinctive helmet and a gladius or short sword. Their normal opponent would be the lightly armoured retiarus. The retiarus was armed with a net, trident and dagger.

Gladiator games continued during the third century and were traditionally held twice a year in December and March while the association with funeral ceremonies disappeared. In the fourth century the growth of Christianity and policies of Constantine I caused their demise, although they continued in reduced form for some time in the West. At the beginning of the fifth century the Western emperor Honorius prohibited them for good.

Around 38 BC the senate had formally banned those from the senatorial class taking part, suggesting such legislation was required. This was followed in 22 BC by a decree banning equestrians too. It would appear some young men of rank were eager to compete, while the social and cultural attitudes were against the practice. No doubt some members of the senate had their own sons in mind when they passed such legislation. Twenty years later Augustus limited games to two munera a year with a maximum of 120 gladiators. By the time of Domitian, only the emperor or appointed official could stage one in Rome. It became customary to set aside ten days at the end of December for such events. Bans on equestrians and women appear to have continued to be flouted. New legislation introduced in AD 11 allowed equestrians and free-born men over the age of 25. Interestingly, free-born women over the age of 20 were also allowed.[12] So we have proof here that female gladiators did indeed exist. A short time later two equestrians volunteered to fight, resulting in one being killed. Tiberius banned the survivor from competing again. By AD 19 the senate once again banned senators or equestrians taking part, although both Caligula and Nero reversed this often forcing men and women to participate. Hadrian forbade the sale of slaves to gladiatorial schools without good cause.[13]

The chief magistrates of a region or town were expected to provide four days of spectacles for the citizens.[14] Despite the evidence for similar numbers of stone amphitheatres in the East, it would seem the Greek speaking areas of the East and the North African provinces were just as fond of gladiatorial spectacles.[15] Beast hunts were extremely popular and there was a thriving trade between North Africa and the rest of the empire in wild animals.

Private hunting corporations were common throughout the empire.[16] This would have made these sort of displays much cheaper for local editores in the North African provinces. We find a number of mosaics depicting such events in the area. At Zliten in modern Libya one example from the second century shows a number of scenes: multiple pairs of gladiators; musicians; condemned prisoners being pushed towards lions and leopards; venatores (beast hunters) fighting various animals; and interestingly, a dwarf and a bear. Another example from the third century from Smirat in Tunisia shows four beast hunters, venatores, pitted against four leopards.

Types of spectacle

The Venatio, beast hunter: elaborate displays involving animals were often held in the morning. Exotic animals like ostriches, giraffes, hippopotamuses, monkeys, elephants and even sea lions were presented to the crowd. Some performed little more than circus tricks but the star attraction was the more dangerous animals. Bears, lions, tigers, bulls, elephants, crocodiles and even rhinoceroses were forced to fight each other as well as men. In 2 BC, twenty-six crocodiles and 260 lions were killed in two separate events in Rome.[17]

Armed men pitched against these animals were called venatores, whereas criminals thrown to the lions, for example, were called 'damnatus ad bestias' – condemned by animal. Lower than the venatores were the bestiarii, who were unarmed and attempted to provoke the animals. The ancient Cretan bull wrestling was introduced by Julius Caesar as *taurocatapsia* where a rider would overtake the bull and jump on its back, pulling it to the ground by its horns. Less dangerous were the hunts using javelins or bows, either on foot or mounted. However, with the more popular contests involving lions, tigers and bears, by the second century the venatores had dropped their heavy armour and wore a simple tunic while armed with a hunting spear. Some individual animals gained a reputation and were given nicknames and saved from death.[18] Elephants were very popular; at one games organised by Pompey they were forced to fight and seemed to beg for mercy, moving the audience to tears.[19]

We can see how ritualised the games were by how they performed executions. The Romans often re-enacted mythological and historical stories.[20] One example was story of Pasiphae, the wife of King Minos of Crete. The god Poseidon wished to punish the king and made his wife fall in love with a bull. The resulting child was the Minotaur. One wonders quite how they managed to perform that for the audience. Another example is the myth of Prometheus who stole fire for mankind only to be punished by the gods. He was tied to a rock and an eagle devoured his liver only for it to regrow and be eaten again the next day. The condemned man was tied to a cross and a bear replaced the eagle, although thankfully he only suffered the once compared to Prometheus's much longer ordeal.

Another example occurred during the reign of Augustus.[21] A Sicilian bandit, Selurus, had been active around Mount Etna for some years. Once captured he was placed on top of a wooden apparatus symbolising the mountain. Underneath were cages with wild animals. Presumably some drama was allowed to build up before the contraption or trapdoor fell casting Selurus to his gruesome death.

We can see here how they might have treated Spartacus if he was captured alive. In fact they never found his body, despite the famous scene in the 1960 film *Spartacus*. The Romans did however crucify the 6,000 prisoners along the Appian Way between Rome and Capua. Some executions under Nero were particularly gruesome.[22] Criminals were wrapped in animal skins and mauled to death by dogs. Others were crucified by day and then burned alive at night. A certain Meniscus, perhaps only guilty of theft, was dressed as Hercules and burned alive.

Both Caligula and Claudius were keen fans of the venatio and regularly threw people to the beasts for entertainment.[23] Caligula was said by Cassius Dio to be 'ruled by charioteers and gladiators', and was the 'slave of actors'. He scandalously forced Roman citizens to fight, and on one occasion twenty-six equestrians were killed. Claudius had an 'excessive fondness' for the games according to Cassius Dio. We hear of 300 bears and a similar number of Africanae, probably lions, being killed between chariot races.

Commodus surpassed both of them. He regularly took part in beast hunts, although often from the safety of a platform built specially around the arena. He was skilled with both the bow and javelin and Ostriches could be decapitated on the run with crescent-shaped arrows. As noted, Titus, celebrating the opening of the Colosseum in AD 80, had 5,000 animals killed in the first 100 days and a further 4,000 over the entire spectacle. The numbers of both beasts and men are often staggering:[24] in AD 70, 2,500 captured Jews were forced into team combats, thrown to the beasts or burned alive. In Athens, thousands of beasts, including 100 lions, were killed. Trajan must hold the record for the bloodiest displays though; following the conquest of Dacia, in games lasting 123 days, 11,000 animals were killed and 10,000 gladiators fought.[25] However, shows would often have been feats of skill to avoid the beasts. Vaulting over them or using tightropes, platforms, false walls or trap doors to evade.

We get some idea of what a day's program at a munus entailed from literary sources.[26] It was the custom to hold beast hunts in the morning, public executions during the lunch break and, perhaps saving the best until last, the gladiators in the afternoon. It is the gladiators whose reputation and fame continued long after the empire ended. They evolved over time to feature distinct types with specific matches preferred. It should be borne in mind that there was a certain amount of convention and ceremony involved.

Types of gladiator

The earliest images of gladiators from the fourth century BC depict pairs of unarmoured fighters protected by just a helmet and round hoplite type shield and armed with spears. Later examples retain the simple loin cloth but add leg greaves. The main point is that the fight was stylised and ceremonial. From being a part of funeral rites it evolved into something quite different, although just as formal. In the republican period we hear of several different types: scissor, eques, thraex, myrmillo, retiareus, sagittarius, veles, hoplomachus, samnis and gallus.[27] However, Commodus reigned from AD 180 to 192 and thus we are interested in the imperial period. There are likely many types, conventions or other aspects of gladiatorial contests that are completely lost to us, however there are enough contemporary accounts, literary records, stone reliefs and archaeological evidence to list the following:[28]

Hoplomachus: He carried a small round shield and in some way represented the ancient Greek hoplite. His helmet had a broad rim and visor with a crest and a feather on either side. He wore high greaves on his legs and a manica on his right arm. Bare chested and wearing a loin cloth and belt. Trousers were worn giving some protection to the thighs. He was armed with a spear and dagger or short sword. Often paired with a myrmillo or thraex.

Thraex: Similar to a hoplomachus with high greaves and leg coverings up to a loin cloth. He also wore a manica on his right arm and a brimmed, crested helmet. The thraex however carried a smaller square curved shield 2ft wide and was armed with a short curved dagger, a sica. The helmet was crested with a griffin's head symbolising the goddess of retribution. He was often paired with a myrmillo or a hoplomachus.

Myrmillo: Wore a broad rimmed helmet with a visor and a crest shaped like a fish with the tail decorated with a plume of feathers. One helmet appears to have a fish scale pattern which would confirm the association with the sea. A greave protected the left leg only, a manica on his right arm. He was armed with a gladius sword and a large scutum shield. The shield was 3ft in length and protected from greave to chin. The myrmillo was classed as a heavy gladiator and fought with forty pounds of equipment. They were never paired with a similar fighter but rather with a thraex or hoplomachus, or occasionally a retiarius. These were the favourite of Emperor Domitian. When a man spoke disparagingly about them in comparison with a thraex Domitian had him thrown to the dogs.

Gallus: possibly an early form of the myrmillo. Carried a scutum shield, greave and helmet. Armed with a gladius. They had disappeared by the first century BC.

Provocator: Wearing a loin cloth and a belt with a metal breast plate. The helmet had a neck guard covering the sides and back. He carried a rectangular shield, perhaps smaller than that of a myrmillo but wore a longer greave on his left leg. The principal weapon was a straight sword. There is one example of a pairing with the heavier myrmillo but generally they were paired with other provocators only.

Dimachaerus: Protected by a broad-rimmed helmet with a visor. Greaves on his legs and a tunic, or more likely mail as he had no shield. He carried two short swords, one possibly curved. Possible paired with another dimachaerus.

Retiarius: This is the iconic gladiator, armed with a fuscina, or trident. He was largely unarmoured with no helmet, shield or greaves. While other gladiator types wore a manica on their right arm the retiarius wore his on the left in which he held his weighted net. On his left shoulder he wore a galerus, a metal plate protecting the left shoulder, neck and head. He also carried a dagger as a back up. A laquerarius was similar but carried a lasso instead of a net. Both were the most lightly armed of the gladiators. A retiarius was often paired with a secutor, who was heavily armed. These were one of the most popular matched pairs throughout the imperial period.

Secutor: Also known as contraretiarius, was designed to fight the retiarius. He was similar to a myrmillo with a large scutum shield, greased left leg, manica on his right arm and wielding a gladius. The helmet, however, was very different. It was smooth and streamlined to prevent the net catching and a visor with small eye holes stopped the points of the trident penetrating. There was a fin-like crest to resemble a fish. The secutor tired quickly and the helmet restricted vision and oxygen.

Arbelas: Also known as scissor, the arbelas wore a helmet and scale or mail armour down to his knees. A manica protected his right arm and short greaves protected both legs up to the knees. The helmet had a visor and often a crest. In his right arm he carried a dagger but in his left was an unusual weapon. Looking rather like a type of pirate's hook, the arbela had a crescent-shaped blade, likely sharpened both sides. There was also what looks like a metal protective tube into which one placed his forearm with presumably a handle at the base or straps to hold into position. He was the most heavily armed and armoured of the gladiators yet carried no shield. Often paired with *retiarius*.

Eques: Mounted gladiators only ever fought each other. Lightly armoured they carried a 2ft diameter round shield similar to cavalrymen of the republican era. The main weapon was a 7 or 8ft long spear, but they also carried a gladius. The helmet had a brim and a visor and often was depicted with a feather either side. Some reliefs show scale armour while others a simple tunic. Many fights appear to have developed into a dismounted phase.

Crupellarius: This type are described by Tacitus as completely covered in steel. They would have been slow moving and though 'ill-adapted for inflicting wounds, they were impenetrable to them'. We read of a battle in AD 21 against a Gallic tribe, the Aedui, as involving men in armour. These proved difficult as 'the iron plates did not yield to javelins or swords'. The legionaries used hatchets, pickaxes, forked poles and pikes to beat them to the ground where they lay 'without any effort to rise like dead men'.[29]

Sagittarius: Protected by a conical helmet and scale armour his principal weapon was the bow.

Samnis: Likely confined to the republican era, Livy describes their appearance: the shield was broad at the top and tapered to the bottom. They wore armour and greave on their left leg. Their helmets were plumed. One fighter had a gold-coloured shield and multi-coloured tunic. His opponent carried a silver shield and white tunic. Other sources suggest an oval shield and armour comparisons of three metal discs. Their weapons were swords or spear.

Essedarius: This is controversial as there is little evidence. However, literary sources suggest a gladiator riding a chariot armed with a spear and round shield, although it is difficult to distinguish such examples from a venatore or bestiarii. One can certainly imagine using chariots as a mobile platform from which to kill animals with bow or javelin. What images do exist of them fighting other gladiators suggest they may have actually fought on foot with a sword. Perhaps they entered the arena in dramatic style.

Veles: Very little is known about veles, but it is thought he was similar to a light infantryman of the republic era. Thus he would have carried a shield, javelin and sword.

Paegniarius: These wore no armour and carried a stick and a whip. The only protection was cloth wrapping on the arms and legs. They were especially popular under Commodus and were likely a warm up act before the more traditional types.

Andabata: It is believed the andabata wore a special helmet with no eye holes and thus fought blind. His opponent would have been another andabata and they would have relied on sound. There are some indications he wore mail armour. Perhaps this was just for novel entertainment value rather than taken as seriously as the more traditional types. This did not appear in the imperial period.

Cestus: These were basically boxers although with a variety of different gloves, some simply padded, others wrapped in iron or even spikes.

Noxxi: These weren't really classed as gladiators but were prisoners or criminals usually matched against animals.

A range of support and other staff were also involved.[30]

Editor: Official or citizen funding the spectacle.

Aedile: Responsible for supervising public games and maintenance of streets and buildings.
Lanista: Trainers and managers of gladiators and gladiator schools.

Familia: Group of arena performers.

Summa rudis and secunda rudis: The first and second stick, senior and junior referees. They used a stick to separate or discipline fighters.

Typically gladiators fought in particular pairs with some matches proving more popular. One of the most iconic fights was between a retiarius and a secutor. Here was matched the lightest armoured gladiator against a heavily armoured one; one with no shield but carrying a net and trident. The other with a large scutum shield, large helmet and gladius sword. No doubt there was an element of cat and mouse in the contest, the lighter gladiator attempting to either lure him into position to throw his net or to tire him out. The secutor attempting to close in to use his sword. The table below shows the most common matches.

Table 6: Common gladiator pairs

Secutor	Retiarius
Scissor or Arbelas	Retiarius
Thraex	Myrmillo, Hoplomachus
Hoplomachus	Myrmillo, Thraex
Retiarius	Secutor, Myrmillo, Scissor/Arbelas
Myrmillo	Thraex, Hoplomachus, Retiarius
Dimachaerus	Dimachaerus
Eques	Eques
Provocator	Provocator

In the first gladiatorial contest of *Gladiator*, Maximus and the other recruits are chained in pairs to fight a group of gladiators in a huge mêlée. This unlikely scenario would be a huge waste of resources; gladiators were expensive to train and maintain. Aside from that, the gladiators are armed and armoured with an odd assortment of helmets, armour and weapons. Plus the contest, while designed to entertain, was expected to follow certain conventions. It would be like a modern boxing audience being confronted with several boxers in the ring at the same time. Pairs from every weight category alongside other disciplines such as wrestlers and martial artists. In reality the contest would have been far more organised and ritualised. A referee would have ensured rules were respected.

Picture 30: Hoplomaches vs Thraex (Wikimedia Commons)

Picture 31: Thraex vs Murmillo (Wikimedia Commons)

Picture 32: Provocator vs Provocator (Wikimedia Commons)

Picture 33: Retiarius vs Secutor (Wikimedia Commons)

Picture 34: Scissor vs Retiarius (Wikimedia Commons)

Picture 35: Eques vs Eques (Wikimedia Commons)

Picture 36: Mounted Eques (Wikimedia Commons)

Life of a gladiator

Gladiators were outsiders from society. the term infamia meant loss of status as well as citizens' rights.[31] Many, such as captives of war, condemned criminals and slaves sold to a ludus or training camp, didn't have rights to begin with. Some poor, destitute or bankrupted individuals saw success in the arena as a desperate way out. They were on the same social level as prostitutes and actors. From the first century BC ex-gladiators were prohibited from holding office, serving on a jury or becoming a soldier. They were also no longer protected from physical abuse or corporal punishment. Seneca records some gladiators swearing an oath agreeing to be burned, chained up or killed.[32]

At the same time, gladiators were extremely popular. Images were common as statues, paintings, mosaics and graffiti. We can see how dangerous it was from Galen, the physician to Emperor Marcus Aurelian. He started his career treating gladiators in Pergamum, modern Turkey, and one example given is of his replacing intestines hanging out of a gaping wound. Keith Hopkins and Mary Beard in their book *The Colosseum*, describe how most training schools were like the one portrayed in *Gladiator*,[33] a small-scale affair ran in the provinces by the ex-gladiator Proximo played by Oliver Reed.

Some prisoners were so terrified of the ordeal that they committed suicide rather than fight.[34] We hear of twenty-nine captured Saxons strangling each other rather than be forced to fight. Another example, given by Seneca, recalls a gruesome method used by a German animal hunter to avoid the arena. His only opportunity came when going to the lavatory; he took a stick with a sponge on the end used by the Romans as a version of lavatory paper and rammed it down his own throat choking to death.

Spectator behaviour occasionally proved problematic. Sometimes prizes were distributed to the crowd ranging from sweets or other food stuffs, to tokens that could be redeemed for more expensive items. Seneca reports that this often produced scuffles. In the early third century under the Emperor Elagabulus, this caused a number of deaths. In AD 59 we hear of a major example of crowd violence at a munus in Pompeii.[35] A number of spectators attended from the neighbouring town of Nuccria. First insults were exchanged then violence ensued and a significant number of spectators died. Rome held an inquiry and Pompeii was banned from holding games for ten years.

Life expectancy

There is enough surviving evidence to piece together some interesting statistics.[36] The average age a man entered the arena was 17 and he would expect to live five-and-a-half years, having fought eight fights. We can see this equates to just one or two fights a year and might be compared to a modern boxing champion. Early in a career one might fight multiple times a year, but a famous fighter might be highly valued and risked only for a big occasion. Some fighters, however, are recorded as fighting more than once in the same games, with one example stating the second fight was seven days later. A small number of fighters had fifty fights in their career and some were able to die of old age in their beds.

Three examples exist from inscriptions: Glauco died at 23 in his eighth fight; a second, aged 27 with eleven fights; and a third aged 34 with twenty-one contests. In contrast, the average life expectancy for Roman males was 31, although the high rate of infant mortality skews this. If one reached the age of 17, then the average age of death rose to 48.

The chances of death per fight are also interesting. In games at Pompeii there were twenty-three bouts with forty-six gladiators. Twenty-one were victorious, suggesting two were draws. Seventeen of the losers survived, while eight gladiators were killed or died from their wounds. This suggests one or two of the winners succumbed to their injuries too. Eight out of forty-six gives a percentage of seventeen, or just under one in six. Augustus stipulated that not all fights were to the death, yet in Campania we find that over four days, out of eleven pairs there were eleven killed, along with ten bears. Approximately three quarters died before their tenth fight. From these examples we can estimated an attrition rate of one-in-six to one-in-eight. In percentage terms this is roughly 13–16 per cent.

Costs

Total numbers of gladiators across the empire and associated costs can also be estimated.[37] Skilled fighters were priced between 3,000 and 15,000 sesterces. Other entertainers and workers in the arena were priced at 1,000 to 2,000 sesterces, similar to an unskilled slave; 500 sesterces could have fed a peasant family for a year. A provincial show might cost 30,000 to 200,000 sesterces, whereas the emperor Hadrian once spent 2 million. Thus, a highly valued gladiator cost the equivalent of thirty times the yearly subsistence of a peasant family.

There were over 200 stone amphitheatres throughout the empire and the estimate of total arenas is around double that. Yet on average, only around five days of the year might have been used for gladiatorial contests. The majority of the usage was for less bloodthirsty shows and entertainment. The total number of gladiators may have been around 12,000, fighting in two shows per year. With a death rate of one in six, 2,000 would need replacing twice a year. We can thus estimate 16,000 fighters in a given year, 4,000 deaths and 4,000 captured prisoners, the condemned, slaves and the desperate, to replace them. Pliny claims that under Caligula there were 20,000 gladiators in training camps, equivalent to nearly four legions.

Estimates of total deaths in the arena may be similar to the gladiators. If we assume 8,000 deaths across the empire of 60 million, we get a fraction of a tenth of a per cent. However, if we consider this is only of fit young men of fighting age, this could be as high as 1.5% of all 20-year-old men, a significant impact on manpower.

Contemporary accounts

One account survives from the time of Titus.[38] Priscus and Verus, possibly fighting or stage names meaning 'ancient' and 'true', fought a long battle that ended in a draw. The crowd demanded an 'honourable discharge' from gladiatorial service and Titus himself sent them rich rewards for their bravery, and palms to mark their joint victory. It was up to the sponsor of the show, the *editor*, to decide if the defeated gladiator was to be killed. This was often the emperor, but a wise man listened carefully to the crowd. The Latin phrase 'pollice verso' means 'thumbs turned', but we don't know what exactly this means or which way the thumbs pointed for life or death.

We get some examples from tombstones. From Trieste we have a tomb provided by Constantius who gave the munus: 'To Decorates the retiarius, who killed Caeruleus and died himself, as both died by the same sword, so the same pyre covers both. Decorates, the secutor, after nine fights left his wife Valeria grieving for the first time.'[39] From Pompeii we find graffiti showing two fighters: A tiro, or novice, Marcus Attilius and Hilarus, winner of twelve out of fourteen fights.[40] It would appear the novice won and his rival 'sent away', meaning although defeated he lived to fight another day.

We get a picture of the customs and ceremony that existed around the games. For example, it was traditional for gladiators to have their last meal in public.[41] The gladiatorial display seems to have been the high point of many games and one could come and view the fighters the night or morning before the fight. We get a vivid portrayal of the crowd from an unlikely source from the fourth century.

In an excerpt from *The Confessions* by St Augustine of Hippo, written at the end of the fourth century, the saint describes the allure of the arena. He tells of young man, Alypius, who arrives in Rome to study law, that he had 'held such spectacles in aversion and detestation', but was persuaded to go by friends. He went, determined to keep his eyes shut and 'forbade his mind to think about such fearful evils'. But the roar of the crowd seduced him: 'A man fell in combat. A great roar from the entire crowd struck him with such vehemence that he was overcome by curiosity.' He soon 'found delight in the murderous contest and was inebriated by bloodthirsty pleasure. He was not now the person who had come in, but just one of the crowd.... He looked, he yelled, he was on fire.' He 'took the madness home with him' and from then on was hooked, returning with others: 'he had been seized by an incredible obsession for gladiatorial spectacles and to an unbelievable degree'.

Colosseum

Construction on the Colosseum began under Emperor Vespasian in AD 72 and it was completed under his son Titus in AD 80. Covering six acres it rose four stories and 157ft in height. The ground floor contained eighty arches, and four tiers of seating accommodated a maximum 87,000 spectators although 50,000 is the more usual estimate. In comparison, the largest premiership stadium, Manchester United's Old Trafford, holds just over 74,000. Wembley stadium holds a little more than the Colosseum at 90,000.

The first point to note is that it was not known as the Colosseum at the time. To the Romans it was 'The Amphitheatre' or 'Hunting Theatre'. By the end of the second century it had become the model for over 200 other amphitheatres throughout the empire. Many others would have been built of wood, or used the natural contours of the land. In Rome, temporary wooden structures were often built and taken down after the games. The Forum was a common location with the audience watching from temporary wooden benches. The Circus Maximus had long been used for chariot races even before the first stone structure was built there in the second century BC.

The Colosseum arena measured 278 x 177ft or 84 x 54 metres. The Circus Maximus, in contrast, was over 2,000ft in length by 387 in width, which was suitable for chariot races. The football pitch at Wembley stadium measures 345 x 225ft or 105 x 68 metres, thus we can see that the arena floor of the Colosseum was slightly smaller. A better comparison is perhaps an American football field which, at 91 x 49 metres, is slightly longer and narrower, but only by between 5 to 7 metres.

The Colosseum became a political as much as a sporting venue. While the seating was strictly hierarchical, the emperor was accessible and visible

Picture 37: The Colosseum (Wikimedia Commons)

Picture 38: The Colosseum Interior (Wikimedia Commons)

to elites and the crowd. As far as is known there was no entrance price. It was provided to citizens at the largesse of the benefactor, usually the emperor. Tokens of wood, bone or lead suggest admission was restricted to certain classes and seating was tightly packed at forty centimetres per person and seventy centimetres leg room.[42]

About a quarter of Rome's population of 1 million would be adult males, and half of those slaves. With a maximum capacity of 87,000, this would have accommodated two thirds of the free adult male population.

Gladiator portrays the spectacle very well, but what is open to question is the scenario. It is unlikely the Romans would waste trained gladiators on a battle re-enactment which would likely result in high levels of injury or death. In this situation it would be preferable to use prisoners or criminals.

The Battle of Zama scene

Another iconic scene in the film is Maximus's first appearance at the Colosseum. He joins a group of fellow gladiators on the arena floor, unaware of what may come through the gates to confront them. They are on foot, armed with spears and shields and mail shirts. Maximus tells the men:

'Whatever comes out of these gates we've got a better chance of survival if we work together.' In reality, for a well known battle the entertainment would likely be rehearsed. Such displays were not unheard of. Pompey had staged an event involving elephants and javelin throwers at the Circus Maximus.[43]

We also see examples of mass combat. In 29 BC Dacian and Suevi prisoners fought a mock battle.[44] On this occasion a Roman senator, Quintus Vitellius, was able to take part despite the earlier ban by Augustus. Both Julius Caesar and Claudius had put on mass combat displays.[45] On another occasion Hadrian had 300 condemned criminals fight wearing distinctive gold cloaks.[46]

In the film what actually came out of the gates were six scythed chariots, each with two horses. They also had a driver and a female passenger in gold coloured armour, armed with bows and javelins. Perhaps surprisingly, the most unlikely part of this scenario is not the use of chariots or female warriors. It is rather that the Romans hadn't attempted to display the battle with some accuracy. Most would have been left scratching their heads wondering where Hannibal's elephants were and why there were chariots at a battle where they played no part.

The fact that Augustus banned women competing in 22 BC suggests women did indeed take part in games. In fact, it may have been the sight of a woman of 'noble rank' participating along with equestrians that caused Augustus to legislate against both.[47] Further evidence of women fighting can be seen when the Emperor Domitian staged events involving women and dwarves, albeit likely for comedic value.[48] Yet not long after, the poet Juvenal is horrified that some women fought as gladiators. Martial tells of a female hunter who rivals Hercules: 'We have now seen such things done by women's valour.'[49] It would appear professional female fighters did compete in games during the second century. The practice was common enough for Septimus Severus to ban female gladiators during his reign (AD 193–211). As he reigned the year after Commodus died, this would strongly suggest the scene involving female gladiators was not in any way improbable.

We have also seen how some fighters used chariots, although it's likely they actually fought on foot. Maximus is able to organise the men into a formation and they manage to defeat the charioteers. We have seen how mock battles were routinely displayed. It's thus not unreasonable or unlikely that someone could have incorporated chariots in a display involving massed ranks of fighters. But let's consider the actual battle of Zama and decide if the film gives a likely representation.

The real battle of Zama

The battle of Zama was fought in 202 BC in modern Tunisia, several miles to the south west of Carthage. It marked the end of the second Punic War between Rome and Carthage. In 219 BC, Hannibal had besieged and sacked the pro-Roman city of Saguntum in eastern Spain causing Rome to declare war. In 218 BC, Hannibal crossed the Alps and invaded the Italian peninsula, famously taking elephants with him. Several famous victories followed at Trebia, 218 BC, Lake Trasimene 217 BC and Cannae in 216 BC, where Hannibal was able to surround a much larger army and destroy it, killing 80,000 Romans. Some Italian cities, Syracuse and Macedonia, joined the Carthiginians. Hannibal was unable to take Rome or defeat the Romans decisively. The war spread to Sardinia and Sicily, but the Carthaginians failed to capture either island. Rome attempted to expand their presence in Iberia, but they too failed. The tide began to turn with the arrival of Publius Scipio in Iberia. He defeated Hasdrubal Barca, Hannibal's brother, and drove the Carthaginians out of Iberia by 206 BC. He then invaded North Africa in 204 BC. The Carthaginians were forced to recall Hannibal from Italy. Thus setting up the fateful battle that ended the war.

The Roman army consisted of around 29,000 infantry and 6,000 cavalry. The Carthaginians had 36,000 infantry, but only 4,000 cavalry. However, they also had eighty war elephants. Hannibal's forces faced north-west on a flat plain. He placed his infantry in three lines. In the first were mercenaries from Gaul, Ligura and the Balearic islands. Second came citizen levies and third, his battle-hardened veterans. In front were his eighty war elephants, which he hoped would be decisive. Scipio's slightly smaller army was also arranged in three main lines. First came the light infantry Hastati, second the heavy Principes, and last the veteran Triarii. In front of all three were lightly armed elites armed with javelins and light spears. To combat the elephants Scipio altered the usual checker-board layout and had his troops deployed with units directly behind each other and gaps between the columns. His light javelin troops were to lure the attacking elephants forward and it was hoped the elephants would avoid the mass of men and advance into the gaps where they could be surrounded and killed. Scipio also flanked his army with cavalry with the majority on his right flank giving it a distinct numerical advantage.

Hannibal started the battle by ordering his elephants and skirmishers forward. Roman skirmishers met them and at the same time Scipio had his cavalry blow horns to frighten the elephants. This caused the elephants on the left to panic and retreat, causing disorder on the Carthaginian left wing. The Roman cavalry on the right saw their chance and attacked the Carthaginian cavalry, who retreated to draw them away from the battle. The cavalry on the Roman left also attacked their mounted opponents. Meanwhile, the remaining elephants had charged straight ahead and been drawn into the gaps by the retreating velites. When they reached the rear of the Roman lines they were met with a wall of spears, javelins and arrows from all sides and were quickly neutralised.

The first line of Roman infantry advanced and pushed the Carthaginians back. This was checked by Hannibal sending in his second line, which in turn pushed back the Hastati. Scipio sent in his Principes. Once again the Romans pushed back their opponents, so Hannibal sent in his final line. While the battle hung in the balance, both wings of Carthaginian cavalry had deliberately drawn away the pursuing Romans only to turn on them and attack. This failed and the Carthaginian cavalry was routed and fled, which ultimately proved decisive

There was a pause in the infantry engagement and both armies redeployed their troops into a single line. The Romans with the Hastati in the centre and Triarii on the wings, Hannibal placing his veterans in the centre. The resulting clash was bloody and could have gone either way. What proved pivotal was the return of the Roman cavalry who attacked the Carthaginian rear. They were encircled and destroyed avenging Rome's defeat against Hannibal at Cannae. Around half the army were killed and the rest captured compared to 2,500 Romans and 2,500 Numidian allied casualties. Carthage was forced to sue for peace. Hannibal survived the battle but later went into exile. Pursued by the Romans, he eventually committed suicide. Fifty years after the battle, in the third Punic War, Carthage was again defeated and the city destroyed.

We note there were no chariots or female Amazonian-like warriors at the battle. How then could the battle have been re-enacted? They certainly were able to represent it. They had elephants and could easily have have used a small number. Of course a mock battle would be better suited to a larger venue. But even so, one or two elephants could have been dispatched as a prelude to the main event. They wouldn't even need to have killed them, simply trained them to follow retreating javelin men out of the arena to represent the initial charge at the start of the battle. The dramatic ebb and flow of three lines of infantry would be a relatively easy display to organise, with the climatic moment being the appearance of the Roman cavalry. Given how much effort they put into recreating Greek and Roman myths and other mock battles, it seems unlikely they would deviate too much from such a well-known battle. A Roman audience watching a recreation of the battle of Zama would expect to see elephants, an infantry battle and a Roman victory at the end.

Map 14: The Battle of Zama 202 BC

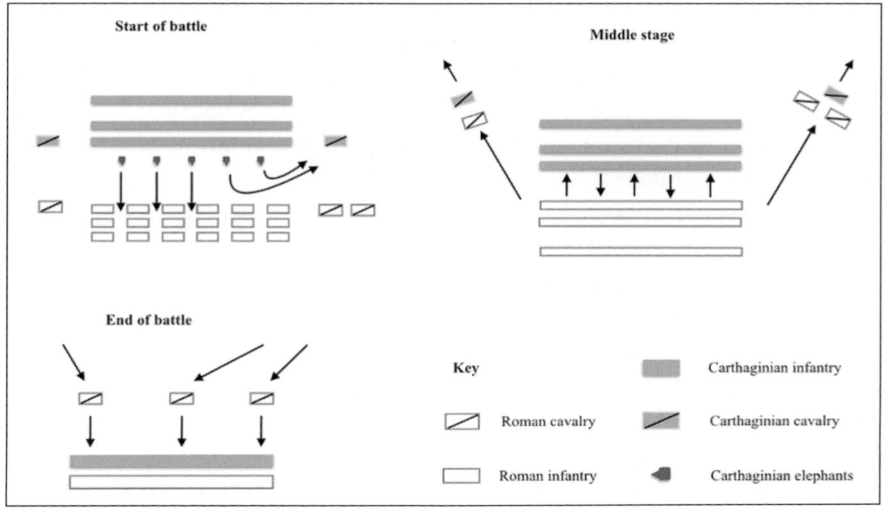

Naumachia, naval battles

Some amphitheatres were specially constructed to hold a body of water. Nero arranged for the Campus Martius to be filled with water. One part of the show involved seeing aquatic animals in their natural habitat. Another allowed a mock naval battle from history involving the Athenians against the Persians. This was then drained quick enough to allow a mock land battle between the same opposing forces. Domitian is said to have staged a smaller version in the Colosseum.

Julius Caesar put on a number of such displays. One in 46 BC involved ships with three or four banks of oars, 2,000 oarsmen and 1,000 warriors. Usually such displays were held on artificial lakes. In 2 BC Augustus used one to recreate the battle of Salamis in 480 BC, between the Greeks and the Persians. Third triremes and biremes were involved along with 3,000 gladiators and likely many more oarsmen and sailors. Two days later a similar contest involved 300 men and resulted in those playing the role of the Athenians, after winning the naval engagement, landing on an island and capturing a fortress.

Perhaps the greatest example of a naval battle was put on by the Emperor Claudius in AD 52 at a natural lake, Faucine, outside Rome. Tacitus describes how 19,000 prisoners performed a mock battle between Sicilains and Rhodians. The lake was surrounded with a raft and breastworks from which the Praetorian Guard could fire ballistas and catapults. The lake itself was big enough to allow the ships to manoeuvre and use their battering rams. It is here we find the only reference to the famous line often assumed to be spoken by gladiators. The prisoners reportedly said '*ave Caesar, morituri the salutant*', which means, 'Hail Caesar. Those who about to die salute you.' There is no record of this being repeated in any other context and certainly not at individual gladiatorial contests at the Colosseum or anywhere else.[50]

The last recorded *naumachia* was in AD 274 under the Emperor Aurelian. There is some dispute about whether the Colosseum was able to be flooded.[51] Cassius Dio records that Titus filled the arena with water and brought in animals to swim for the crowds followed by a mock naval battle. Suetonius claimed they took place away from the arena. The Romans often used examples of historical battles from Greek history. They didn't always end as expected though, which suggests it was not always possible to choreograph and manage such an event. Perhaps this is why they were reluctant to use examples of Roman battles. A Roman defeat, even in a mock battle, would not go down well with the audience, let alone a possibly vengeful emperor.

Single combat

After the epic Battle of Zama scene, Maximus is matched against Tigris the Gaul. He is armed with round shield, what looks like a leather cuirass body armour and a gladius. Tigris is armed with sword and axe and has metal greaves, large metal shoulder pads and a helmet with a face covering. During the battle several tigers are released from the arena floor, although still attached to long chains. Tigers were a novelty when Augustus exhibited one in 11 BC.[52] However, they were more common by the time of Marcus Aurelius, though likely far more expensive than the usual lions and bears. Maximus, of course, prevails, but the whole scenario is unlikely. The whole point of a matched pair was to see the skill of the fighters. Displays involving tigers or other wild animals usually included prisoners or beast hunters, venatores. The final combat scene pits our hero against Commodus himself. In fact, as we shall see, Commodus did indeed fight in the arena. What he didn't do is put himself in any danger.

Chapter 6

Commodus

Joaquin Phoenix was 25 years old when *Gladiator* was released. In contrast, Commodus was 18 when his father died and 31 when he was killed. Phoenix did a fine job of portraying the complex character for which he was nominated an Academy Award for Best Supporting Actor. Lucius Aurelius Commodus was born on 31 August, AD 161. Named after Lucius Verus, who had been called Commodus himself before taking the title Augustus. Commodus's older brother, Hadrianus, died the following year, and his twin brother, Antoninus, also died when he was 5. A younger brother, Annius Verus, died aged 7 in the same year that his uncle Lucius Verus died. One can only speculate what effect this had on the young Commodus, although this level of infant mortality was common at that time.

This left Commodus the sole male survivor. He had five surviving sisters: Lucilla, born AD 150, married to co-emperor Lucius Verus then to Claudius Pompeianus, and later executed by her brother; Faustina, born AD 151 and married to Gnaeus Claudius Severus, a friend and advisor to her father; Fadilla, born AD 159, with whom he remained close; Annia Cornificia, AD 160, married a Marcus Petronius who was later executed by Commodus, though Annia was spared; Sabina, born c. AD 170, whose husband Burrus was executed by Commodus while she was allowed to marry an obscure equestrian. Despite the many plots against Commodus, it is perhaps noteworthy that only Lucilla was implicated.

Commodus received a similar education to his father and uncle: the Latin Classics, grammar, Greek language and literature, law, rhetoric and philosophy. We get differing accounts of Commodus.[1] Dio Cassius refers to him as 'guileless' and 'a slave to his companions', and states that his mother Faustina thought her son 'simple minded'. Yet Marcus gives thanks his children are 'neither stupid nor deformed'. From a young age Commodus was viewed by some as 'cruel and dishonourable', with a 'lewd, foul-mouthed debauched character'.[2] One telling example survives. Aged 12, on finding his bath water too cold, he ordered the slave responsible to be burned alive. The other servants conspired to fool him by placing a sheepskin in a fire, but it demonstrated what he might do once unconstrained by the adults around him. This could be a story invented by his many enemies, Cassius Dio certainly had good cause to dislike him. As a senator he must have wondered if he too would fall to Commodus's ire. As we shall see, Commodus also had good cause to distrust the senate.

However, all that was in the future and at the age of 5 he accompanied his father and uncle in their triumph over the Parthians in AD 166. The empire was immediately beset by two major problems. The first was the devastating plague that swept westward, likely brought back by returning soldiers. The second was the invasion of the northern border by various Germanic tribes.

At the start of AD 168 the two emperors set off for the Danube border. This was the last time the 7-year-old Commodus would have seen Lucius Verus, who died in early AD 169. Marcus dismissed nearly all of his brother's freedmen, perhaps as a response to the rumours of influence they had on his behaviour. Fatefully, he left Eclectus, who later served Commodus and was directly responsible for his assassination twenty-three years later.

When Commodus was about 9 years old he was 'seized by a hot fever'.[3] Galen diagnosed an inflammation of the tonsils and was able to cure him using among other things, honey and rose water. We can see how fragile life was when in AD 170, his younger brother Annius Verus died in an operation to remove a cyst behind his ear. His father allowed himself five days' mourning before returning to the war, remaining on the border for two years. We cannot be certain, but it would seem his personality was far more like his charismatic uncle Lucius Verus than his sombre philosophical father.

In AD 172, Commodus was present in Carnuntum when his father received the title Germanicus and the acclamation of the legions. Herodian states that Marcus would bring his son with him when he was a small boy. Presenting his son to the army was an attempt to illicit trust and loyalty. In January AD 175, Commodus was enrolled in all of the colleges of priests, an event commemorated on coins. All these acts suggest that Marcus was proactively grooming Commodus for the throne. Avidius Cassius revolted in the East and Commodus was summoned to the border, leaving Rome in the May. In July AD 175 he received the toga virilis a month short of his fourteenth birthday, suggesting there was some urgency. Marcus formally announced that Commodus was his heir and successor. One wonders what effect the betrayal of a once loyal general had on 14-year-old Commodus. He would, no doubt, have been keenly aware what this could mean for his own future. Perhaps the seeds of mistrust of those around him were planted at that point.

Both Cassius Dio and the *Historia Augustus* are hostile to Commodus. Yet Dio states that Commodus was 'not naturally wicked' and only later turned to 'lustful and cruel habits'.[4] Both sources also implicated Faustina in the plot with Avidius and we are left to speculate what affect this had on Commodus, even if it was just cruel gossip. With Avidius dead and the Marcomanni, Quadi and Sarmatians all defeated, Marcus decided to use the opportunity to travel east anyway and he took Commodus and Faustina with him. Pertinax, Claudius Severus and Pompeianus accompanied the party. As the party crossed the Taurus mountains in southern Turkey, Faustina fell ill and died. Dio suggests she may have committed suicide, fearful of her role in the plot being uncovered, but there is no evidence to support this. The fact that Marcus brought her along and was reportedly genuinely grief-stricken suggests the rumours may be just that. Whatever the cause, Commodus was 14 when his mother died. He followed his father across the eastern provinces. He would have witnessed his father's approach to the rebellion and how he refused to execute those senators implicated. He did, however, issue a decree prohibiting senators from serving as governors in their own provinces. This wasn't an example Commodus chose to emulate during his reign.

On their way home in AD 176, both Marcus and Commodus visited Athens and were initiated into the Eleusian Mysteries. A Christian writer of the time, Athenagoras, wrote that the emperors were 'in every way, by nature and by upbringing, good, moderate, beneficent and deserving of kingship'.[5]

In the autumn of that year they returned to Italy, surviving a violent storm on the way. On 23 December Marcus arranged for a triumph for the German and Sarmatian wars, and requested the senate grant Commodus *imperium*, or magisterial authority. Marcus also appointed him consul from 1 January AD 177. This required the senate to relax the laws regarding age, making him the youngest consul in history. At the triumph, the sight of Commodus controlling the reins of a chariot with his father walking alongside was a clear sign to the people of Rome of who Marcus intended to succeed him. Coins appeared showing Commodus as Caesar and associating him with Hercules. Lucius Verus and been similarly associated with the Greek hero and his later behaviour suggested Commodus had a great affection and admiration for the former emperor and adoptive uncle.

Marcus fell ill in AD 177 and this hastened him to grant Commodus the title of Augustus. Marcus retained the title of Pontifex Maximus, but Commodus was now officially joint emperor at the age of only 15. All the evidence suggests that Marcus was a loving father who groomed his son for the role of emperor. In an age where child mortality was high, once he reached his teens it was likely he would survive to a good age. If Marcus had adopted someone else, as Hadrian and Antoninus had done, this may have put his son in danger. No doubt his ill health, and the youth of Commodus, gave Marcus some concern, but he had clearly made a decision, if not in AD 175 after the revolt of Avidius, then certainly by AD 177.

Part of his continued education involved hearing petitioners and dealing with legal matters. One area in which he later significantly differed from his father was in dealing with the senate. Marcus feigned equality and treated and spoke to them accordingly. Commodus rejected this, which was one reason why the senate turned against him. In AD 177 conflict once again appeared on the northern frontier. Maximus Valerius was sent to Lower Moesia, Pertinax to Dacia and Julianus to Dalmatia to quell the unrest. The following year Marcus brought forward the marriage of his son to the 14-year-old Bruttia Crispina. She was the daughter of a powerful senator who had been friends with Marcus and the previous two emperors. He received the consulship as a reward. At 17, Commodus was younger than most Roman bridegrooms. Marcus appears to have been in a hurry to secure his position and build a dynasty.

On 3 August AD 178, the emperors set out on the next stage of the German wars. Accompanying them were Claudius Pompeianus and Bruttius Praesens, Commodus's new father-in-law. Also there were the two praetorian prefects, Perennis and Paternus, who played important parts later. They went on the offensive in AD 179 with Valerius Maximianus leading Legio I Adiutrix. Paternus led another army and won an initial victory. As the tide turned some German tribes and the Iazyges sent ambassadors to the two emperors at Vindobona. They now concentrated on destroying the Quadi and Marcomanni. The scenes on the column of Marcus Aurelius suggest he had lost patience with repeated raids and treaty breaking. Panels show villages burnt, beheadings, women and children killed and lines of chained captives. The 18-year-old Commodus could see the Roman army on the verge of a great victory, but the following spring his father fell ill. Given his actions, he must have realised the seriousness of the situation. First, he urged his son to continue the campaign; next he commended his son to his generals and advisors and finally to the army. Dio suggests foul play may have been at work, but neither Herodian or the Historia Augusta back this up. Most historians give the reason as natural causes. We can thus dismiss the scene in the film where Commodus strangles his father and seizes the throne. Dio records that Marcus died leaving Commodus many advisors and guardians, 'among whom were numbered the best men of the senate'. But Commodus ignored their counsel and, after negotiating a truce with the barbarians, rushed to Rome, 'for he hated all exertion and craved the comfortable life of the city'.[6] So Cassius claimed.

Generals such as Maximianus and Pompeianus, along with the praetorian prefects Perennis and Paternus, remained loyal and presented the young Commodus to the army. Despite the scathing assessment of Cassius Dio, it would seem Commodus remained on the front line throughout the campaigning season of AD 180 and some later historians report he conducted a successful campaign in this period.[7] In fact, he refused peace terms with the Buri twice and prosecuted the war until he was satisfied with the terms, which involved hostages, the return of 15,000 prisoners and a five-mile strip of land on the northern border with Dacia. Claudius Pompeianus had argued against the ending of the war, but remained a senior advisor despite the new emperor's decision. At the same time the tribes of northern Britain raided over Hadrian's Wall.

Sources report conflict in Dacia in which Albinus Clodius and Prescinnius Niger 'won fame'.[8] But the greatest struggle was apparently in Britain. Tribes crossed Hadrian's Wall and 'proceeded to do much mischief and cut down a general together with his troops'; Commodus sent Ulpius Marcellus and 'he ruthlessly put down the barbarians of Britain'. By AD 184 the title Britannicus appeared on coins. Back in October of AD 180 Commodus had returned to Rome. Much to the disgust of senators, Commodus elevated freedmen such as Saoterus and Cleander. However, the source of the first serious plot came from much closer to home. The contemporary sources all blame Lucilla for the events. First, animosity developed between her and the empress Crispina. Second, Commodus had refused her a divorce from her hated husband Pompeianus. She had taken a lover, who Dio names as Quadratus. Herodian gives him the same name as her husband, Claudius Pompeianus. Historians identify him as Claudius Pompeianus Quintianus, who was betrothed to Lucilla's daughter and a friend to the emperor. Cassius Dio claims that as Commodus entered the hunting-theatre, Claudius Pompeianus leapt out, thrusting out a sword in the narrow entrance. 'See! This is what the senate has sent you', he is reported to have shouted. The assailant had been betrothed to Lucilla's daughter, but allegedly 'had intimate relations both with the girl herself and with her mother'.[9]

Herodian goes into more detail. Born c. AD 170, and writing c. AD 240, he lived through the events, but without the fear of execution Cassius likely experienced. It paints Lucilla in a poor light, but may go some way to explain the behaviour of Commodus towards the senate and the subsequent bad press he received. Lucilla had been allowed to retain 'all the privileges of her imperial position', having been married to Lucius Verus and being the daughter of Marcus Aurelius. After her father's death, Commodus continued this policy. She was allowed 'to retain the imperial honours; she continued to occupy the imperial seat at the theatres, and the sacred fire was carried before her'. But things changed when Commodus married Crispina. Custom demanded that the front seat at the theatre be assigned to the empress and Lucilla found this difficult to accept. She took any honour paid to Crispina as an insult to herself. Herodian tells us that, unlike in *Gladiator*, the General Pompeianus was devoted to Commodus. This might explain why Lucilla kept it from him and he wasn't implicated in the plot. She turned elsewhere for help:

> She tested the sentiments of a wealthy young nobleman, Quadratus, with whom she was rumoured to be sleeping in secret. Complaining constantly about this matter of imperial precedence, she soon persuaded the young man to set in motion a plot which brought destruction upon himself and the entire Senate.
>
> Herodian, 1.8.3/4

Herodian describes the assailant as a rash youth, while the *Historia* dismisses him as a fool. He certainly failed, as his shout allowed Commodus to defend himself and his bodyguards to reach him in time. An investigation was held and we see just how murderous and treacherous Roman politics was. The praetorian prefects Paternus and Perennis saw how powerful and hated Saoterus had become and arranged for his murder. Paternus was then promoted to the senate, but this had the result of making him more vulnerable. Without the protection of the Praetorian Guards he too was less of a danger and was soon accused of being part of the plot and executed. This resulted in Perennis becoming the sole commander of the Guard and Cleander rising in power as a freedman advising the emperor. The implication being that one, or both, of these figures were instrumental in their colleagues' deaths. Further executions followed which no doubt caused more animosity in the senate. Commodus, however, didn't stop there.

> Commodus also put Crispina to death, having become angry with her for some act of adultery. But before their execution both women were banished to the island of Capreae.
>
> Cassius Dio book 73.4

There is some dispute about Crispina as some evidence suggests she was still alive in AD 187.[10]

Many of Marcus's old amici were caught up in the purge. Pertinax, however, went on to be appointed governor of Britannia, Maximianus became consul in AD 186 and Pompeianus was allowed to retire to his estates. His son with Lucilla was able to have a political career until he too was murdered by the emperor Caracalla in AD 212.

The effect on Commodus was enormous. If the senators felt put out by the rise of powerful freedmen, this was only exacerbated by the emperor's reaction. It's worth recalling the words of the would-be assassin: 'This is what the senate has sent you.' It is no wonder Commodus became suspicious and less trusting. Roman patronage was based on a reciprocal beneficia and amicus. In return the emperor expected gratia and fides. Commodus would have seen this informal arrangement as broken. He could no longer expect loyalty and increasingly turned to men who relied upon him for patronage rather than the elite. This meant the equestrians he had promoted, such as Perennis, or freedmen such as Cleander, derived their power completely from the emperor.

He reversed many of his father's policies, reintroducing the charge of majestas, which included treason. He also stopped senators trying their own and set up his own court. Sentences included exile or execution, the confiscation of property and damnatio memoriae, where all records and inscriptions were erased. Ironically, this last fate is what befell Commodus after his murder. What made matters worse was the fact a successful prosecution meant the accuser kept half of the condemned's estate, with the rest going to the emperor. This predictably led to a frenzy of vicious accusations and counter accusations, made worse as a failed prosecution by a delatores (denouncer) often led to their execution.

Two future emperors escaped just such an accusation during his reign: Didius Julianus and Septimus Severus. Both accusers were executed with the latter example being crucified. Commodus no doubt felt he was entirely justified in his behaviour. Not only had he seen his father's friend Avidius betray him, but his own mother was rumoured to be implicated in a plot that could have resulted in his death. Then, within two years, his own sister and several senators conspired to have him murdered. An act performed by a supposed loyal supporter who had made it quite clear he was acting on behalf of the senate. We can also see where some of the hostility came from as Cassius Dio complains about increased taxes. Commodus ordered the senators, wives and even children to contribute two gold pieces each year on his birthday. He also ordered the senators in all the other cities to give five denarii apiece. He spent this 'disgracefully on his wild beasts and his gladiators'.[11]

Bad enough that he taxed the rich and promoted low-born men, but he wasted his time and money on games. Although perhaps this shows resentment at what was likely a popular policy with the people of Rome. His closest adviser was widely resented by the senate. Cleander 'sold senatorships, military commands, procuratorships, governorships, and, in a word, everything'. He appointed twenty-five consuls in one year, which was unheard of. He amassed 'more wealth than any who had ever been named cubicularii'.[12]

Commodus had a private arena in which he trained and fought as a gladiator. His preferred type was a secutor. We recall this type was designed to fight the lightly armoured retiarius. Carrying a large scutum shield, and gladius he was protected by a greave on his left leg and manica on his sword arm. He also wore the large finned helmet with a small visor or eye holes. His opponent would likely be a retiarius armed with a trident but with no helmet, shield or greaves. Two important points are worth noting: first, in his early reign he confined these fights to private bouts; second, his opponents used wooden or blunted weapons and he was never in any actual danger.

Cassius Dio complains that Commodus was interested only in games, in particular chariot racing. He confined acting as a charioteer away from the public gaze, often at night, so as to avoid the shame Cassius suggests would follow such behaviour of an emperor in public. He even adopted the green uniform of one of the teams. He killed many wild beasts in private and in public. But it was perhaps his performance as a gladiator that shocked the most. In private he was said to have 'sliced off the noses of some, the ears of others, and sundry features of … others'. He even managed 'to kill a man now and then'. However, in public he 'refrained from using steel and shedding human blood'.[13]

We must remember Commodus was 21 at the time of the attempted assassination. It is not unusual for a young man with riches and power thrust upon him to indulge in particular pursuits, nor is it unusual, given his close shave with a dagger-wielding attacker, to wish to be able to defend himself. Indeed, later would-be assassins were well aware of Commodus's physical prowess and ability, hence their decision to try to poison him.

Meanwhile, by AD 184 Ulpius Marcellus had restored order in Britannia. We saw how Dio described this as 'the greatest struggle', and the province was soon plunged into further unrest. This time it was the army that mutinied. Marcellus is described as strict, arrogant and unpleasant, and this may have been a contributing factor.[14] Interestingly, Dio states the troops blamed Perennis in Rome as he was seen as making decisions on behalf of the emperor. The soldiers declared a lieutenant, Priscus, as emperor. This is not Statius Priscus of Parthian War fame, but likely Caerellius Priscus. Priscus declined, apparently stating: 'I am no more an emperor than you are soldiers.' Perennis removed the *legates* of each legion who would have been senators and replaced them with equestrian subordinates. There is then a curious incident.

We hear that the 'lieutenants' in Britain sent 1,500 'javelin men' and sent them to Rome. Commodus met them outside the city. They inform the emperor they came because Perennis was plotting against him and planned to make his son emperor. Commodus believed them and he was egged on by Cleander because, concerning Perennis, 'he hated him bitterly'. Commodus handed Perennis over to the 1,500 men and he was 'maltreated and struck down'. Sadly, his wife, sister, and two sons were also killed.[15]

We are left to wonder who led these 1,500 men. Were they vexillations from the three legions? Perhaps led by the three demoted legates? Auxiliary troops often numbered 500 or 1,000 per unit so these could represent three units, one from each legion. The legates would have had to return to Rome anyway and could not withdraw legionaries. Yet they would need a bodyguard, as there was serious unrest in Gaul at that time. Given Commodus had access to nine cohorts of Praetorians, not to mention the Urban Cohorts, it is unlikely he felt immediately threatened. Perhaps he really wasn't aware of his prefect's actions and sided with the legates. He certainly was not compelled to grant an audience. The clear winner from the death of Perennis was Cleander, whose influence increased even more. Commodus would have been well aware that promoting men like Cleander and giving them so much power would alienate the senators, but he clearly did not care. Around this time Commodus took a mistress, Marcia, who would have a significant part to play in his assassination. She likely came from the household of Verus.[16]

The fall of Perennis allowed significant figures to return to favour. Maximianus received a suffect consulship; Pertinax replaced Marcellus as governor of Britain; Julianus become governor of Bithynia; Severus of Lugdunensis; and Clodius Albinus to a province in Gaul. The latter four of these all went on to become emperor in the year of the five emperors, along with Niger, after the death of Commodus. At this time was a revolt known as 'the deserters' war', led by a certain Maternus, who headed a disparate group in Gaul and the Iberian peninsula. They rebels attacked 'the largest cities' and released prisoners, 'no matter what the reasons for their imprisonment'. In return for their freedom, they joined the rebels. The bandits 'roamed over all Gaul and Spain' Burning and sacking cities.[17]

In the summer of AD 186, Niger and Severus had all but destroyed the rebellion. Maternus planned one last desperate throw of the dice to murder Commodus during the festival of Hilaria in March AD 187. It is interesting to read that Commodus appeared popular, despite the sources' usual hostility. Maternus decided he could not fight Commodus on equal terms and in open battle. We read that 'the majority of the Roman people were still well disposed toward Commodus'. Importantly, he also had the support of the Praetorian Guard. Maternus hoped to use guile and cunning.[18] He attempted to infiltrate the city and assassinate Commodus.

Unfortunately for Maternus, and perhaps many senators, he was betrayed, captured and beheaded. Herodian claims that after this latest attempt Commodus was rarely seen in public. To make matters worse, a plague struck Italy followed by a famine. Commodus left Rome for Laurentum, a few miles to the south west on the coast. Cleander remained in Rome and Commodus ordered him to secure the grain supply. Shortages of labour pushed up wages and reduced rents further, thereby reducing imperial tax receipts. Herodian reports that Cleander took advantage of the situation. He bought up most of the grain supply and put it in storage, hoping to control the people and army with future generous distributions of grain. He hoped he might win the support of the people if he timed his apparent generosity correctly. However 'the Romans … hated the man and blamed him for all their difficulties; they especially despised him for his greed.'[19]

There is evidence at this time of the organisation of an Egyptian grain fleet, plus the securing of more supply from Carthage in North Africa. At the same time, the imperial revenue was in serious trouble. One of the reasons for the unrest in the legions of Britain was the inability to pay the expected donative. Such was the problem that all the sources show Commodus attempting to raise revenue.[20] Charges were brought against senators and then dropped for a price. The *Historia Augusta* states some were accused simply for not being willing to name Commodus as the heir in their will.

This came to a head in AD 189–190. Pertinax, having suppressed the mutinous legions in Britain, was now sent to quell unrest in North Africa as governor in AD 188–189. By AD 190 he was back in Rome. Papyrius Dionysius, a distinguished equestrian, had been appointed to the post of Prefect of Egypt. Cleander rescinded this and kept him as Prefect of *Annona* in Rome. This proved to be a fatal mistake for Cleander. The population of Rome was nearly 1 million, and 200,000 households were entitled to free grain. This required 300 million tonnes of grain a year to be transported and stored. It was Dionysius who stirred up the mob against Cleander, blaming him for the shortages.

Cassius Dio tells of a curious and dramatic event at a horse race in the Circus Maximus. A crowd of children ran in, led by a 'tall maiden of grim aspect', who was taken to be a divinity. The children shouted 'bitter words' about Cleander, which was taken up by the mob. They then marched out in search of Commodus who was at the nearby Quintilian suburb, 'invoking many blessings' on Commodus, but 'many curses' on Cleander. There must have been more behind this event as it does sound rather staged. Whatever the case, Cleander's response made matters worse. He sent soldiers against the crowd and many were killed or wounded. These soldiers are likely to have been an elite cavalry unit, the Equites Singulares Augusti, who numbered around 1,000 and reported directly to Cleander. Dio reports that the mob was supported by the Praetorian Guard, but it is unclear whether they responded to the bloodshed or were part of a wider conspiracy. Whatever the case, the sources agree it was directed at Cleander and not Commodus. The emperor, however, was not to know this when he heard the roar of the mob.

His sister Fadilla rushed to warn her brother. Herodian has her telling Commodus that Cleander armed the people and the soldiers against him. His supporters and the 'entire imperial cavalry' were reported to be fighting with 'those who hate him … killing each other and choking the city with blood'. She warns 'the fury of both factions will fall upon us unless you immediately hand over to them for execution this scoundrelly servant of yours.'[21]

Cassius Dio claims it was Marcia who told Commodus, and continues with the events. Commodus was so terrified, 'he was ever the greatest coward', that he immediately ordered Cleander, and even his son, to be killed. The boy must have been young because we hear he was being reared in the emperor's charge. Sadly, the boy was 'dashed to the earth and so perished'. The Romans took the body of Cleander, dragged it away and 'abused it and carried his head all about the city on a pole'. We also read that many who had 'enjoyed great power' under Cleander were also killed.[22]

Herodian gives a similar but perhaps more dramatic end. Commodus was terrified because the danger was 'already upon him'. We have an image of the mob at the palace gates. Commodus panicked and sent for Cleander. The unsuspecting prefect appeared and the emperor ordered him 'seized and beheaded, and, impaling his head on a long spear, sent it out to the mob'.[23]

There is some debate over whether this occurred in the autumn of AD 189 or the spring of AD 190. Commodus then purged all those with links to Cleander, even his wife Damostratia, who had once been a lover of Commodus. Herodian writes that this was a turning point for Commodus. He gave himself totally to 'licentious pleasures'. Men of 'intelligence and … even a smattering of learning' were driven out and replaced by 'the filthy skits of comedians and actors'. He turned his attention to the games, taking lessons in driving the chariot and training for beast fights.[24]

This was the third major threat the emperor had survived. The first by Lucilla, the second from Maternus, and now the Roman mob. It was also the latest in a number of advisors who had met an untimely death. First, Saoterus was murdered, followed quickly by Paternus, the praetorian prefect being executed as a result of the subsequent investigation into Lucilla's plot. This allowed the rise of Perennis as the sole praetorian prefect who himself was alleged by the British Legions to have been the cause of their rebellion and plotting against Commodus. His execution allowed the rise of Cleander. With Cleander gone another freedman, Eclectus, was able to rise to prominence. However, Dionysius, the man who had incited the mob against Cleander, was himself executed.

Commodus appears to have increased his devotion to games, but in truth he was always an eager spectator and participant. There are several depictions of him associated with gladiatorial games as well as with with Hercules. Cassius Dio records that one of his many titles was 'The Roman Hercules', and statues were erected depicting him in this way. A lion-skin and club were paraded before him and placed on a chair in the amphitheatre. Commodus would enter the arena in the 'costliest finery available'.[25] On other occasions he was dressed as the god Mercury. A coin from AD 182 has him on horseback fighting a lion, but by AD 192 we see Commodus as Hercules wearing a lion skin, and on the reverse holding a club and dragging a lion. The sources record the Colossus statue outside the Colosseum had the face of Sol replaced by that of Commodus and an inscription added: 'Champion of the secutores; only left handed fighter to conquer a thousand men.' His image changed over time, with busts of a young Commodus, another of a bearded young man, and the last depicting him as Hercules.

On one occasion, Commodus opened a games by killing a hundred bears with spears from a walkway.[26] The following day he killed a variety of domestic animals, followed by a tiger, a hippopotamus and an elephant. In the afternoon he began the gladiator contests armed with a shield and wooden sword against a man with just a wooden pole. After his predictable victory he relaxed to watch the more bloodthirsty bouts. As a gladiator he continued to perform as his his favoured type, the *secutor*. In addition to

Picture 39: A young Commodus (Wikimedia Commons)

Picture 40: Commodus as an adult (Wikimedia Commons)

those above, animals he is said to have killed include lions, elephants, rhinoceroses and a giraffe. Dio describes how he had condemned men dressed up as giants and then personally killed them, acting out stories from Greek myths.

When Commodus fought, senators and equestrians felt obliged to attend. On one such occasion, Commodus killed an ostrich then held aloft its head in front of the senators, grinning as he did so.

Dio explains the danger they felt by this act: 'many would have died by the sword, there and then, for

Picture 41: Commodus as Hercules (Wikimedia Commons)

laughing at him'. A fate they avoided by chewing on some laurel leaves. After AD 190, that images of Hercules on coinage increased significantly. Dio tells of a Julius Alexander in the Eastern provinces who had emulated Commodus by killing a lion with a javelin from horseback. Commodus had him killed, perhaps in a fit of jealously. The *Historia Augusta* suggests this was a serious rebellion. Whatever the case, Commodus isolated himself from the senators and it becomes harder to excuse his actions.

The sources, biased as they are, all record an increase in executions and despotic behaviour. He ordered Rome be renamed Commodiana, the legions Commodian, and a day of Commodiana to celebrate this 'elevation'. He titled himself as follows: Emperor Caesar Lucius Aelius Aurelius Commodus Augustus Pius Felix Sarmaticus Germanicus Maximus Britannicus, Pacifier of the Whole Earth, Invincible, the Roman Hercules, Pontifex Maximus, Holder of the Tribunician Authority for the eighteenth time, Imperator for the eighth time, Consul for the seventh time, Father of his Country. Next he insisted the months be renamed in honour of this, thus calling them: Amazonius, Invictus, Felix, Pius Lucius, Aelius, Aurelius, Commodus, Augustus, Herculeus, Romanus, Exsuperatorius. Dio remarks 'so superlatively mad had the abandoned wretch become'.

So, by the summer of AD 192 he was identifying himself as Hercules and asking the senate to rename Rome, the army and the months of the year after himself. The *Historia Augusta* claims the suggestion of deification came from the senate, but it was a brave senator who argued against this.

The *Historia Augusta* also lists a long line of high-ranking people killed by Commodus, suggesting there was possibly another plot.[27] His victims included two Silani, Servilius and Dulius; Antius Lupus and two Petronii, Mamertinus and Sura, and also Mamertinus's son Antoninus (his own nephew); six former consuls (Allius Fuscus, Caelius Felix, Lucceius Torquatus, Larcius Eurupianus, Valerius Bassianus and Pactumcius Magnus); Sulpicius Crassus; the proconsul Julius Proculus; Claudius Lucanus, a man of consular rank; and his father's cousin, Annia Faustina and 'innumerable others', along with many of the families of some of those mentioned.

These suffered damnatio memoriae and had their estates confiscated and children left destitute. Many had their names restored by the Emperor Pertinax, but we can immediately see the contrast with Marcus Aurelius who vowed never to execute a senator. Even when compelled, he resorted to exile and did not punish the offender's family. One notable casualty is Mamertinus, Cornificia's husband, and thus Commodus's step-brother.

Antoninus, his nephew, also was killed. Crispina may have still been alive because it was around this time the *Historia Augusta* claims that she was accused of adultery and exiled, later being put to death in AD 191–2.

The survivors included Pertinax, who was now praetorian prefect and consul elect for AD 192, sharing the latter post with Commodus himself. Laetus, friend of Eclectus, was appointed as praetorian prefect in AD 191. Eclectus and Maria were also safe for now, but one wonders how they felt; should a plot be successful it could easily be fatal for both of them too. On the other hand, given recent history they must have been conscious of the precariousness of their position. Narcissus also remained, fatefully as it turned out for Commodus. Clodius Albinus was made governor of Britain, Pescennius Niger was given the powerful province of Syria. Severus was governor in Pannonia Superior and his brother Geta in Moesia Inferior. All these figures were to play a key role after Commodus's death and the chaos that resulted.

The last year of his life started badly with a devastating fire in Rome that burned a significant part of the city, including the Temple of Peace, and left many destitute. It might have been at this time that he introduced his higher taxes for the rich, taking two gold pieces from each senator and their family each year on his birthday in August. Senators from other cities had to give five denarii each. A major rebuilding program was undertaken, but he also erected a number of statues dedicated to himself often in the garb of Hercules. Under Commodus, many equestrians and freedmen were elected to the senate. There were only around 100 senatorial and equestrian appointments each year and these had been controlled by Cleander. He appointed twenty-five suffect consuls in one year before his death. The wealthy aristocrats were resentful, and no doubt this was reciprocated by Commodus after the attempts on his life.

One interesting fact is worth noting regarding Lucilla's son, named after his father, Tiberius Claudius Pompeianus; an inscription suggests he was at one point named Aurelius Commodus Pompeianus. This would suggest he was named this under Commodus, but dropped it after the emperor's murder. It is possible that the childless Commodus had singled out his nephew and the son of his father's amici. This alone may have made him a target under the subsequent emperors, which might explain why he reverted back. The young man was able to develop a political career and obtained the consulship in AD 209 under Severus, but ultimately was murdered by Caracalla in AD 212. Yet the indications are that both he and his father Pompeianus remained in favour through the reign of Commodus and subsequent emperors.

At the same time, the grain supply was restored and the damaged parts of the city rebuilt. Commodus also arranged a series of races in the Circus Maximus. He took the unusual step of appearing in the arena in exhibitions, something he charged the state a million sesterces for. Combatants were armed with wooden or blunt weapons. Many senators trained and fought in private just as Commodus had done, yet there was still a certain stigma attached which prevented their appearance in public. Unlike gladiatorial, contests there was no legal or social penalties for appearing in chariot races.

So far, Commodus had taken part in private bouts, opening ceremonies and beast hunts. Scandalous as this was for the Roman senators, now he planned something far more outrageous. Commodus is recorded as fighting in the public in the arena at the end of AD 192.[28] His intention must have been to put on a display like no other, and what better way than to appear and fight himself. The emperor was said to have cast aside 'all restraint' and took part in 'public shows'. He promised 'to kill with his own hands wild animals of all kinds and to fight in gladiatorial combat'. The way it is described suggests it was something completely novel. When people heard they 'hastened to Rome from all over Italy and from the neighbouring provinces to see what they had neither seen nor even heard of before'. We read of the 'skill of his hands' and that he never missed with either bow or javelin.[29]

The event opened in the amphitheatre with Commodus again dressed as Hercules. A raised platform had been erected and the arena divided into four parts. The emperor demonstrated his skill using spear and bow. Deers, gazelles, lions, leopards, an elephant and a tiger were all killed, each reportedly with a single shot. Even Herodian, usually critical, joined the crowd in appreciating the feat. Sometimes he descended to the arena floor to kill the less dangerous animals, and on one occasion he killed a hundred lions with the same number of spears. After his morning exertions he rested for lunch. When he fought as a gladiator it would seem he fought with wooden swords, although Herodian claims he did wound some of his opponents. What seems clear is that Commodus was never actually in any danger; it was more like an exhibition match before the main event.

When the paired gladiators came out they fought with sharpened blades and Commodus now looked on, dressed as the god Mercury. When some fighters were reluctant to kill their opponents, Commodus had them chained together and fight on. We hear of him descending to the floor and plunging his hands into the wound of a defeated gladiator and wiping the blood on his head. It is also at these games we hear from Cassius Dio, of the emperor killing an ostrich and waving its severed head and his sword at the watching senators. However, regardless of how appalled the senators were and how the sources record these events, what is clear is the crowd in general loved it.

During the games he honoured Laetus, the praetorian prefect, and Eclectus, his steward, by embracing them and kissing them in the arena in public. This would have again upset the senators, who would view this show of equality as disrespectful and unbecoming an emperor. Importantly, it shows that right up to the end, these two men and Marcia were held in high esteem. All three would be instrumental in his murder. The emperor now planned some form of ceremony for the festival of Saturnalia in mid- to late December. This included staying at the gladiator barracks and arriving at the arena dressed as a secutor and accompanied by gladiators. He also planned to kill the two consuls, Clarus and Falco. Herodian tells how Marcia pleaded with him not to debase the imperial image and he angrily dismissed her and called for Laetus and Eclectus to make arrangements. They too protested and he threw them out.

Commodus then retired to bed for a sleep, 'for this was his custom in the middle of the day'. But before doing so he took a wax tablet and allegedly 'wrote down the names of those who were to be put to death that night'.[30] Top of the list was Marcia, Eclectus and Laetus, followed by a number of senators, elder statesmen and advisors appointed by his father. It is possible Pompeianus was included too. Commodus then went to 'his usual baths and drinking bouts' and we hear of a remarkable twist of fate. In the palace was a very young boy, 'one of those who went about bare of clothes but adorned with gold and costly gems'. Commodus was apparently very fond of the child and 'often slept with him'. The boy was playing about the palace and wandered into the emperor's bedroom. He picked up the wax tablet and by a momentous stroke of fate walked off with it only to bump into Marcia.[31]

One can only wonder at the panic such a discovery might have created. Yet if we believe Herodian, this happened before Saturnalia (around 17 December) and the murder did not take place until the last day of the festivities on New Year's eve. Perhaps the plotters were walking on eggshells during the festivities, with Commodus unaware of their discovery; or he may have simply forgotten his angry outburst. It is possible there were other motives at play. Ecelctus and Marcia were rumoured to have been lovers, and it may be telling that they married shortly after the murder. It is also possible this was simply a story created by the senators to cover up a successful plot that was less rushed and far deeper than they wished to admit. The *Historia Augusta* states Pertinax was in on it, although Cassius Dio, an admirer of Pertinax, does not.

Interesting, too, that Pompeianus was in Rome on the night of the murder. He had retired to his estates and did not attend the senate after his wife's failed plot ten years earlier. One can only conclude he had a good reason to be there on that particular occasion. Timing was vital. Commodus was still very popular with the Praetorian Guard, the wider army and the people of Rome. On the last day of festivities much of the Praetorian Guard would have been taking part, and perhaps the worse for drink. Much of the senate too would be on hand in Rome. Commodus was also physically fit, strong and skilled with weapons, so an attack by one or even two persons might not succeed. On the final evening, 31 December, Marcia attempted to poison him. Cassius Dio claims she put it in his beef while Herodian says it was the wine. Unfortunately it didn't work and Commodus vomited. In some pain he went to the bath house where he was sick for a second time.

Marcia and Eclectus now panicked, thinking he might survive and suspect them. They approached the freedman Narcissus who was Commodus's personal wrestling partner. He entered the bath house and strangled Commodus to death. Herodian states: 'Narcissus rushed in where the emperor lay overcome by the poisoned wine, seized him by the throat, and finished him off.' While Dio has Commodus suspecting the truth: 'he indulged in some threats. Then they sent Narcissus, an athlete, against him, and caused this man to strangle him while he was taking a bath.' This is obviously far removed from the depiction in films.

After the murder Laetus and Eclectus conferred with Marcia about the next move. The story they agreed was that the emperor had died suddenly of apoplexy. They hoped this would be believed by the people and soldiers due to his 'endless and excessive orgies had prepared them for such an outcome'.[32]

What happens next shows just how nervous the killers were of what the response would be. There is every indication that, far from being universally loathed, the murder of Commodus would have angered many. Two slaves wrapped the body up and carried it through the palace, past guards who were sleeping, drunk from the festivities or simply uninterested in what the slaves were carrying. It was then loaded onto a cart and taken to the suburbs, far enough to lay undiscovered, but close enough to be viewed when necessary. The body was handed over to the Pontifex Minor, Livius Larensis. Laetus and Eclectus went to the house of Pertinax. The sources claim Pertinax was still up and expected the late visit to augur his arrest by Commodus. After being reassured he sent out a trusted man to view the body. This being done Laetus and Pertinax then sent messengers to all the senators, most of whom were still in Rome.

We are presented with two likely narratives. First, the sources describe how the plot was a rushed and panicked affair brought about by the angry reaction of Commodus to his closest advisors criticising his plans for Saturnalia. The two-week duration of the festivities is glossed over and the act placed on the last day. With the poisoning unsuccessful, they were forced to approach the wrestling partner of Commodus, who fortunately agreed to their designs and was able to finish the job. Having committed murder, the conspirators then approach an apparently unknowing Pertinax, the praetorian prefect, and presented him with a fait accompli in the hope he wouldn't kill them on the spot, or turn them in later. The senators were assembled that very night and supporters of Pertinax, such as Pompeianus, just happened to be in the city. 'And it was at this time, under Pertinax, that I myself saw Pompeianus present in the senate for both the first and the last time.' (Cassius Dio book 74.3.)

On the other hand, we have the possibility of a deeper plot set in motion in late AD 192, with Commodus's inner circle becoming increasingly disillusioned and frightened by their emperor's actions. If the sources contain an element of truth, then perhaps we can speculate a likely timeline. During the games in late AD 192 Marcia, Laetus and Eclectus were all still in favour. The argument over the festival of Saturnalia in December might have convinced them they were likely to eventually suffer the same fate as Cleander and Perennis. If Commodus did drunkenly write a list, then we are asked to accept that he forgot all about it, or this list was compiled on the last night of Saturnalia – two weeks after the initial argument. It is possible the sources invented this tale as a pretext to excuse the murder; it is more likely that Pertinax was already involved and the sources are absolving the future emperor of any guilt.

As word got out, much of the senate reacted with jubilation. Herodian claims the people, too, were 'in a frenzy of joy', although especially the wealthy and those with positions of influence, as these were always in particular danger from Commodus. Cassius Dio also claims that both the senate and populace joined in shouting 'bitter words' and insults. However, the sources also make clear the Praetorian Guard were still loyal to Commodus and their support was vital. Herodian reports that 'all the people therefore went out to the camp to force the praetorians to submit'. Laetus, Eclectus and Pertinax arrived and Laetus ordered the praetorians to assemble.[33]

In his address, Laetus explained that Commodus had died of apoplexy and presented them with Pertinax, describing his illustrious career, reminding them that many had fought with him on campaigns in Parthia and along the Danube, and promising his reign would please them. The assembled crowd proclaimed him emperor but the guard, ominously, were restrained. Dio remarks that the soldiers were quiet and it was only the promise of 12,000 sesterces each that placated them. However he adds:

> they suspected that all the privileges granted them by Commodus in violation of precedent would be abolished, and they were displeased; nevertheless, they remained quiet, concealing their anger
>
> Cassius Dio book 74.1

Pertinax then went to the senate house 'while it was still night', and told the assembled elite he had been proclaimed emperor by the soldiers but he immediately offered his resignation, saying: 'I do not want the office and shall resign it at once, this very day, because of my age and feeble health, and because of the distressing state of affairs.' Whether this was false modesty or his genuine sentiment, the senate proclaimed him as well and declared Commodus a public enemy.

With Commodus suffering damnatio memoriae, a law was passed restoring the name of many of his victims. Those convicted of majestas were now allowed to be reburied and their names restored, both figuratively and in inscriptions. Pertinax indicated he wished to work with the senate and took a formal oath never to sentence one of their number to death. In short, he seems to have presented himself as a restoration to the type of rule of Marcus Aurelius and a complete break from Commodus. He also had Pompeianus and Acilius Galbrio sit with him on the imperial bench, signifying joint rule.

Pertinax also praised Laetus and retained Eclectus and Marcia in service. This was too much for some, and they expressed their views in the senate. We must remember, many senators owed their positions to Commodus and would have been nervous at the turn of events. The praetorians too were uneasy and must have been horrified that their favoured emperor was being denigrated and his statues torn down. To make matters worse, Pertinax increased discipline and they saw some of their perks being curtailed. However, for the time being at least, there was the semblance of stability. Some may well have suspected the truth about Commodus's death, others may have worried about their position under a new regime. But for the most part, many more must have been relieved.

In summary, Commodus was a complex character and well portrayed by Joaquin Phoenix in *Gladiator*. He didn't, however, die in the arena at the hands of a 'father to a murdered son, husband to a murdered wife'. Rather, he died in the bath, strangled to death, after being poisoned by his lover and closest advisor. It is possible history has been unkind. Becoming emperor at the age of 18 was difficult enough, being nearly murdered two years later in a plot arranged by his own sister must have been even harder to bear. The would-be assassin had cried, 'See! This is what the senate has sent you', and Commodus seems to have neither forgotten nor forgiven them. He certainly never trusted them again.

The change in roles and increased power for equestrians and freedmen increased friction. Much of those changes may have occurred without Commodus as the empire expanded and evolved. It is possible that some of the criticisms and allegations against Commodus were exaggerations or lies from his political enemies, many of which were in the senate. Perhaps his more outlandish behaviour was simply designed to demonstrate his power rather than a true belief he was the god Mercury, or the reincarnation of Hercules. He may have had senators executed, but it is also a fact that many of them would have killed him given the chance. Yet some of his actions in the latter part of his reign are harder to justify. Renaming Rome and the army after himself seems particularly narcissistic.

What we can say is that after Commodus, Rome did not return to the republic. There were no kindly, conscientious group of senators standing by to restore stable competent government. None of his surviving sisters gave rousing speeches in the Colosseum, unlike in *Gladiator* where, as Commodus and Maximus lie dead on the arena floor, Lucilla turns to Senator Gracchus and says, 'Is Rome worth one good man's life? We believed it once. Make us believe it again.' The film ends with the implication that with a tyrant dead, there is at least the chance of a restoration to 'good government'. Yet Rome was never a democracy or some ideal utopia. Certainly not for the bulk of ordinary people, let alone the large percentage who were slaves.

Nor were there generals such as Lucius Quinctius Cincinnatus, who was appointed dictator twice during the early republic but retired from public life when his duty was served. There was a chance the empire may have returned to the stability of Marcus Aurelius. Pertinax is treated well by the sources. Unfortunately, his reign was cut short and the empire descended into arguably worse turmoil than under Commodus.

Chapter 7

After Commodus

Cassius Dio describes Pertinax as an 'excellent and upright man'. He certainly had a remarkable career. He was born on 1 August AD 126, the son of a freed slave in Liguria, north-east Italy. Pertinax initially worked as a teacher but relatively late in life, in his mid-thirties, he began a career in the army with the help of patronage, which also elevated him to the equestrian class. He served as a cavalry officer in the Roman-Parthian War, AD 161–166. His next appointment was as a military tribune in legio VI Victrix, based at York in Britain. The next step was as a commander of an auxiliary unit, I or II Tungrorum, also in northern Britain, and then in charge of a unit in Moesia in the Marcomannic Wars.

He served as procurator in Dacia before falling foul of palace intrigue and being recalled to Rome. His new patron, Pompeianus, resurrected his career, and he served with distinction on the Danube. In AD 175 he received a suffect consulship, a remarkable achievement on its own for a son of a slave. He then served as governor of various provinces, Moesia, Dacia and Syria. He had briefly been forced out of favour by Perennis under Commodus, but was recalled to Britain to pacify the three mutinous legions. In AD 185 the legions of Britain rebelled and attempted to appoint their own emperor. The legates were removed and a contingent of 1,500 javelin men travelled to Rome from Britain and convinced Commodus to remove Perennis. The legions tried to declare Pertinax emperor too but he refused, and for his pains was ambushed and nearly killed. In AD 187 he resigned, stating the legions were hostile to his rule. He was still in favour with Commodus, as he was appointed proconsul of

Picture 42: Emperor Pertinax (Wikimedia Commons)

Africa. He served as consul for a second time alongside Commodus and then was appointed praetorian prefect.

Unfortunately, the Praetorian Guard felt rather differently. It did not take long for the first attempt of regime change to be uncovered. While he was in nearby Ostia in early AD 193 he was informed of a plot by a group of praetorian officers to replace him with the consul Quintus Sosius Falco. Pertinax rushed back to Rome and the senate declared Falco a public enemy. The emperor kept his promise not to execute a senator and merely banished him to his estates. On 28 March he heard of further unrest in the praetorian camp and sent his father-in-law and Urban Prefect, Sulpicianus, to their camp. Unfortunately this did not prevent around 300 armed Praetorians marching on the palace. The sources claim that many of the palace staff favoured Commodus and so allowed the guards entry. Laetus, the sole praetorian prefect, refused to intervene.

Map 12 shows a plan of Rome and what is immediately clear is how compact it was. The city had spread beyond its original Servian Wall, built in the early republic over 500 hundred years before. We get a hint at how extensive it was in the second century by the dotted line representing the later Aurelian Wall, built c. AD 275. One could walk between the palace buildings, forum, senate house and Colosseum in a matter of minutes. The praetorian camp, outside the original city walls, was less than two miles from the palace. In the second century it was likely the Urban Cohorts were also barracked there. Also marked is the location of the fire of AD 192. Galen, who was out of the city at the time, records the areas damaged: a storeroom building on the Via Sacra (between the senate and the Colosseum); the Temple of Peace; and the libraries on the Palatine, presumably in front of the palace complex. We can also imagine how Commodus would have heard the mob from the Circus Maximus a short distance away, which ended with the death of Cleander.

Pertinax apparently had the opportunity to escape but chose to leave his rooms and meet the guards face to face, with Eclectus at his side. In the dramatic stand off that followed, Pertinax addressed them and all but one of the guards were shamed into sheathing their swords. Tausius from Gaul, however, struck the emperor down, causing many others to join in the carnage. Eclectus bravely wounded some of the assailants before he too was killed. They then cut off the emperor's head, stuck it on a spear and marched back to their camp. There seems to have been nothing planned about the murder as there was no candidate waiting in the wings. This led to what was described as one of the most disgraceful episodes of Roman history, and the cause of the 'year of the five emperors'.

Map 15: Rome c. AD 192

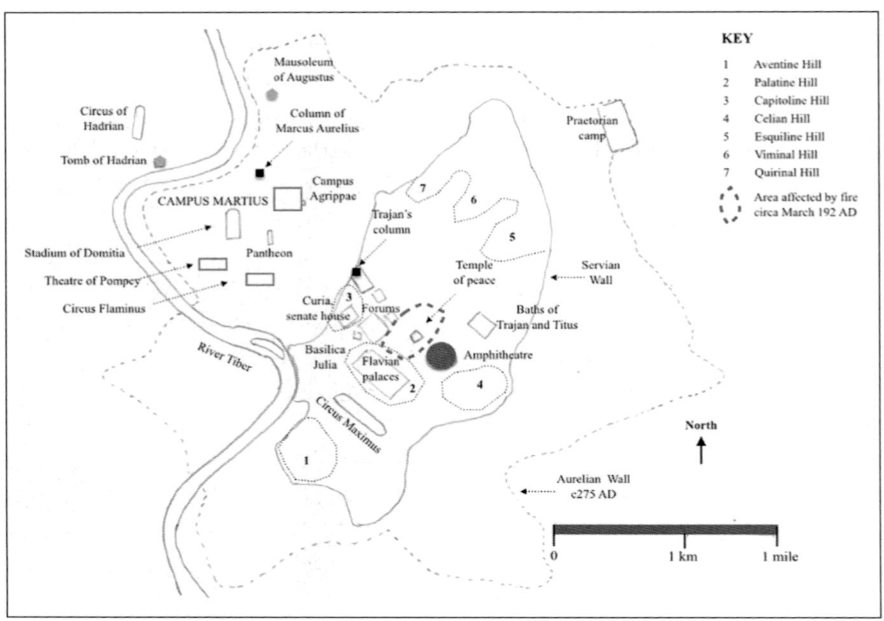

As word got out, many senators feared the guard would hunt them down for their support of Pertinax and death of Commodus. Back in the camp Sulpicianus saw an opportunity and on their return offered them a donation to secure their support for the throne for himself. He wasn't alone; Didius Severus Julianus, urged on by his guests at a dinner party, rushed to the praetorian camp only to be refused entry. He was forced to shout out his own offer. The praetorians quickly realised their position as middle men and went back and forth encouraging higher bids. Sulpicianus got to 20,000 sesterces. Julianus reminded them that the son-in-law of Pertinax might take revenge on his murders, promised he would restore the name of Commodus and the Guards' privileges and raised his offer to 25,000, promising the cash immediately. This was enough and they escorted their new emperor to the senate who endorsed him through gritted teeth being surrounded by armed praetorians. Laetus was removed from post and, along with Marcia, soon executed.

The Roman citizens responded negatively, calling him a thief and murderer. Julianus might just have survived without the initial support of much of the senate and the hostility of the mob, but he quickly lost support of the army and that proved fatal. Pescennius Niger commanded the legions of the East, Septimius Severus the legions of the Danube and Clodius Albinus the three legions of Britain. All three declared themselves emperor. Niger was especially popular with the populace, and the mob in Rome were heard chanting his name. Severus, however, was the closest.

Severus secured his western flank by agreeing to declare Albinus Caesar in return for his support for Severus. Then he marched on Rome. Meanwhile, the increasingly desperate Julianus realised he had little support and the Praetorian Guard might not be a match against several battle-hardened legions from the north, let alone the threat from Niger or Albinus. He summoned Pompeianus to Rome and asked him to take the throne. Pompeianus refused, perhaps because of old age or more likely he saw it as a poisoned chalice that would result in his death and that of his son.

Picture 43: Didius Julianus (Wikimedia Commons)

Picture 44: Pescennius Niger (Wikimedia Commons)

Picture 45: Clodius Albinus (Wikimedia Commons)

Picture 46: Septimius Severus (Wikimedia Commons)

Senator Quintillis was married to Fadilla, sister to Commodus. He had returned to Rome after the death of Pertinax and his words proved pivotal when Julianus came to the senate. The emperor proposed he lead the senate, the priests and the Vestal Virgins out of Rome to meet Severus on the road. He probably saw this as his only chance of saving his skin. Quintillis opposed the motion and declared that if he could not withstand Severus by force of arms he had no right to rule. Julianus was humiliated and retreated to the palace, where the praetorians refused to force the senate to do anything. Julianus was forced to recall the senate to propose Severus as joint emperor, which was agreed.

Unfortunately, things quickly unravelled for the emperor. Severus had promised no harm to the Guard so long as the murderers of Pertinax were handed over. The senate was recalled by the two consuls, Severus declared sole emperor and Julianus condemned to death. A tribune found the emperor alone in the palace and his last words were: 'But what evil have I done? Whom have I killed?' Severus wasted no time after entering Rome. He hunted down all the remaining conspirators of the murders of Pertinax and Commodus. Narcissus the wrestler was thrown to the beasts in the arena.

Severus assembled the praetorians in ceremonial dress without their armour and weapons. He harangued them for their disloyalty and their actions in murdering Pertinax and selling the empire. They had their ceremonial daggers removed and were dismissed and forbidden from within 100 miles of Rome on pain of death. Civil war soon erupted, with members of the senate supporting one of the now three claimants.

Severus first turned his attention on the approaching Niger defeating him several times before he was captured and beheaded after the battle of Issus in AD 194. Severus declared his son Caracalla as his heir. Albinus in Britain now realised he had been duped by Severus, his title of Caesar had meant nothing. He declared himself emperor and crossed to Gaul taking control over much of Iberia too. Severus then turned his attention west and finally defeated Albinus at the battle of Lugdunum in Gaul on 19 February AD 197. In captured papers there were letters from various senators offering support. Severus sent the head of Albinus on to Rome as a message. Those senators who had openly supported Albinus he pardoned, but those who had conspired in secret, he condemned to death. Sulpicianus, the father-in-law of Pertinax who was beaten to the prize of emperor by Julianus, was executed, along with twenty-nine others.

Severus proved to be a strong and able ruler. The empire reached its greatest extent under his rule. The Severan dynasty lasted until AD 235 and its end occurred on the northern frontier where our story began, and coincidentally where Septimius Severus began his march on Rome after the murder of Commodus's successor. Pertinax himself had spent much of his time fighting along the Danube under Marcus Aurelius, and alongside two men whose career most closely resembled our fictional hero, Maximus. First, his friend and mentor Pompeianus, and second, Marcus Valerius Maximianus.

Septimius Severus was the only Severan to die of natural causes. His son Caracalla killed his own brother, Geta, a year after their father's death. Caracalla was himself murdered five years later. Macrinus lasted a year before being executed. His 9-year-old son, Diadumenian, was caught within a month and beheaded. Elagabalus was murdered at 18 and his body thrown in the Tiber. Severus Alexander managed to last thirteen years before he too was killed.

Just as in the time of Marcus Aurelius there was war in the East. The Romans had been partially victorious despite suffering heavy losses. Severus, though, claimed victory and held a triumph. In AD 234 Germanic warriors once more crossed the Rhine and Danube. The Emperor attempted to bribe the Germans and this seems to have been the final straw. The legions rebelled and Severus Alexander was murdered while at a meeting with his generals at Moguntiacum, modern-day Mainz, on the Rhine. So ended the Severan dynasty. His successor was Maximinus. His reign is generally seen as the start of the 'Crisis of the Third Century'. This was a period lasting nearly five decades, racked by civil wars, barbaric invasions and migrations, and political instability. It ended with the reign of Diocletian who imposed a series of political, administrative and military reforms to bring a level of order back.

Gladiator won a well-deserved Oscar for best film. But we started off this book with the question: would we have been just as entertained if this, and other films, were more historically accurate? I would argue we would. The bloody war on the northern frontier included dramatic victories over Rome by both Germanic and Sarmatian armies. The Column of Marcus Aurelius shows vividly the devastating response. The opportunity to show shields and armour behaving as they should, would not detract from fighting scenes. Nor would more realistic battle tactics. We have also seen how the political intrigue and friction between the senate, equestrians, the emperor, army and others is interesting and dramatic enough for any audience. From the revolt of Avidius Cassius under Marcus Aurelius to the many plots against Commodus. The last plot, which resulted in the year of the five emperors, could be a film all on its own. Full of betrayal, double crossing and murder. I hope I have convinced the reader that the real history is every bit as entertaining as anything the film industry has produced.

Sources and citations for maps and pictures not by author

Maps

Map 1: Roman Empire c. AD 117. Image from Wiki commons. Roman Empire during reign of Trajan. Roman dependencies in light grey. Author: Tataryn77. CC BY-SA 3.0, https://commons.wikimedia.org/w/index.php?curid=17030479

Map 2: Imperial and Senatorial provinces AD 117. Image from wiki commons. Author: Andrei nacu. Public domain https://commons.wikimedia.org/w/index.php?curid=23100228

Map 5: Barbarian tribes and Roman provinces, second century. Image adapted from wiki commons. Roman Empire at the time of Hadrian c. AD 125. Author: Furfur, German localization (with minor changes) of the original Image:Roman_Empire_125.svg, made by Andrei nacu - Own work, CC BY-SA 3.0, https://commons.wikimedia.org/w/index.php?curid=6358523

Map 6 First Marcomannic War. Image adapted from from wiki commons. CC BY-SA 3.0, https://commons.wikimedia.org/w/index.php?curid=1644381

Map 7 Second and Third Marcomannic Wars AD 177-180, AD 180-182. Image adapted from from wiki commons. Map of Roman Empire. CC BY-SA 3.0, https://commons.wikimedia.org/w/index.php?curid=1644381

Map 8: Roman road network second century Image amended from wiki commons. Author: Furfur, German localization (with minor changes) of the original Image: Roman_Empire_125.svg, made by Andrei nacu - Own work CC BY-SA 3.0, https://commons.wikimedia.org/w/index.php?curid=6358523

Sources and citations for maps and pictures not by author

Pictures

Picture 1: Roman onager. Image from wiki commons. Author: Hermann Diels (1848-1922) - Antike Technik: Sechs Vorträge, Public domain https://commons.wikimedia.org/w/index.php?curid=37717934

Picture 2: Reproduction of Roman ballista. Image from wiki commons. Photograph by Rolf Krahl - dsc_3735, CC BY-SA 2.0, https://commons.wikimedia.org/w/index.php?curid=42587336

Picture 3: Roman sling bullet from a scorpion. Image from wiki commons. Photograph by Peter van der Sluijs - Own work, CC BY-SA 3.0, https://commons.wikimedia.org/w/index.php?curid=24023723

Picture 4: The Column of Marcus Aurelius. Image from wiki commons. Author: Photo by giggel. CC BY 3.0, https://commons.wikimedia.org/w/index.php?curid=58997430

Picture 5: Detail from The Column of Marcus Aurelius. Image from wiki commons. Author: Jebulon - Own work CC0, https://commons.wikimedia.org/w/index.php?curid=30857810

Picture 6: Roman carroballista from column of Marcus Aurelius. Image from wiki commons. Matthias Kabel, Own work CC BY-SA 3.0, https://commons.wikimedia.org/w/index.php?curid=6077612

Picture 7: The Miracle of the Rain scene. Image from wiki commons. Detail from the Column of Marcus Aurelius in Rome. The event in the picture is the so-called 'rain miracle in the territory of the Quadi', in which a rain god, answering a prayer from the emperor, rescues Roman troops by a terrible storm, a miracle later claimed by the Christians for the Christian God. Author: Barosaurus Lentus. Own work, CC BY 3.0, https://commons.wikimedia.org/w/index.php?curid=7268210

Picture 8: Soldiers wearing lorica segmentata. Image from wiki commons. Detail from Column of Marcus Aurelius in Rome. Photo by Barosaurus Lentus. Own work, CC BY 3.0, https://commons.wikimedia.org/w/index.php?curid=7268320

Picture 9: Soldiers wearing lorica squamata and lorica hamata. Image from wiki commons. Detail from Column of Marcus Aurelius, Rome. Photo by Barosaurus Lentus -Own work, CC BY 3.0, https://commons.wikimedia.org/w/index.php?curid=7268351

Picture 10: Captured woman scene. Image from wiki commons. Detail of the Column of Marcus Aurelius, Rome. Author: Carole Raddato CC BY-SA 2.0, https://commons.wikimedia.org/w/index.php?curid=45976585

Picture 11: Roman and Sarmatian cavalry. Image from wiki commons. Cavalry battle against Sarmatians, scene xxxvii, Trajan's Column. Author: Attributed to Apollodorus of Damascus - Conrad Cichorius: "Die Reliefs der Traianssäule", Erster Tafelband: "Die Reliefs des Ersten Dakischen Krieges", Tafeln 1–57, Verlag von Georg Reimer, Berlin 1896 Public Domain, https://commons.wikimedia.org/w/index.php?curid=5118017

Picture 12: Replica Roman gladius sword. Image from wiki commons. 'Albion Augustus Roman Gladius 2'. Author: Søren Niedziella, Denmark. CC BY 2.0, https://commons.wikimedia.org/w/index.php?curid=21501182

Picture 13: Roman pila. Image from wiki commons. Public Domain, https://commons.wikimedia.org/w/index.php?curid=465215

Picture 14: Roman plumbatae. Image from wiki commons. Author: Faganarms Inc. CC BY-SA 3.0, https://commons.wikimedia.org/w/index.php?curid=19658481

Picture 15: Roman legionary wearing lorica segmentata. Photograph by permission of Matthew Parkes of Petuaria Revisited and the Legio VI Victrix, Eboracum re-enactment group

Picture 16: Roman legionary wearing lorica hamata. Photograph by permission of Matthew Parkes of Petuaria Revisited and the Legio VI Victrix, Eboracum re-enactment group

Picture 17: Roman centurion with scutum shield and pilum. Photograph by permission of Matthew Parkes of Petuaria Revisited and the Legio VI Victrix, Eboracum re-enactment group

Picture 18: Late Roman soldiers wearing lorica squamata. Photograph by permission of Ross Cronshaw of Magister Militum reenactment group

Picture 19: Reproduction Roman gladius sword. Photo by permission of Matthew Parkes of Petuaria Revisited

Picture 20: Reproduction Centurion helmet. Photo by permission of Matthew Parkes of Petuaria Revisited.

Picture 21: Reproduction Roman legionary gallic helmet. Photo by permission of Matthew Parkes of Petuaria Revisited

Picture 22: Reproduction Roman ballista. Photo by permission of Matthew Parkes of 'Petuaria Revisited'.

Picture 23: Emperor Hadrian. Image from wiki commons. Bronze bust of the Roman Emperor Hadrian 2nd century AD at the Greco-Roman Museum in Alexandria Egypt AG. Author: Allan Gluck. CC BY 4.0, https://commons.wikimedia.org/w/index.php?curid=87621520

Picture 24: Emperor Antoninus Pius. Image from wiki commons. Portrait bust of Antoninus Pius (A.D. 138-161). Inv. No. S 2436. Athens, Ancient Agora Museum (1-2-2020). Author: George E. Koronaios. CC0, https://commons.wikimedia.org/w/index.php?curid=86576398

Picture 25: A young Marcus Aurelius. Image from wiki commons. Bust of Marcus Aurelius, first half of the 2nd century CE, white marble. Author: Yair Haklai - Own work, CC BY-SA 4.0, https://commons.wikimedia.org/w/index.php?curid=80049978

Picture 26: Emperor Marcus Aurelius. Image from wiki commons. Portrait of Emperor Marcus Aurelius. Discovered at Acqua Traversa, near Rome, 1674. Author: Marie-Lan Nguyen (2011), CC BY 2.5, https://commons.wikimedia.org/w/index.php?curid=12915724

Picture 27: Lucius Verus. Marble portrait of the co-emperor Lucius Verus. Image from wiki commons. Author: Pierre Selim. Lent by Musée du Louvre, Département des antiquités grecques, étrusques et romaines. CC0, https://commons.wikimedia.org/w/index.php?curid=21497084

Picture 28: Annia Aurelia Galeria Lucilla Image from wiki commons. Head of Annia Aurelia Galeria Lucilla (148 or 150 - 182) (?), daughter of emperor Marcus Aurelius; marble; Roman art; Collections of the Musée de Mariemont, Belgique. Author: JoJan. Public Domain. https://commons.wikimedia.org/w/index.php?curid=74033483

Picture 29: Lucilla or her mother Faustina. Image from wiki commons. Marble bust : Faustina Minor or her daughter Annia Lucilla. About 162-170 AD. From the house of Jason Magnus, at Cyrène (Libia). Room 70, British Museum, GR 1861.11-27.18 (Sculpture 1468). Author: Vassil. CC0, https://commons.wikimedia.org/w/index.php?curid=79362590

Picture 30: Hoplomachus vs Thraex. Image from wiki commons. Detail of the Gladiator mosaic floor, a Hoplomachus fighting a Thraex, Römerhalle, Bad Kreuznach, Germany. Author: Carole Raddato from FRANKFURT, Germany. Uploaded by Marcus Cyron, CC BY-SA 2.0, https://commons.wikimedia.org/w/index.php?curid=30157029

Picture 31: Thraex vs Murmillo. Image from wiki commons. Detail of Gladiator mosaic, a Thraex (left) fighting a Murmillo (right), Römerhalle, Bad Kreuznach, Germany. Author: Carole Raddato from FRANKFURT, Germany. Uploaded by Marcus Cyron, CC BY-SA 2.0, https://commons.wikimedia.org/w/index.php?curid=30157015

Picture 32: Provocator vs Provocator. Image from wiki commons. Author: Gladiatorenschule Berlin - Own work, CC BY-SA 4.0, https://commons.wikimedia.org/w/index.php?curid=87589097

Picture 33: Retiarius vs Secutor. Image from wiki commons. Mosaic showing a retiarius (net-fighter) named Kalendio fighting a secutor named Astyanax. The lanista, master of gladiators, cheers them on. The outcome is shown above and confirmed by the inscriptions; the word VICIT appears beside Astyanax, and beside Kalendio's name is an O with a line through it, an abbreviation for Obiit or death. 3rd century AD, National Archaeological Museum of Spain, Madrid. Author: Carole Raddato from FRANKFURT, Germany -, CC BY-SA 2.0, https://commons.wikimedia.org/w/index.php?curid=37878968

Picture 34: Scissor vs Retiarius. Image from wiki commons. Retiarius and Scissor in a show fight in Carnuntum 2015. Author: MatthiasKabel - Own work, CC BY-SA 4.0, https://commons.wikimedia.org/w/index.php?curid=59809470

Picture 35: Eques vs Eques. Image from wiki commons. Detail of Gladiator mosaic, two Eques fighting equipped with lance, sword and the traditional small round shield, Römerhalle, Bad Kreuznach, Germany. Author: Carole Raddato from FRANKFURT, Germany. Uploaded by Marcus Cyron, CC BY-SA 2.0, https://commons.wikimedia.org/w/index.php?curid=30157041

Picture 36: Mounted eques. Image from wiki commons. Gladiator eques during a show in Carnuntum. Author: MatthiasKabel - Own work, CC BY 2.5,https://commons.wikimedia.org/w/index.php?curid=2325276

Picture 37: Colosseum. Image from wiki commons. Author: Andreas Ribbefjord, sv:Bild:Colosseum-2003-07-09.jpg, CC BY-SA 3.0, https://commons.wikimedia.org/w/index.php?curid=51319

Picture 38: Colosseum Interior. Image from wiki commons. CC BY-SA 3.0, https://commons.wikimedia.org/w/index.php?curid=132875

Picture 39: A young Commodus. Image from wiki commons. Commodus - bust in the Louvre (Ma 1123), Paris.Author: ChrisO - Transferred from en.wikipedia, CC BY-SA 3.0, https://commons.wikimedia.org/w/index.php?curid=240331

Picture 40: Adult Commodus. image from wiki commons. Bust of Commodus Museum Ephesos/Turkey. Author: Segafredo18 - Own work, CC BY-SA 3.0, https://commons.wikimedia.org/w/index.php?curid=4448976

Picture 41: Commodus as Hercules. Image from wiki commons. Bust of Commodus as Hercules, hence the lion skin, the club and the golden apples of the Hesperides. Found in an underground chamber in the area of the Horti Lamiani, 1874. Author: Marie-Lan Nguyen (2006), Public Domain, https://commons.wikimedia.org/w/index.php?curid=54636971

Picture 42: Emperor Pertinax. Image from wiki commons. Possible statue of Roman Emperor Pertinax, originating from Apulum (modern Alba-Iulia, Romania). In display at National Museum of the Union. Author: Codrin.B - Own work, CC BY-SA 3.0, https://commons.wikimedia.org/w/index.php?curid=16920962

Picture 43: Didius Julianus. Image from wiki commons. Bust of Didius Julianus (cropped), Residenz Museum, Munich. Author: © José Luiz

Bernardes Ribeiro, CC BY-SA 3.0, https://commons.wikimedia.org/w/index.php?curid=62416650

Picture 44: Pescennius Niger. Image from wiki commons. Pescennius Niger, 193-194, Aureus, Antioch. Aureus Obv: IMP CAES C PESC NIGER IVST AVG - Laureate, draped and cuirassed bust right. Rev: IOVICAPPRVRB - Jupiter seated left, holding Victory and scepter. Unlisted RIC, Calico 2406. Author: Numismatica Ars Classica NAC AG - http://www.dirtyoldcoins.com/roman/id/niger/niger021.jpg, CC BY-SA 3.0 de, https://commons.wikimedia.org/w/index.php?curid=32922120

Picture 45: Clodius Albinus. Image from wiki commons. Denarius of Clodius Albinus as consul and caesar. Author: Nicolas Perrault III - Own work, CC0, https://commons.wikimedia.org/w/index.php?curid=73050207

Picture 46: Septimius Severus. Image from wiki commons. Bust of Septimius Severus (reign 193–211 CE). White, fine-grained marble, modern restorations (nose, parts of the beard, draped bust). Palazzo Becquavila in Verona; purchased in Rome in 1822. Author: Bibi Saint-Pol, own work, 2007-02-08, Public Domain, https://commons.wikimedia.org/w/index.php?curid=1959071

References

Aurelius, Marcus, *Meditations*, (Penguin Classics, London, 2006).

Beard, Mary, *SPQR A History of Ancient Rome*, (Profile Books, London, 2016)

Birley, Anthony, *The Roman Government of Britain*, (Oxford University Press, Oxford, 2005).

Bishop, M.C., Gladiators, *Fighting to the Death in Ancient Rome,* (Casemate, Oxford, 2017).

Bishop, M.C., *Lucius Verus and the Roman Defence of the East*, (Pen and Sword, Barnsley, 2018).

D'Amato, R. and Negin, A., *Decorated Roman Armour, from the Age of the Kings to the Death of Justinian the great*, (Frontline Books, Barnsley, 2017).

D'Amato, Raffaele and Sumner, Graham, *Arms and Armour of the Imperial Roman Soldier, from Marius to Commodus, 112 BC – AD 192*, (Frontline Books, London, 2009).

Dando-Collins, Stephen, *Legions of Rome*, (Thomas Dunne Books, New York, 2010).

Davenport, Caillan, *A History of the Roman Equestrian Order*, (Cambridge University Press, Cambridge, 2019).

De La Bedoyere, Guy, Gladius, *Living Fighting and Dying in the Roman Army*, (Little Brown, London, 2020).

Elliott, Simon, *Romans at War*, (Casemate, Oxford, 2020).

Epplett, Christopher, *Gladiators and Beast Hunts*, (Pen and Sword, Barnsley, 2020).

Esposito, Gabriele, *Armies of the Late Roman Empire AD 284–476, History Organisation and Equipment*, (Pen and Sword Books, Barnsley, 2018).

Ferris, Ian, *Hate and War, The Column of Marcus Auelius*, (The History Press, Stroud, 2009).

Goldsworthy, Adrian, *Pax Romana*, (Weidenfeld and Nicolson, London, 2016).

Goldsworthy, Adrian, *The Fall of the West,* (Phoenix, London, 2010).

Goldsworthy, Adrian, *The Complete Roman Army,* (Thames and Hudson, London, 2003).

Goldsworthy, Adrian, *Roman Warfare* (Phoenix, London, 2000).

Grant, Michael, *The Antonines*, (Routledge, London, 1994).

Hamilton, Walter, *Ammianus Marcellinus, The Later Roman Empire AD 354–378* (Penguin Books, London, 1986).

Hopkins, Keith and Beard, Mary, *The Colosseum*, (Profile Books, London, 2005).

Kershaw, Stephen, *Barbarians, Rebellion and Resistance to Ancient Rome*, (Robinson, London, 2019).

Levick, Barbara, *The Government of the Roman Empire*, (Routledge, London, 2000).

Low, D.M., *Gibbon's The Decline and Fall of the Roman Empire,* (Chatto and Windus, London, 1981).

McHugh, John, *The Emperor Commodus, God and Gladiator*, (Pen and Sword, Barnsley, 2015).

McLynn, Frank, *Marcus Aurelius, Warrior, Philosopher, Emperor*, (Vintage, London, 2010).

Milner, N.P., *Vegetius: Epitome of Military Science 2nd Ed* (Liverpool Universety Press, Liverpool, 2011).

Mortimer, Paul and Bunker, Matt, *The Sword in Anglo-Saxon England from the 5th to 7th Century*, (Anglo-Saxon Books, Ely, 2019).

Mortimer, Paul, *Woden's Warriors, Warriors and Warfare in 6th-7th Century Northern Europe*, (Anglo-Saxon Books, Ely, 2011).

Moscsy, Andras, *Pannonia and Upper Moesia, A History of the Middle Danube Provinces of the Roman Empire*, (Routledge, Abingdon, 2014).

Nossov, Konstantin, *Gladiator, The Complete Guide to Ancient Rome's Bloody Fighters*, (Lyons Press, Guilford, 2011).

Penrose, Jane, *Rome and Her Enemies*, (Osprey Publishing, Oxford, 2005)

Pollard, Nigel and Berry, Joanne, *The Complete Roman Legions*, (Thames and Hudson, London, 2015).

Procopius (translated by Williamson, G & Sarris, P.), *The Secret History,* (Penguin Books, London, 2007).

Rivet, A.L.F and Smith, Colin, *The Place-Names of Roman Britain,* (Batsford, London, 1982).

Salway, Peter, *A History of Roman Britain,* (Oxford University Press, Oxford, 2001).

Scarre, Chris, *Chronicle of the Roman Emperors*, (Thames and Hudson, London, 2007).

Southern, Patricia, *Roman Britain, A New History 55 BC- AD 450*, (Amberley Publishing, Stroud, 2013).
Tacitus, *Agricola and Germanis*, (Penguin Classics, London, 2009).
Taylor, Don, *Roman Empire at War*, (Pen and Sword, Barnsley, 2016).
Travis, Hiliary and Travis, John, *Roman Body Armour*, (Amberley, Stroud, 2012).
Travis, Hiliary and Travis, John, *Roman Helmets*, (Amberley, Stroud, 2016).
Travis, Hiliary and Travis, John, *Roman Shields*, (Amberley, Stroud, 2016).
Underwood, Richard, *Anglo-Saxon Weapons and Warfare,* (Tempus Publishing Ltd, Stroud, 1999).
Webster, Graham, *The Roman Imperial Army*, (A & C Black, London, 1981).

Websites

Tod's Workshop https://www.youtube.com/channel/UCWnlQMQ-ACfhpD68yWRsnJw
Lindybiege https://www.youtube.com/user/lindybeige
Skallagrim https://www.youtube.com/user/SkallagrimNilsson
Shadiversity https://www.youtube.com/user/shadmbrooks
Metatron https://www.youtube.com/channel/UCIjGKyrdT4Gja0VLO40RlOw
ThegnThrand https://www.youtube.com/channel/UCNz5BlP5XafcfOWGbxCAgxQ
scholagladiatoria https://www.youtube.com/channel/UCt14YOvYhd5FCGCwcjhrOdA

Endnotes

Chapter 1

1. Beard, 2016: 59
2. Beard, 2016: 60
3. Beard, 2016: 56
4. Beard, 2016: 91
5. Beard, 2016: 218
6. Beard, 2016: 373
7. Beard, 2016: 422
8. Scarre, 2007: 90
9. Scarre, 2007: 94
10. Scarre, 2007: 96
11. Scarre, 2007: 98
12. Cassius Dio book 69.23.2
13. Scarre, 2007: 105
14. Historia Augusta: Life of Hadrian 25.8
15. Scarre, 2007: 106
16. Scarre, 2007: 107
17. Historia Augusta: Life of Antoninus 13.3
18. McLynn, 2009: 3-4
19. McLynn, 2009: 6
20. McLynn, 2009: 10
21. Levick, 2000: xix
22. McLynn, 2009: 13
23. McLynn, 2009: 10
24. McLynn, 2009: 87
25. McLynn, 2009: 88
26. McLynn, 2009: 90
27. McLynn, 2009: 80
28. McLynn, 2009: 177

Chapter 2

1. Ammianus Book 23.14-15
2. Goldsworthy, 2003: 192
3. Goldsworthy, 2003: 244
4. Ammianus Book 23.4
5. Bedoyere, 2020: 212
6. Milner, 2011: 89
7. Milner, 2011: 24 & 80-81
8. Milner, 2011: 10
9. D'Amato and Sumner, 2009: 65
10. Halsall, 2003: 173
11. Milner, 2011: 98
12. Caesar Gallic Wars book VII 87-88
13. Tacitus, Book 2.14
14. Elliott, 2020: 202
15. Goldsworthy, 2000: 175
16. Cassius Dio book 54.20
17. Davidson, 1998: 189
18. Davidson, 1998: 189
19. Davidson, 1998: 192
20. Davidson, 1998: 189
21. Hughes, 2020: 50-51
22. Penrose, 2005: 210
23. Mocsy, 1974: 109
24. Mocsy, 1974: 103
25. Mocsy, 1974: 183
26. Mocsy, 1974: 184
27. Mocsy, 1974: 184
28. Dio Cassius book 72.2
29. Elliott, 2020: 203
30. Dio Cassius 72.7
31. Elliott, 2020: 204
32. Taylor, 2016: 176
33. Elliott, 2020: 206
34. Elliott, 2020: 206
35. Ferris, 2009: 42
36. https://orbis.stanford.edu

Chapter 3

1. Webster, 1981: 109
2. Webster, 1981: 113
3. Webster, 1981: 109
4. Milner, 2011: 72
5. Milner, 2011: 44
6. McLynn, 2009: 325
7. Webster, 1981: 146
8. Webster, 1981: 150
9. Cassius Dio book 60.20
10. Webster, 1981: 152
11. Elliot, 2020: 151
12. Milner, 2011: 13
13. Davidson, 1998: 197
14. Davidson, 1998: 197
15. Travis, 2012: 125
16. Caesar, Gallic wars book 1.25
17. https://www.youtube.com/watch?v=EfgMfSZiQSU
18. Underwood, 1999: 25
19. https://www.youtube.com/watch?v=uDRBw1Hl_Qg&t=261s
20. https://www.youtube.com/watch?v=jr9-uT58Z08&t=1497s
21. https://www.youtube.com/watch?v=ni-h8SH1yUw
22. Lindybiege: https://www.youtube.com/watch?v=afqhBODc_8U
23. Underwood, 1999: 32-34
24. Esposito, 2018: 111
25. Goldsworthy, 2003: 180
26. https://www.youtube.com/watch?v=eYsr81y0Aeo
27. https://www.comitatus.net/bows.html
28. https://www.youtube.com/watch?v=VvIzvUYdeKY
29. https://www.warhistoryonline.com/ancient-history/archers-roman-army.html
30. Travis, 2012: 125
31. Marren, 2006: 10
32. Travis, 2012: 116
33. Webster, 1981: 151
34. Mortimer, 2011: 169
35. https://www.youtube.com/watch?v=VtJS1MziI98
36. https://www.youtube.com/watch?v=RO_nG6OpCKg
37. Marren, 2006: 10
38. Underwood, 1999: 119

39. Underwood, 1999: 94
40. Esposito, 2018: 93
41. Hughes, 2020: 45
42. Evans, 2000: 136
43. Esposito, 2018: 93
44. Polybius, book 6.23
45. Underwood, 1999: 77
46. Underwood, 1999: 63
47. Legio V Macedonia: https://www.youtube.com/watch?v=jnoiTX0xZ0Y
48. https://www.youtube.com/watch?v=65n3PpjPK04
49. https://www.youtube.com/watch?v=Xu8QGkqLjno
50. Travis, 2015: 113
51. Pollard and Berry, 2015: 172
52. Milner, 2011: 50
53. Milner, 2011: 95-6
54. Milner, 2011: 97
55. Milner, 2011: 26
56. Milner, 2011: 98
57. Milner, 2011: 112
58. Plutarch, The life of Crassus, 25
59. Arrianus, Ektaxis kata Alanon
60. Milner, 2011: 104
61. Esposito, 2018: 71
62. McLynn, 2009: 351
63. Tacitus, Annals, book 14, chapters 36-7
64. Cassius Dio, book 56.20
65. Paterculus, Roman History, 2.119.2-5
66. Cassius Dio, book 56.20
67. Paterculus, Roman History, 2.119.2-5
68. Tacitus 1.61
69. Taylor, 2016: 106
70. Clarkson, 2019: 17
71. Hamilton, 1986: 435
72. Goldsworthy, 2000: 175
73. Elliott, 2020: 202
74. Davidson, 1998: 189
75. Davidson, 1998: 189
76. Davidson, 1998: 189
77. Hughes, 2020: 50-51
78. Davidson, 1998: 192

Chapter 4

1. Beard, 2016: 401
2. McLynn, 2009: 21
3. McLynn, 2009: 24
4. McLynn, 2009: 27
5. McLynn, 2009: 32
6. McLynn, 2009: 46
7. Beard, 2016: 411-2
8. Beard, 2016: 411
9. McLynn, 2009: 72
10. McLynn, 2009: 101
11. McLynn, 2009: 123
12. Hopkins and Beard, 2011: 82
13. Cassius Dio, book 72.36
14. McLynn, 2009: 153
15. McLynn, 2009: 185
16. Beard, 2016: 439
17. Beard, 2016: 439
18. Mocsy, 1974: 183
19. Taylor, 2016: 110
20. McLynn, 2009: 341
21. McLynn, 2009: 353
22. McLynn, 2009: 360
23. Cassius Dio book 72.22
24. McLynn, 2009: 374
25. Hopkins and Beard, 2011: 90-1
26. McLynn, 2009: 418
27. Bishop, 2018
28. Bishop, 2018: 132

Chapter 5

1. Hopkins and Beard, 2011: 54
2. Nossov, 2009: 12
3. Nossov, 2009: 14
4. Epplett, 2020: 3
5. Epplett, 2020: 10
6. Nossov, 2009: 16-7
7. Nossov, 2009: 15

8. Hopkins and Beard, 2011: 98
9. Nossov, 2009: 20
10. Hopkins and Beard, 2011: 42
11. Epplett, 2020: 64
12. Epplett, 2020: 36
13. Epplett, 2020: 64
14. Epplett, 2020: 70
15. Epplett, 2020:73-4
16. Epplett, 2020: 85-6
17. Epplett, 2020: 34
18. Nossov, 2009: 32
19. Nossov, 2009: 33
20. Hopkins and Beard, 2011: 45
21. Epplett, 2020: 31
22. Epplett, 2020: 51
23. Nossov, 2009: 38
24. Nossov, 2009: 38
25. Hopkins and Beard, 2011: 51
26. Hopkins and Beard, 2011: 55
27. Nossov, 2009: 45
28. Bishop, 2017: 84-98
29. Nossov, 2009: 71
30. Epplett, 2020: xii
31. Epplett, 2020: xii
32. Hopkins and Beard, 2011: 77
33. Hopkins and Beard, 2011: 76
34. Hopkins and Beard, 2011: 85
35. Epplett, 2020: 79
36. Hopkins and Beard, 2011: 86-9
37. Hopkins and Beard, 2011: 90-4
38. Hopkins and Beard, 2011: 49
39. Epplett, 2020: 98
40. Epplett, 2020: 99
41. Hopkins and Beard, 2011: 56
42. Hopkins and Beard, 2011: 109
43. Epplett, 2020: 23
44. Epplett, 2020: 31
45. Epplett, 2020: 45
46. Epplett, 2020: 64
47. Epplett, 2020: 32
48. Epplett, 2020: 60-1

49. Epplett, 2020: 104
50. Hopkins and Beard, 2011: 60
51. Hopkins and Beard, 2011: 43
52. Epplett, 2020: 33

Chapter 6

1. McHugh, 2015: 2
2. McLynn, 2009: 401
3. McHugh, 2015: 13
4. McHugh, 2015: 18
5. McHugh, 2015: 30
6. Cassius Dio book 73.1.2
7. McHugh, 2015: 57
8. Cassius Dio book 73.8
9. Cassius Dio book 73.4
10. McHugh, 2015: 76
11. Cassius Dio book 73.16.3
12. Cassius Dio book 73.12
13. Cassius Dio book 73.10
14. McHugh, 2015: 97-8
15. Cassius Dio book 73.9
16. McHugh, 2015: 10
17. Herodian 1.10.2
18. Herodian 1.10.4
19. Herodian 1.12.4-5
20. McHugh, 2015: 126
21. Herodian 1.13.3
22. Cassius Dio book 73.13.6
23. Herodian 1.13.3
24. Herodian 1.13.8
25. Epplett, 2020: 67
26. Hopkins and Beard, 2011: 115
27. McHugh, 2015: 167
28. McHugh, 2015: 192
29. Herodian 1.15.1
30. Herodian 1.17.1
31. Herodian 1.17.3-4
32. Herodian 2.1.3
33. Herodian 2.2.5

Index